Llewellyn's

2006

Witches' Spell-A-Day Almanac

Holidays & Lore   Spells & Recipes
Rituals & Meditations

Editing/Design: Michael Fallon
Cover Design: Lisa Novak; Background Photo: © PhotoDisc
Interior Art: © 2005, Terry Miura (illustrations: pp. 9, 29, 49, 71, 91, 113, 133, 153, 173, 193, 215, 235); © Eris Klein (holiday and day icons)

ISBN 0
Llewellyn is a registered trade
PO Box 64383,
St. Paul

Table of Contents

About the Authors

Elizabeth Barrette serves as the managing editor of *PanGaia* and assistant editor of *SageWoman.* She has been involved with the Pagan community for more than fifteen years, and in 2003 earned ordination as a priestess through Sanctuary of the Silver Moon. She lives in central Illinois and enjoys herbal landscaping and gardening for wildlife. Visit her website at http://www.worthlink.net/~ysabet/index.html.

Nancy Bennett's work has appeared in such publications as *Silver Wheel,* several *We'Moon* magazines, and several of Llewellyn's annuals. She lives on Vancouver Island with her animals and family and strives to balance a writing life with a love of nature and a historical sewing habit.

Stephanie Rose Bird enjoys a rich life as an artist, writer, herbalist, healer, mother, and companion. Her art work is included in several significant art collections around the world, and she is a faculty member at the School of the Art Institute of Chicago. Currently, she leads herb craft workshops at the Chicago Botanic Gardens and writes a column for *SageWoman* magazine.

Boudica is reviews editor and co-owner of the *Wiccan/Pagan Times* and owner of the *Zodiac Bistro,* two online publications. She is a teacher with CroneSpeak, teaching both on and off the net, and guest speaker at many festivals and gatherings. A former New Yorker, she now resides with her husband in Ohio.

Emely Flak has been a practicing solitary witch for eleven years, and is a freelance writer in Daylesford, Australia. She is also employed as a development professional, and much of her work is dedicated to embracing the wisdom of Wicca for the personal empowerment of women in the competitive workplace.

Lily Gardner-Butts is a lifelong student of folklore and mythology. In addition to writing for Llewellyn, she writes short stories and teaches creative writing. Lily has been practicing witchcraft in Portland, Oregon, for twelve years and is a member of the Power of Three coven.

James Kambos is a writer and folk artist. He holds a degree in history and has had a lifelong interest in folk magic. He has authored numerous articles on the folk magic traditions of Greece, the Near East, and the Appalachian region of the United States. The beautiful hill country of southern Ohio is where he calls home.

Lady MoonDance is a Pagan priestess who leads community events and rituals and teaches workshops.

Kristin Madden is a homeschooling mom and author of several books on shamanism, paganism, and parenting. She is dean of Ardantane's School of Shamanic Studies and is a Druid and tutor in the Order of Bards, Ovates, and Druids. In her spare time, Kristin rehabilitates wild birds. Visit her online at http://www.kristinmadden.com.

Sharynne NicMhacha is a Celtic priestess and Witch. She has studied Old Irish, Scottish Gaelic, and Celtic mythology at Harvard University where she has published a number of research papers. She teaches workshops and plays music with the group Devandaurae.

Olivia O'Meir has been published in the *Beltane Papers, newWitch,* and Llewellyn's *Magical Almanac*. She is a feminist Dianic Witch and ordained reverend, and she runs Diana's Den in the Philadelphia area. She is a member of many women's spirituality and Goddess-focused groups on- and offline. Visit her at www.geocities.com/medusa_athene.

Laurel Reufner has been a solitary Pagan for over a decade now. She is active in the local CUUPS chapter, Circle of Gaia Dreaming, and is often attracted to bright and shiny ideas. Southeastern Ohio has always been home, where she currently lives in lovely Athens County with her wonderful husband and two adorable heathens, er, daughters. Her website may be found at www.spiritrealm.com/Melinda/paganism.html.

Gail Wood started practicing Wicca in 1984. She is cofounder of the Web, a Pagan circle with members nationwide. She teaches Wicca, tarot, shamanic journeywork, and alternative spiritual practices.

Luci Sophia Zain is a lifelong spiritual aspirant. She has studied with a wide variety of spiritual groups, and has as well spent much time in solitary spiritual pursuit. She is currently working on establishing a new spiritual group.

S. Y. Zenith is three-quarters Chinese, one tad Irish, and a lifelong solitary eclectic Pagan. Based in Australia, her time is divided between constant travel, writing, experimenting with alternative remedies, and teaching the use of gems, crystals, holy beads, and sacraments from India and the Himalayas. She is also a member of the Australian Society of Authors.

Introduction

A Note on Magic and Spells

The spells in the *Witches' Spell-A-Day Almanac* evoke everyday magic designed to improve our lives and homes. You needn't be an expert on magic to follow these simple rites and spells; as you will see if you use these spells through the year, magic, once mastered, is easy to perform. The only advanced technique required of you is the art of visualization.

Visualization is an act of controlled imagination. If you can call up in your mind a picture of your best friend's face or a flag flapping in the breeze, you can visualize. In magic, visualizations are used to direct and control magical energies. Basically, the spell-caster creates a visual image of the spell's desired goal, whether it be perfect health, a safe house, or a protected pet.

Visualization is the basis of all good spells, and as such it is a tool that should be properly used. Visualization must be real in the mind of the spell-caster so that it allows him or her to raise, concentrate, and send forth energy to accomplish the spell.

Perhaps when visualizing you'll find that you're doing everything right, but you don't feel anything. This is common, for we haven't been trained to acknowledge—let alone utilize—our magical abilities. Keep practicing, however, for your spells can "take" even if you're not the most experienced natural magician.

You will notice also that many spells in this collection have a somewhat "light" tone. They are seemingly fun and frivolous, filled with rhyme and colloquial speech. This is not to diminish the seriousness of the purpose, but rather to create a relaxed atmosphere for the practitioner. Lightness of spirit helps focus energy; rhyme and common language help the spell-caster remember the words and train the mind where it is needed. The intent of this magic is indeed very serious at times; and magic is never to be trifled with.

Even when your spells are effective, magic won't usually sparkle before your very eyes. The test of magic's success is time, not immediate eye-popping results. But you can feel magic's energy for yourself by rubbing

your palms together briskly for ten seconds, then holding them a few inches apart. Sense the energy passing through them, the warm tingle in your palms. This is the power raised and used in magic. It comes from within and is perfectly natural.

Among the features of the *Witches' Spell-A-Day Almanac* are an easy-to-use "book of days" format; new spells specifically tailored for each day of the year (and its particular magical, astrological, and historical energies); and additional tips and lore for various days throughout the year—including color correspondences based on planetary influences, obscure and forgotten holidays and festivals, and an incense-of-the-day to help you waft magical energies from the ether into your space.

In creating this product, we were inspired by the ancient almanac traditions and the layout of the classic nineteenth-century almanac *Chamber's Book of Days,* which is subtitled *A Miscellany of Popular Antiquities in connection with the Calendar.* As you will see, our fifteen authors this year made history a theme of their spells, and we hope that by knowing something of the magic of past years we may make our current year all the better.

Enjoy your days, and have a magical year!

2006
Year of Spells

January is the first month of the Gregorian calendar. Its name comes from the two-faced Roman god Janus, ruler of gates and doorways. Its astrological sign Capricorn, the goat (December 21–January 20), is a cardinal earth sign ruled by Saturn. January is a time of new beginnings. New Year's Day brings with it the tradition of making resolutions for the year. Popular customs include opening the front and back door of the home, a symbolic way of letting the new year in and the old year out. Epiphany, or Twelfth Night, falls on January 6 and is the final night of the Christmas season. This night is a time to gather family and friends near a crackling fire, enjoying food and sweets and sharing hopes and wishes for the coming year. January's Full Moon was known as the Wolf Moon, a time when the hungry pack would search for food. In many regions, snow blankets the ground, icicles hang from the eaves, and the night sky is spangled with starlight. Evergreen trees, symbols of eternal life, stand out now in the winter woodland. Blue jays and cardinals brighten the winter landscape. Traditionally during this month Pagans perform purification magic using seasonal scents such as pine and ginger. The ritual burning of written charms so that their magic may be released is also popular in January.

  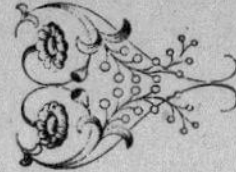 

January 1
Sunday

New Year's Day – Kwanzaa ends

1st ♑
☽ → ♒ 7:14 am

Color of the day: Yellow
Incense of the day: Poplar

Lasting Resolutions Spell

The new year is associated with resolutions to kick bad habits or to establish good new ones. But why do so many of our New Year resolutions last only a few days? Usually, this is because we set our standards too high. Today, set a realistic goal by making sure it's achievable. For example, if you love chocolate, it would be unrealistic to expect yourself to give it up totally. A more realistic goal is to reduce your chocolate consumption rather than abstain from your pleasure. Focus on making improvement rather than extreme change. This way you stand a good chance of achieving your goal with a sense of accomplishment. Also, don't forget to pat yourself on the back when you achieve it. As you state your goal, light a gold candle to attract success.

Emely Flak

Notes:

Holiday lore: New Year's Day calls for safeguards, augurs, charms, and proclamations. All over the world on this day, people kiss strangers, shoot guns into the air, toll bells, and exchange gifts. Preferred gifts are herring, bread, and fuel for the fire.

January 2
Monday

1st ♒

Color of the day: Gray
Incense of the day: Maple

Make a Wish Spell

Today is the eighth day of Christmas. Traditionally, this is a time for each member of the household to make a wish for the coming year. To do this, take a good quality sheet of white stationery or artist's watercolor paper. Using a black-ink calligraphy pen, let each person in your family write down wishes for the year. The wishes could be in the form of a spell, an affirmation, or a prayer. Be sure to write as neatly as possible. As you write, think of the white paper as representing the New Year—clean, pure, and full of possibilities. Concentrate while writing your wish, knowing that each wish will become a reality. Keep the wish list out for all to see, so family members can recall the goals and work toward them.

James Kambos

 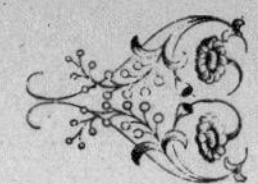  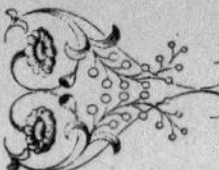 

Notes:

January 3
Tuesday

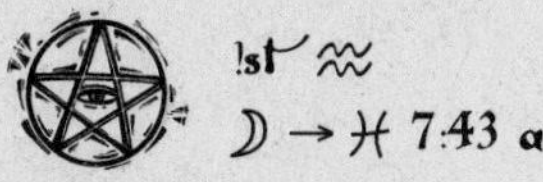

1st ♒
☽ → ♓ 7:43 am

Color of the day: Red
Incense of the day: Gardenia

Hogmanay Purification Spell

In parts of Scotland, the Gregorian New Year was called Hogmanay. This was a special time when people gathered at sacred sites such as stone circles to sing and dance in the moonlight. Bonfires were lit, and warm spiced ale and special cakes were served. This new year purification spell originates from Hogmanay traditions. Decorate the doorways of your home with holly, hazel, or rowan. After sunset, take a vessel of pure spring water and drink from it, thanking the gods, the ancestors, and the spirits of the land. Sprinkle the water in every room of your house. Afterward, carefully light dried juniper branches or sprigs, and carry them around the house saying:

> Welcome in, New Year!
> When ye come,
> Bring good cheer!
>
> Well may we a' be,
> Ill may we ne'er see.
>
> The gude New Year
> It is begun!

Sharynne NicMhacha

Notes:

January 4
Wednesday

1st ♓

Color of the day: Brown
Incense of the day: Cedar

Holy Day of Apollo Spell

To open yourself to new business possibilities, try this spell. Write the name of a desired new endeavor on a paper plate. This could be a new career or a new investment. Make a hole in the middle of the plate and pass a string through it. Twirl the plate clockwise, and say:

> Wheel of fortune,
> Spinning round,
> This is where my future
> is found.

  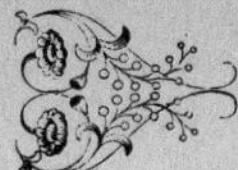 

Grant me courage to
step forth
And change for better
my life's course.

Place the plate where you will see it each day. Visualize yourself happy with this new choice each time you see the plate. Decorate it and add to its magic. Note: Today is one of the celebration days of Apollo, who is the god of prophecy. Ask for his guidance if you're unsure of your future. Seek him in your sleep and dream of new destinies.

Nancy Bennett

Notes:

January 5
Thursday

1st ♓
☽ → ♈ 9:44 am

Color of the day: Green
Incense of the day: Evergreen

Money Bag Spell

Make a "money bag" by combining a piece of silver (an old coin made of silver will do) or some shredded money (available from the mint and at specialty stores), some chamomile, and a piece of malachite in a small spell bag. Carry this in your purse or pocket so you will never be without "pocket change."

Boudica

Notes:

January 6
Friday

1st ♈
2nd Quarter 1:56 pm

Color of the day: White
Incense of the day: Ginger

Renewal Spell

This spell is aimed at renewing and refreshing your mind, body, and soul. First, find a place to meditate. Place three candles in front of you—one each of red, black, and white. Put the black candle on the left. It represents any stress and tension you might be feeling. Place the white one on the right. This candle symbolizes tranquility and peace. The

   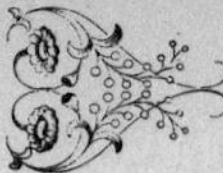 

red one, which is placed in the center, symbolizes you, full of life. First, light the black one. As you light it say: "I remove all stress surrounding me." Light the white candle and say: "I affirm the peace inside me." Then, light the red center candle and say: "I am full of energy and vitality." When you are ready, extinguish the candles and say: "With harm to none, so mote it be!"

Olivia O'Meir

Notes:

Holiday lore: Twelfth night and the night following it are when wassailing used to take place. The word "wassail" comes from the Anglo-Saxon words *waes heil,* meaning "to be whole or healthy." People drank to each other's health from a large bowl filled with drink such as "lamb's wool," which was made of hot ale or cider, nutmeg, and sugar with roasted crab apples. In some parts of Britain, trees and bees are still wassailed to ensure a healthy crop. Having drunk to the tree's health, people fire shotguns into the branches. Different regions sing different wassail songs to the tree. Here's one from Worcestershire:

Here's to thee, old apple tree,
Whence thou mayest bud,
Whence thou mayest blow,
Whence thou mayest bear
apples enow.

January 7
Saturday

2nd ♈

☽ → ♉ 2:09 pm

Color of the day: Blue
Incense of the day: Jasmine

Computer Guardian Spell

Many of us are more than a little lost without our trusty old computers, myself included. With the usual precautions of battery backups, surge protectors, and virus protection, this spell creates a helpful metaphysical guardian to keep watch over your computer. You will need a small air fern, available in many garden centers, and a red and a yellow candle. Place the plant between the two lit candles, and while reciting the chant below charge the plant watching over your computer and all of its paraphernalia.

Mercury, Mercury,
Hear my plea.
Guard my computer both
night and day,
While I am here and
while I'm away.

Keep the plant in your work area near your computer. The lovely thing

about an air fern is that it will grow in just about any kind of light and doesn't require watering. Mist it every so often, and it will be fine.

Laurel Reufner

Notes:

January 8
Sunday

2nd ♉

Color of the day: Orange

Incense of the day: Cinnamon

Life Everlasting Mojo

It is the beginning of the year, a time to take stock of our lives. Use the healing power of the Sun to create a mojo bag for longevity, prosperity, and love. This mojo features the yellow blossoms of life everlasting and jasmine flower oil along with an Egyptian ankh amulet in honor of Sun Ra. Crumble a handful of life everlasting herb in a bowl. Toss in three shiny pennies. With your hands, mix these two ingredients together as you wish for good health, love, and a long life. Gaze at the bright pennies and colorful flowers, and think of love, health, and longevity thrice. Into the bowl, add three drops of jasmine oil. Swirl the bowl to mix the ingredients. Take deep cleansing breaths. Focus on love, health, and longevity multiplying before your eyes. Pour the ingredients into a sky blue mojo bag. Tie three knots to secure the drawstring. To the string tie on a silver ankh talisman, a symbol of longevity to ancient Egyptians. Draw an ankh on front of the mojo bag with red paint if a metal talisman is not available. Always keep the Life Everlasting Mojo close to your person. Feed it twice a month on a Friday with three drops jasmine or rose oil and a smattering of magnetic sand.

Stephanie Rose Bird

Notes:

January 9
Monday

2nd ♉

☽ → ♊ 8:58 pm

Color of the day: Lavender

Incense of the day: Lilac

Appreciate the Pleasures Spell

January reminds us to hold close those we love and cherish the

   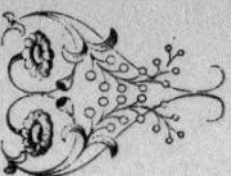 

things we have. We appreciate the sturdy walls of the house more when we hear cold winds howling outside. This ritual is not about asking for something new, but about appreciating the little pleasures and the security in your life. You will need a favorite book, a good number of candles, and a lighter. Gather your family together and light the candles. Turn off any electric lights, then say:

Hold us near,
Family dear,
As these words we say.

Candlelight,
Winter's night,
Keep the cold away.

Take turns reading aloud, choosing from your favorite passages in the book. Reading by candlelight creates a very cozy, magical atmosphere and strengthens family bonds. When finished, share a hug and then blow out the candles.

Elizabeth Barrette

Notes:

January 10
Tuesday

2nd ♊

Color of the day: White
Incense of the day: Honeysuckle

A Spell for Harmony and Peace

On a violet-colored cloth with a pleasing pattern, place a purple candle. Next to it, place a small, flat dish of salt. Light some lavender incense and breathe deeply, then let out your breath in a lovely tone. As you breathe and intone, light the candle. Still your voice and draw a pentacle in the salt as you say:

By air, fire, water,
earth, and spirit
Hearken my prayer, all
those who hear it.
Let there be peace and
let there be harmony.
Blessed be.
Wild and free.

Chant the verse nine times, and then return to your single tone. Breathe deeply and envision being filled with this peace and harmony. Extinguish the candle in thankfulness.

Gail Wood

Notes:

   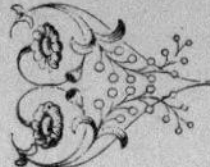 

January 11
Wednesday

2nd ♊

Color of the day: Yellow
Incense of the day: Maple

Flying Creatures Blessing

Today, look at the sky and observe. What kind of flying weather is it today? Consider all creatures that fly, and how they will deal with today's weather. Light some incense, and get out your favorite feather or air talisman, saying:

> Let all who fly be safe
> and free. May my heart
> soar as my feet are firmly
> grounded on the earth.
> Blessed be the creatures
> of the air. I celebrate the
> skies and its creatures!

Wave your feather in the air, breathe deeply, and proclaim: "So mote it be." Wear something yellow today for the element of air, or something blue or gray for the sky. Focus on breathing as you go about your day, and be joyful for the ability to breathe.

Luci Sophia Zain

Notes:

January 12
Thursday

2nd ♊
☽ → ♋ 5:50 am

Color of the day: Turquoise
Incense of the day: Vanilla

Money Bowl Spell

For ensuring a smooth, continuous flow of money for household bills and expenses, unforeseen circumstances, a special gift for a loved one, or for gradual improvements in your home or premises, create your very own money bowl. Take a brass or copper bowl and shine it up with some polish and cloth. Name it the "Bowl of Plenty," and fill it with a handful of cinquefoil or five-finger grass. Add a fistful of silver coins, gold coins, and a few dollar notes. Say the following nine times each morning and each night at exactly the same hour each time:

> O Bowl of Plenty!
> Ever generously flowing
> to me.
>
> And as I will,
> So mote it be!

Each day, keep adding coins and bills until the bowl is full. Once a month, transfer the bowl's contents into a cash box or piggy bank and begin this same ritual afresh.

S. Y. Zenith

 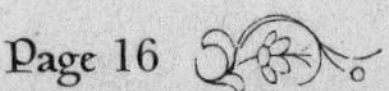

 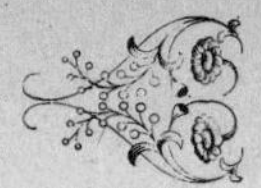   

Notes:

January 13
Friday

2nd ♋

Color of the day: Pink

Incense of the day: Parsley

Crystal Seed Planting Spell

To bring your family blessings and protection in the year to come, plant a crystal seed. Purify a clear quartz crystal by soaking it in salt water for seven days. Leave it out in the moonlight overnight. Smudge yourself and the crystal in sagebrush and cedar. Hold the crystal in both hands, and imagine that it contains your home and land. See yourself and your family members coming and going, all within the crystal. Call upon the spirit of the crystal and of your home. Ask for their blessings and protection. Look deeper within the crystal. Visualize a happy family—people sharing great successes and delightful times. Feel how wonderful this is and return the energy to the crystal. Thank the spirits, and plant this crystal into a houseplant or in the dirt by your front door.

Kristin Madden

Notes:

January 14
Saturday

2nd ♋

3rd Quarter 4:48 am

☽ → ♌ 4:31 pm

Color of the day: Indigo

Incense of the day: Violet

Magical Cooking Spell

The Full Moon in Cancer brings with it an upwelling of emotions combined with the desire for home, security, and comfort. Now that the flurry of the holidays is over, indulge your natural desire to hibernate during cold winter months. To support this process, make your home a comfortable and creative place, filled with light and warmth. Decorate it with items of your own creation. Set aside time to enjoy cooking, cross-stitch, knitting, sewing, quilting, drawing, or other arts and crafts, remembering that everything you create contains a bit of your

 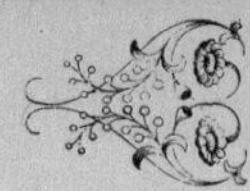  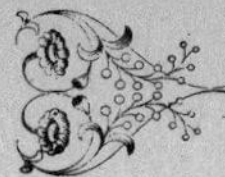 

energy. Whenever you begin a new project, ask yourself what kind of energy you wish to put into the finished item. Before you begin, then, visualize or speak aloud the energy that you want to create. Pause periodically as you work and revisualize the energy, while thinking of things you want to remove (hunger, anger, poverty, miscommunication, sadness, loneliness, sickness, and the like) as well as the things you want to grow (love, friendship, prosperity, happiness, community, health).

Lady MoonDance

Notes:

January 15
Sunday

3rd ♌

Color of the day: Gold
Incense of the day: Sage

Carmentalia Divination

Today we celebrate the feast day of Carmenta, the ancient Italian goddess of divination. Augury was an ancient method of divination practiced by the Romans, which foretold one's future from the activity of birds. As you prepare your spell, think of a question you wish to pose. Using a wand, describe a circle beginning in the east. Light a candle in each of the four directions. On a square of silk in the middle of your circle, place a small bowl of walnuts and a vase of bird feathers as an offering to Carmenta. Light incense and say:

> **Carmenta, all-seeing
> goddess, let my prayer
> rise to you on this smoke.
> Reveal an answer to my
> query.**

Hold the feathers in your left hand and let them drop to the square of silk at your feet. The patterns that the feathers make should point to an answer of some sort.

Lily Gardner-Butts

Notes:

January 16
Monday

Martin Luther King, Jr. Day

3rd ♌

Color of the day: White
Incense of the day: Coriander

Smooring Ritual

In ancient times, the hearth-fire was rarely allowed to go out, especially in winter. When the fire had burned down to an ember, it was carefully preserved under a blanket of ashes. In Scotland, this was called "smooring," and it was done in a ritualistic way. The embers were arranged in a circle divided into three parts, with an ember in the middle known as Tula nan Tri (Hearth of the Three). You can perform this fire magic with three candles, with a fourth in the center symbolizing what you wish to preserve and encourage in the season to come. Close your eyes and pass your hand over the candles, saying:

> I am smooring the fire
> As Bridget would smoor.
> The gods' protection
> Be upon the flame.
>
> I will build this power
> As I build the hearth
> At the dawn of the red
> sun of day.

Sharynne NicMhacha

Notes:

January 17
Tuesday

3rd ♌
☽ → ♍ 4:49 am

Color of the day: Black
Incense of the day: Poplar

Holy Day of Osiris Spell

Today was one of the holy days of Osiris in ancient Egypt. To raise energy today, take some broth, such as chicken broth, and warm it over a stove. As the broth heats, stir it clockwise. Inhale the essence, and repeat this phase three times:

> Steam will rise and
> broth will warm.
> Keep my body safe from
> harm.
> Magic mixture, energy
> rise,
> With this spell I
> internalize!

Pour the broth into a favorite mug. Sip it slowly and visualize the broth feeding you strength with each swallow. To harness the energy further, make yourself a talisman with herbs and feathers or chicken bones and carry it with you in a small bag. Osiris is the god of resurrection. You can ask for his help to aid in a new beginning. Ask with an honest heart, for he also serves as a judge of the worthiness of the recently dead.

Nancy Bennett

Notes:

January 18
Wednesday

3rd ♍

Color of the day: Topaz
Incense of the day: Pine

Psychic Communication Spell

This spell will help increase your long-distance psychic abilities. For it, you'll need a like-minded partner who does not live with you. Set a time when you can perform this ritual with your friend. You'll both need a white candle and charged amethyst stone. At the designated time, each of you should light your candle and gaze at the flame. Handle the amethyst stone. Concentrate on one thought; visualize a blue-white light surrounding the candle. Then, project your thought in the direction of your partner. Limit this exercise to about ten minutes. Extinguish the candle and call your friend. Tell each other what you felt, thought, or any images you saw. Perform this ritual at least once a month and you will increase your psychic awareness.

Ideally, this spell should be worked on Mondays or Wednesdays, during a waxing Moon.

James Kambos

Notes:

January 19
Thursday

3rd ♍
☽ → ♎ 5:24 pm

Color of the day: Purple
Incense of the day: Sandalwood

Thor's Sacred Day Ritual

The sacred day of Thor, Norse god of war, thunder, and lightning, falls on this date. And to add to the energy, this year his sacred day occurs on a Thursday, which is named after Thor. In Norse mythology, Thor destroyed his enemies with his magic hammer while he acted in the best interests of his people. Although he was the god of war, he was also known for his fair and good nature. Thor's hammer is widely used today as a symbol of protection and as a business charm to improve reputation and authority. The energies today are ideal for spells requiring

 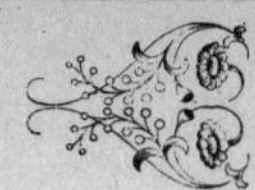   

resilience, protection, and personal strength. On a white candle, use a pin to engrave Thor's hammer and lightning symbols. Light the candle, saying:

With the power of Thor
I empower this spell
To protect and help me
Manage my challenges
well.

Emely Flak

Notes:

January 20
Friday

2nd ♎

☉ → ♒ 12:15 am

Color of the day: Rose
Incense of the day: Rose

Banish Baggage Spell

Banish old, negative baggage from your life and make yourself more receptive to love. For this spell, dress up a bit. Set your table with a treat you enjoy. Add some red candles, a red rose, a heat-resistant bowl with water, and paper and pen. Settling yourself at the table, light the candles. Now, write down all the obstacles you put up to keep yourself from love: such as self-doubt, feelings of unworthiness, and so on. When finished, light the paper from a candle. Let the paper burn a bit and then drop it in water to extinguish the flame. Enjoy your treat and leave the rose where you can enjoy it, using it as a reminder of the negative energies you have banished from your life. You are now ready for love to come to you.

Laurel Reufner

Notes:

January 21
Saturday

3rd ♎

Color of the day: Brown
Incense of the day: Cedar

Focusing Spell

Need to clear your mind for an exam or some other kind of very involved project? You will need a spell bag or cauldron, a citrine crystal for clarity, a piece of silver thread to tie yourself down to earth, a quartz crystal for further clarity, some honeysuckle for wisdom, some thyme to repel negativity, some salt for grounding, some

holy thistle for strength, and some rosemary for remembrance. Place these items in your cauldron near where you are working on your project, or in a spell bag to carry around with you as you work on your project. Create a positive attitude by repeating to yourself: "I can do whatever I need to do!" Keep the cauldron near your work, or feel the spell bag in your pocket as you work on your project.

Boudica

Notes:

Holiday lore: Feast Day of Saint Agnes of Rome. Since the fourth century, the primitive church held Saint Agnes in high honor above all the other virgin martyrs of Rome. Church fathers and Christian poets sang her praises, and they extolled her virginity and heroism under torture. The feast day for Saint Agnes was assigned to January 21. Early records gave the same date for her feast and the Catholic Church continues to keep her memory sacred.

January 22
Sunday

2nd ♎

☽ → ♏ 5:28 am

4th Quarter 10:14 am

Color of the day: Amber
Incense of the day: Basil

Sun Shower Spell

Imagine you are standing outside on a beautiful, sunny day. If you can stand outside in the Sun for this visualization, it will be even more powerful. Feel the warmth of the Sun on your body and its light on your closed eyelids. Imagine its rays pouring over you. The light and warmth covers you and soaks in through your pores, eyes, and mouth. Feel the light wash away tension, illness, and discomfort. These spiral away from you and are absorbed into the earth for purification. The light turns to red. As it flows over you, your root chakra energizes. The light then becomes orange, then yellow, green, indigo, and violet, energizing your chakras as it changes. It becomes golden-white again, balancing your energy field.

Kristin Madden

Notes:

   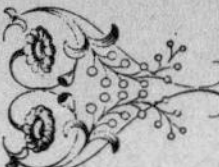 

January 23
Monday

4th ♏

Color of the day: Silver
Incense of the day: Myrrh

Black Cat Hoodoo Trick

This is the time to honor the Egyptian cat goddess Bastet, who manifests either as a cat or as a cat-headed woman. She is goddess of joy, music, dance, pleasure, sunrise, family, fertility, and birth. A great way to engage the blessings of Bastet is a Black Cat Hoodoo Trick. In Hoodoo, the word "trick" means "a spell." Take a black cat-shaped candle and set it outside after sunset on a fireproof holder. Trim the wick to one-half inch. Write out a petition on brown paper with a sharpened pencil. Ask Bastet for what you need in writing. Set your request next to the burning candle. Hold it down with a stone that is special to you. The black cat candle brings good fortune in games of chance, sport competitions, and other risk-taking. It also aids invisibility, returns lost objects and lovers, and brings prosperity. After the candle has burned for about ten minutes and you have read your petition aloud three times, extinguish the flame. Take some of the melted candle wax off the candle while it is still soft but not hot, and roll it into a ball. Wrap the petition, with words facing inward, around the wax. Tie the mass firmly with a red ribbon, and place the bundle under your bed. As you fall asleep each night, reflect on the candle ritual. Within seven days, Bastet's spirit will help your wish come true—if it is meant to be.

Stephanie Rose Bird

Notes:

January 24
Tuesday

4th ♏
☽ → ♐ 1:38 pm

Color of the day: Gray
Incense of the day: Juniper

Mars Protection Spell

In the ancient Indian astrological system of Jyotish, the planet Mars is also regarded as the ruling planet for Tuesday. Red coral, which is governed by the planet Mars, is one of nine precious gems useful for Jyotish

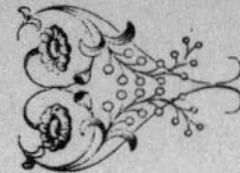

remedies. Persons wishing to gain the blessings of Mars and attract its strong protective energies will find the wearing of red coral very useful. This is especially true when you wear it against the skin after invoking Lord Mars on a Tuesday. The mantra for Lord Mars should be repeated at least nine times. Practitioners familiar with Hinduism or Hindu pantheons should chant the relevant mantra 108 times for maximum effect:

Om bhaum bhaumaye
namah Om.

S. Y. Zenith

Notes:

January 25
Wednesday

4th ♐

Color of the day: White
Incense of the day: Neroli

Banishing Obstacles Spell

In honor of poet Robert Burns' birthday, here's a spell to help remove any blockages that might stop the creative flow. This spell calls on the Hindu elephant god Ganesha, who is known for bringing good luck and banishing obstacles. Keep his image wherever you pursue your creative dream. Place a rutilated quartz, citrine, opal, or agate near the image. Burn some nag champa, sandalwood, patchouli, cinnamon, and laurel incense. Light the incense and say: "Ganesha, remove any creative blockages, so that I may create and express my soul." Take a few deep breaths. With each breath, see the block crumbling apart, eventually disappearing completely—allowing you to start creating.

Olivia O'Meir

Notes:

Holiday lore: Burns' Night is a key event in Scotland that has been observed for about 200 years in honor of Robert Burns, who was born on this day. One of Scotland's most beloved bards, Burns immortalized haggis in a famous poem. This a Scottish dish of animal organs boiled in a sheep's stomach with suet and oatmeal. "Burns' Suppers" are celebrated not only in Scotland but wherever patriotic Scots or those of Scottish descent live.

January 26
Thursday

4th ♐
☽ → ♑ 5:31 pm

Color of the day: Crimson
Incense of the day: Carnation

Aquarian World Healing Ritual

In honor of the sign of Aquarius, drape your altar in purple or put out an amethyst stone. Though an air sign, Aquarius is also the water-bearer. Place a small pitcher or goblet of water on your altar as well. Aquarius is the sign of the humanitarian. Today, let your spell be for world healing:

> Let there be harmony in
> the world. Let there be
> loving intent. May all our
> hearts be lifted to healing
> the wounds of Mother
> Earth and of her people.
> Father Sky, please send
> your blessings to us today.

Ask yourself what one act can you perform to show your commitment to world healing. Then do it. Also, wear something purple today to reinforce your commitment.

Luci Sophia Zain

Notes:

January 27
Friday

4th ♑

Color of the day: Purple
Incense of the day: Dill

Ice Shrink Spell

Today, look outside at the fairyland of ice and snow. Sunlight glitters in the crystal teeth hanging from the eaves. White waves hang motionless, frozen in the moment of cresting. Frost-feathers decorate the windows. In winter, ice fairies are everywhere, but as the weather warms they disappear. You can give them a place to spend the summer by making an ice shrine. You will need a plain mirror, at least twelve inches across, for the base, and an assortment of quartz crystals, glass lozenges, and other sparklies. Place the mirror shiny side up, and arrange the other items on it as a wintry wonderland. Invite ice fairies to move in with this verse:

> When spring comes,
> never fear.
> Ice and snow will stay
> right here.
> Jack Frost's kin have
> their home
> In this shrine of glass
> and chrome.

Keep the shrine in a safe place through the year.

Elizabeth Barrette

Notes:

January 28
Saturday

4th ♑

☽ → ♒ 6:09 pm

Color of the day: Black
Incense of the day: Patchouli

Dark Moon Meditation for Beginnings and Endings

Burn some patchouli incense, and settle yourself into a comfortable meditative state. Breathe deeply and see yourself in a doorway between two rooms. Look into the room behind you, and that everything is put away neatly. Take notice of all that the room contains. Take a deep breath and say goodbye. Shut the door on all the things ended and taken care of. Turn around and go forward into the brightly lit room. As you walk around the room, you notice that on a desk by the window is a book titled "My New Beginning." Open the book and begin to read. After reading, close the book and put it back on the desk. Take a deep breath and open your eyes. Adjust to being back in your circle. You will remember what you read, and you are ready to begin.

Gail Wood

Notes:

January 29
Sunday

Chinese New Year (dog)

4th ♒

New Moon 9:15 am

Color of the day: Orange
Incense of the day: Coriander

Honoring Friendship Spell

This New Moon in Aquarius also begins the Chinese Year of the Dog. Like Aquarians, dogs are the most humanitarian of the signs. Dogs are both idealistic and imaginative. Compassionate companions, they are loyal, honest, and brave. Since the Chinese New Year is a time for new beginnings and sets the tone for the year ahead, embrace the Year of the Dog by sharing a New Year's treat of moon cakes with friends. While traditional cakes are embossed with intricate designs, the following recipe is a fun and easy substitute.

  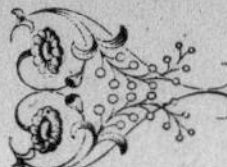 

Easy Moon Cakes

1/2 cup salted butter
1/4 cup sugar
2 egg yolks
1 cup all-purpose flour
1 cup jam or red bean paste

Preheat the oven to 375 degrees. Stir together the butter, sugar, and one of the egg yolks. Mix in the flour, and form the dough into a large ball. Wrap it in plastic and refrigerate for half an hour. Beat the second egg yolk in a bowl, and set it aside. Unwrap the chilled dough and form it into small balls. Make a hole with your thumb in the center of each ball. With a teaspoon, fill each ball with a small amount of jam and close it shut again. Dip each ball into the beaten yolk and place on a greased cookie sheet. Bake for twenty minutes or until edges are slightly brown.

Lady MoonDance

Notes:

January 30

Monday

1st ♒

☽ → ♓ 5:32 pm

Color of the day: Ivory
Incense of the day: Chrysanthemum

Wandering Pet Protection Spell

Spread out a white handkerchief. On it, place a clipping of your pet's hair and a picture of your home or one of you and your pet together. Imagine your pet back in its favorite inside place, sleeping contentedly. Keep this image in mind and say:

From this place you will
not roam,
For you are safe and
loved at home.

Whenever you leave,
Return to me,
From this dawn onward.
So mote it be!

Wrap the photo and hair in the hankie and tie it securely. Place it near your pet's favorite inside place.

Nancy Bennett

Notes:

   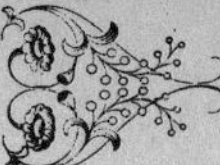 

January 31

Tuesday

Islamic New Year

1st ♓

Color of the day: Maroon

Incense of the day: Poplar

Spell for Artists

Sarasvati, Hindu goddess of letters, music, and magic, is honored today. Her images portray her holding a book, a sitar, and prayer beads. For inspiration, on a white square of cloth place pearls, a white flower in a glass bowl of water, a bottle of ink, a pen, and a sheet of new paper. If you wish for inspiration of another sort, use symbols for your corresponding art. Burn a white candle and a stick of incense, and pray:

> O Mother Sarasvati,
> Remove the darkness
> from my mind
> And bless me with eternal
> knowledge.

Meditate using the following mantra:

> Om aing Sarasvati
> namaha Om.

It is said that if you say this mantra 500,000 times, all knowledge will be revealed.

Lily Gardner-Butts

Notes:

February is the second month of the Gregorian calendar, and the year's shortest month. It is named for Februa, an ancient purification festival, and its astrological sign is Aquarius, the water-bearer (January 20–February 18), a fixed air sign ruled by Uranus. In February, Mother Earth begins to stir; daylight lasts a little longer, and the first crocuses begin to peek through the snow. The major holiday of the month, Imbolc or Candlemas, celebrates the strengthening Sun. This is a day of purification and banishment; candles are lit and Yuletide greenery is burned in a ritual fire to illuminate the waning darkness of winter. Corn dollies, called Corn Maidens, are dressed in scraps of white lace and ribbons. The maiden is placed in a basket, called the Bride's Bed, with a small ribbon-entwined wand representing the God. Romance is celebrated on Valentine's Day, February 14. Magical activities include love divinations of all types, and, of course, treating your romantic partner to chocolates is a common custom. Long ago, February's Full Moon was called the Snow Moon, and the month is still known for powerful snow storms. Still, nature begins to sense the turning of the year. House finches begin looking for nesting sites, and in the still-frozen woodland foxes begin searching for a mate.

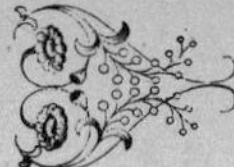

February 1
Wednesday

1st ♓

☽ → ♈ 5:46 pm

Color of the day: Yellow
Incense of the day: Sandalwood

Spicy Business Potpourri

How about a spicy, magical potpourri to bring in some new business at this dark time of year? In a small jar place three tablespoons of orris root or cellulose fiber fixative, along with one teaspoon of amber, sandalwood, or orange-spice fragrance oils. Allow this to sit overnight. To two cups of small pine cones add one cup rose petals and buds, one-half cup of orange peel ribbons, and each of the following: a whole star anise, several basil leaves, two whole nutmegs, several bay leaves, two cinnamon stick pieces, and several small to medium sea shells. Gently combine all the ingredients in a glass or ceramic bowl. Add the ingredients of the jar from the night before. Store the contents in a glass or plastic jar in a cool, dry, dark place for one week, and it is ready to use.

Laurel Reufner

Notes:

February 2
Thursday
Imbolc – Groundhog Day

1st ♈

Color of the day: Brown
Incense of the day: Sandalwood

Dream Tending Spell

This is a truly special day for Wiccans and some Witches. It is Imbolc, a high holiday that honors the triple goddess Brigit and one of the eight sabbats that mark the turning of the wheel of the year. Groundhog day is also observed today. This holiday incorporates the seasonal divination of the more ancient Imbolc, which uses the movement of a snake rather than the shadow of a groundhog to divine how much longer winter will remain. It is the beginning of the Storm Moon and also the time of the Feast of Oya, the orisha of weather and changes. To the Iroquois people, it is Midwinter Ceremony, a time to bless the fields, tell your dreams, and pay tribute to your ancestors. Today is also the birthday of Marie Laveau II, New Orleans' Voodoo Queen and diviner extraordinaire. At bedtime now, light a braid of sweet grass. Extinguish the flame but allow the braid to smolder. Wave the braid lovingly and with great care around your bedroom, motioning with your hand to encourage the smoke to drift in a snake-like stream over your

bed and pillow. Dip the braid in springwater, making absolutely sure no flame remains. Then put the braid away. Pour lavender water in a large bowl. Put your favorite seashell inside the bowl of water. As you sleep, the bowl will act as a conduit for messages from the ancestors, nature spirits, and the great beyond. Place this under your bed or on your bed table. Replenish the water as needed over a period of two weeks. Write down your dreams in a journal. Read over them frequently. Messages revealed in the darkness of winter have special meaning. Work each day to lift the shroud of darkness so you can glimpse new growth and the coming light of spring. Understanding the mysteries of winter is at the heart of Imbolc and its celebrations.

Stephanie Rose Bird

Notes:

Holiday lore: On Imbolc, a bundle of corn from the harvest is dressed in ribbons and becomes the Corn Bride. On February 2, the Corn Bride is placed on the hearth or hung on the door to bring prosperity, fertility, and protection to the home.

February 3
Friday

1st ♈

☽ → ♉ 8:31 pm

Color of the day: White
Incense of the day: Thyme

Love Oil Spell

Feeling neglected by a loved one? A personalized love oil can be created and used for reminding the other person that you are there—even when you're not actually physically around. In a sterilized glass jar, add two parts rose essential oil, one part jasmine essential oil, and one part neroli or orange blossom oil. You can adjust the ingredients to suit your own tastes—but do not let any one element overwhelm the others. Then, add six parts of a base oil such as sweet almond or virgin olive. Place two fresh rose petals and two lodestones in the jar. Gently mix the ingredients together, seal the jar, and let it stand for three weeks in a cool, dry, and dark corner. On the third week, shake the jar, strain the ingredients through muslin, and decant the liquid into an attractive glass bottle. Apply a drop of each at the base of the throat, behind each ear, and

on the wrists when dating. The oil can also be dabbed on to cushions, pillows, linen, curtains, and furnishings.

S. Y. Zenith

Notes:

February 4
Saturday

1st ♉

Color of the day: Brown

Incense of the day: Lilac

Growth of Light Spell

Continue your celebration of the growing hours of daylight. For today, place on your altar a white or gold cloth and something silver to represent the Moon. Turn out all of the lights, and light a candle, saying:

> O Moon, whose silver
> light illumines my night,
> I thank thee for thy
> wisdom. Although the
> days grow longer, I do
> recall thy lovely light.
> New Moon, Crescent,
> First Quarter, Gibbous,
> Full, Disseminating, Last
> Quarter, and Balsamic,
> I adore thee in all thy
> phases.

Lift your Moon symbol, and say:

> Bless me, O Silver
> Mother, and teach me
> your shadow wisdom.
> Let me not dwell too
> much in the Sun, but
> always balance sunlight
> and moonlight.

Snuff your candle, and be still and silent in the darkness.

Luci Sophia Zain

Notes:

February 5
Sunday

1st ♉

2nd Quarter 1:29 am

Color of the day: Yellow

Incense of the day: Clove

Serpent Healing Spell

One of the symbols of the goddess Bridget was the serpent, which represented healing and transformation.

As water arises from beneath the ground, the serpent emerged from the underworld, bringing the healing power of the spirit realm and signalling the approach of spring. In Scotland and Ireland, a divination ceremony called the Rite of the Serpent was performed in early February. Use this spell to encourage the arrival of spring and increase life energies and blessings in your own life. Light a green candle and set it on a white cloth. Meditate on the image of the serpent. Offer it honor and devotion, and ask for a sign of what is to come, saying:

The Serpent shall come
from the hole.
The Queen shall come
from the mound.
I will not harm the serpent,
Nor will she harm me.

Sharynne NicMhacha

Notes:

February 6
Monday

2nd ♉
☽ → ♊ 2:32 am

Color of the day: Lavender
Incense of the day: Daffodil

Aphrodite Self-Love Ritual

Today is the sacred day of Aphrodite, Greek goddess of love and beauty. Celebrate your own beauty with self-love and with the freedom and energy of a sacred dance. For tens of thousands of years and across many cultures, dance has been a way to energize, to heal, and to commune with the spirits. Try a dance such as a sensual belly dance that honors your feminine essence. Play music that makes you feel sexy and primal. Dance barefoot. Express your sensuality in any way you wish, through your own unique movement. Don't worry about technique; just let your body express its mood. Feel your worries subside Let yourself feel energized as goddess energy pumps through your veins.

Emily Flak

Notes:

 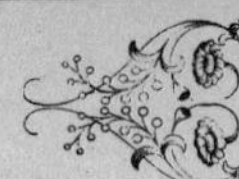   

February 7
Tuesday

2nd ♊

Color of the day: Red
Incense of the day: Evergreen

Home Protection Spell

The best protection for your home is to lock up when you are away. Lock the windows, the doors, and any other openings. When going away for the weekend on vacation, a protection spell works best if no one knows you are away except a trusted friend. Stop the mail, don't order things that may be delivered while you are gone, or have someone check for packages. Once the prep work is done, place a black stone such as onyx, jet, or smoky quartz under the doormat or near the door, and say:

> I ward this house
> By the power of Vesta.
> Those who would harm
> Will not enter.

Pieces of elder over the doorways and on windowsills give added protection.

Boudica

Notes:

February 8
Wednesday

2nd ♊
☽ → ♋ 11:33 am

Color of the day: Brown
Incense of the day: Coriander

Wish-Upon-A-Star Spell

The Chinese celebrate the Star Festival today. Begin this spell by taking a walk in the starlight tonight. First note the constellations that you recognize, then take in the entire sky, its vastness and beauty. Visualize the light that you see as a shower of creative energy raining down onto you. Return to your sacred space where you have set up 108 tea lights. That's a lot of candles, but worth going to the trouble—the number 108 is of great significance in sacred rituals all over the world. In numerology, its digits added become nine, the Goddess number, and 108 multiplied by 4 becomes 432, the number the ancients described as the cosmic cycle of time. As you light each of your 108 tea lights, quietly call out the name of the Goddess. Imagine that the energy you have drawn from the night-time stars, as well as the white beauty of the Goddess, is pulsing within you. After you have finished lighting the lights, take a breath. Now make a wish.

Lily Gardner-Butts

Notes:

Holiday lore: Today is the Buddhist Needle Memorial. On this day, as part of the principle of endless compassion espoused by the Buddhist faith for all sentient and nonsentient beings, all the sewing needles that have been retired during the year are honored. That is, needles are brought to the shrine and pushed into a slab of tofu that rests on the second tier of a three-tiered altar. Priests sing sutras to comfort the needles and heal their injured spirits.

February 9
Thursday

2nd ♋

Color of the day: White
Incense of the day: Geranium

Fox Power Spell

In February, the quiet darkness of a midwinter night can be shattered by the yelping of a fox searching for a mate. Foxes do not hibernate and this is their mating season. With grace and speed, foxes move through the shadows of the winter woodland. Their powers of cunning and agility have been invoked by shamans for centuries. To expand your powers of intelligence and energy, call upon Fox as a power animal. Since this is a Thursday before a Full Moon, it is a favorable time to call upon Spirit Fox. To do so, place a photo or artwork depicting a fox on your altar. Scent the room with a woodsy fragrance such as pine. Hold the image of a fox in your mind and say: "Swift as wind, quiet as night, Spirit Fox help me with my urgent need." Let the power of the Fox aid in bringing a swift solution to any problem.

James Kambos

Notes:

February 10
Friday

2nd ♋
☽ → ♌ 10:44 pm

Color of the day: Pink
Incense of the day: Sandalwood

   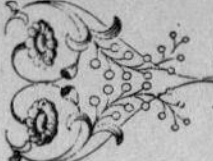 

Rosy Beauty Spell

The entire month of February is sacred to all goddesses of love and beauty. Beauty is not just a physical trait, but also is spiritual. The way of beauty sees every life as sacred and unique. Roses are the symbols of beauty and its ideals. Take time now to surround yourself with this flower. Burn rose incense, splash on rose water, anoint yourself with rose oil, or buy yourself a rose bouquet. Anytime you see life as dull or gray, think about the rose and repeat the following chant:

> May I walk the way of beauty.
> May I see the sacred all around.
> May I see beauty within.
> May I see beauty without.
>
> May I be blessed with roses,
> And walk the way of beauty always.

Olivia O'Meir

Notes:

February 11
Saturday

2nd ♌

Color of the day: Gray
Incense of the day: Juniper

Releasing Limitations Ritual

On a clean white sheet of paper, make a list of all the things you think are holding you back from obtaining all that you desire in this life. Then make a second list of reasons why these limitations exist in your life or why you have not yet released them. Take a good look at your lists and allow all the thoughts and emotions they evoke to come up. See these energies drain from you and flow into the paper. Place the paper in a fireproof container. As you light it on fire, say simply: "I release anything and everything that limits my joy, health, and success." Watch the paper burn and imagine the fire releasing and transforming these energies. Feel your spirit purified and transformed. Then flush the ashes down the toilet. As they spiral away, see and feel the limitations leave you for good.

Kristin Madden

Notes:

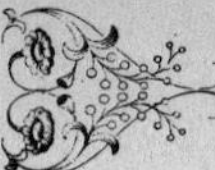

February 12
Sunday

2nd ♌

Full Moon 11:44 pm

Color of the day: Gold
Incense of the day: Poplar

Build Your Confidence Spell

Whether you are preparing for a job interview, or working up your courage to approach your favorite valentine, there are times that we all need a little added confidence. The Full Moon in Leo is the perfect time to embrace the vibrant self-assurance of this fiery Sun sign. On days like this, make getting yourself ready a ritual in itself. Set up a small altar beside your bathroom mirror, or on your dresser or vanity. Light an orange candle and take a few deep breaths before you begin. In the shower or bath, feel the water removing your fears and holding and supporting you. Know that you can accomplish your goal. See yourself dressing as the best side of yourself, the side that you want the world to see today. As you finish, sniff a bottle of bergamot essential oil and dab a bit of it over your ear. For added confidence, courage, and success in business, place a yellow/brown tiger's-eye in your pocket, or wear one on a pendant or in a pouch over your heart. As you notice yourself having moments of courage and confidence, place some of this energy back into the stone, so that you can draw on it later.

Lady MoonDance

Notes:

Holiday lore: Lincoln is called the Great Emancipator and is thought of as one of our great presidents. Know this, however: Lincoln was a rather unknown figure until the age of forty, when he first entered the Illinois state legislature. His later assassination threw the country into widespread mourning, inspiring Walt Whitman to write:

Coffin that passes
through lanes and street,
through day and night
with the great cloud
darkening the land . . .
I mourned, and yet shall
mourn with ever-
returning spring.

February 13
Monday

3rd ♌

☽ → ♍ 11:13 am

Color of the day: Gray
Incense of the day: Rose

Lupercalia Ritual

On this day, the Romans celebrated Lupercalia in honor of Faunus and Flora. Across the empire, young men dressed up in furs and capered in the streets, carrying handfuls of goatskin thongs with which they swatted other citizens. Because these figures represented male goats, their activities promoted fertility and plentiful sexual energy. In addition, young girls put their names into a lottery, and the boys would draw a name to choose their partner for the festival. Temporary girlfriends and boyfriends exchanged gifts such as candy and flowers. These rites provided a kind of healthy outlet for youthful exuberance and romance, without letting things get too serious or overwhelming. Lupercalia is the rowdier Pagan ancestor of Valentine's Day. Celebrate this time by holding a feast and serving some goat stew and lots of finger foods for couples to share. Trade stories with each other. What was your greatest endeavor in love, or what was your most awkward romantic moment?

Elizabeth Barrette

Notes:

February 14
Tuesday
Valentine's Day

3rd ♍

Color of the day: Black
Incense of the day: Sage

A Couples Spell

Life is hard on relationships. The demands of career, kids, and different work schedules all add up and often it's the relationship you treasure most that suffers. Ennui sets in, creating a distance between loving partners, and if you aren't careful you're soon taking each other for granted. Fight back with this fun spell, for which you will need some chocolate and something sparkling to drink, such as wine, carbonated water, or sparkling juice. Perhaps the two of you have a favorite chocolate dessert that you can make together. If not, buy some good chocolates that you both will enjoy. Pick a time when the two of you can be together and alone without interruption. Wear a little something you know your part-

 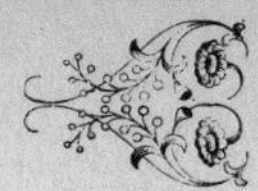   

ner enjoys seeing you in. Light some candles, and snuggle up together and feed each other chocolates. While doing so, be mindful of just how much you care for this other person, and how much you enjoy sharing your life with him or her.

Laurel Reufner

Notes:

February 15
Wednesday

3rd ♍

Color of the day: White
Incense of the day: Eucalyptus

Winter Blues Banishment

Winters can be long and spring can seem far away in February. Confined indoors by the cold and inhospitable weather, we can become depressed and lethargic. We neglect ourselves, and leave a dusty and cluttered household. Despite that it lifts the spirits to clean out all the physical and mental cobwebs, we still find it hard to do this basic task. To start, simply choose one room, preferably the room where you spend the most time. Burn some lavender incense. Smudge the corners of the room and yourself. Then open the blinds or drapes and call out: "Go, snow, go. Come, Sun, come!" Keep the incense burning, and with your broom walk deosil while sweeping the ceilings. Chant: "Sun and broom, sweep the room. Fill us with spring perfume." Continue cleaning from top to bottom. When the room is finished, take a deep breath and fill your lungs with the clean lavender scent. Envision your inner room as clean and full of spring's perfume.

Gail Wood

Notes:

February 16
Thursday

3rd ♍

☽ → ♎ 12:09 am

Color of the day: Purple
Incense of the day: Musk

Money Spell

To gather money for a property or a business you want to invest in,

  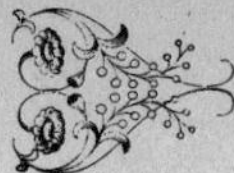 

take four stones and place them at each directional corner. Take silver coins and join them with these to form a square. Write what you want on a piece of paper and place it in the center. See yourself in this new opportunity. Trace coins with your finger, starting in the east, and say:

East by south,
My choice is made.
South by west,
My futures laid.

West by north,
Let fortune come.
North by east,
My will be done.

If you can, leave this altar up. Every time you go by it, envision yourself in your new home or life. This spell is in honor of Terminus—an old and important deity. His festival, the Terminalia, was held in February. Landowners laid sacrifices at the boundary stones of their property.

Nancy Bennett

Notes:

February 17

Friday

3rd ♎

Color of the day: Rose

Incense of the day: Ylang-ylang

Rose Quartz Love Spell

For healing frayed emotions, patching up after a tiff with a lover, or embarking on a journey within to find self-love, rose quartz is ideal due to its natural sympathetic nature when attuned with its owner's emotions. It assists in diffusing negative stimuli and unpleasant memories. Working on a subtle level, rose quartz stimulates love, self-acceptance, forgiveness, and a gentle appreciation of all things. Obtain a pair of small, smooth, rose quartz tumbled stones, and have them set in silver to wear as a pendant against your skin. Or, alternatively, you can use a heart-shaped rose quartz pendant. Rose quartz may also be placed around the home for enhancing loving energies. Compose and recite each day a concise and personal affirmative chant.

S. Y. Zenith

Notes:

 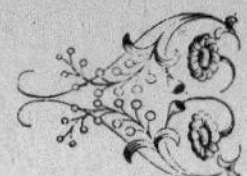  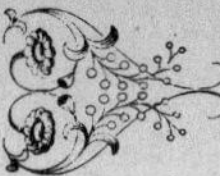 

February 18
Saturday

3rd ♎

☽ → ♏ 12:11 pm

☉ → ♓ 2:25 pm

Color of the day: Blue
Incense of the day: Pine

God and Goddess Purification Rite

This is the time of year to honor the Roman god Februus and the goddess Februa, spirits of February. These two are symbolic spirits of purification. We honor their spirit by cleansing the home and hearth. One of the better ways of doing this is using hyssop herb, frankincense, and myrrh. All have a lengthy history as purifying herbs. Heat your cauldron up on a stovetop or over an open fire, as you prefer. Add in a cup of fresh or one-half cup dried hyssop. When the cauldron bubbles, remove it from the heat. Cover, and steep the potion for twenty-five minutes. Strain, cool for ten minutes, and add eight drops frankincense essential oil and four drops myrrh. Swirl the whole gently to mix. Dip your besom into the potion, and sweep your house from the front to back while saying the following incantation: "Peace this way flow. Negative energy go!" Afterward burn a peacefully scented incense to thank Februus and Februa for their divine inspiration and their cleansing energy.

Stephanie Rose Bird

Notes:

February 19
Sunday

3rd ♏

Color of the day: Amber
Incense of the day: Cinnamon

Minerva Honoring Spell

The Roman goddess of wisdom, arts and crafts, and medicine, Minerva, is honored on this day. This is an ideal time to ensure that the tools of our own craft are in good order. Most of us, in this busy and connected millennium, rely on computers to help us perform our jobs, to communicate with others, and pursue our various interests. In fact, it's difficult to imagine our lives without this technology. Because of the deep importance of computers, we need to take steps to protect our computer and keep the work area around it

cleansed. Place a clear quartz crystal near your computer to absorb negative energy and to protect you from stress. Clear quartz is known for its balancing and protective qualities. Dilute a few drops of eucalyptus or pine oil with water to wipe your keypad and areas around the screen. While emitting a pleasant smell, the oil solution cleanses and enhances mental clarity.

Emely Flak

Notes:

February 20

Monday

Presidents' Day (observed)

3rd ♏

☽ → ♐ 9:38 pm

Color of the day: Silver
Incense of the day: Frankincense

Veiled One Power Ritual

In Irish and Scottish folklore, the spirit of winter was personified as an ancient figure known as the Cailleach, or Hag. Her name means "Veiled One," and she is a mysterious figure indeed. As springtime approaches and retreats in cycles, the Cailleach is said to be using her wand to prevent the arrival of spring. Winter is her season of power, so she hopes to extend her reign as long as possible. Perform this ceremony to honor the Cailleach, Veiled One of Winter. Place a gray or purple cloth on your altar, and light a white candle. Make an offering of juniper, mistletoe, and club moss while saying:

Spirit of winter,
Season of the sleep of
death
And season of rebirth,
I call you, Veiled One,
Ancient One,
You who guards the
powers of the wilderness.

Honor to you, and rest
for three seasons,
Until your time of power
shall come again!

Sharynne NicMhacha

Notes:

February 21
Tuesday

3rd ♐

4th Quarter 2:17 am

Color of the day: White
Incense of the day: Musk

Honor the Ancestors Spell

Today ends the ancient Roman observance of Feralia, a festival that honored the dead. Romans believed family ghosts would not rest until they were given small gifts—seeds, a flower, or a bit of grain were common. To honor your ancestors, on your altar place one yellow candle and a small saucer. In front of the candle place a photo of the deceased. Also on hand have a pinch of salt, some grain, a small piece of bread, and some red wine. Light the candle and begin placing the other items in the saucer.

James Kambos

Notes:

February 22
Wednesday

4th ♐

Color of the day: Topaz
Incense of the day: Cedar

Honesty of our Fathers Spell

Today is George Washington's birthday, considered by many to be the father of the United States. Today, we give thanks to all of our fathers—our biological fathers, ancestral fathers, cultural fathers, and spiritual fathers. George Washington was reputed to be exceptionally honest. Today let us make a renewed commitment to honesty. If you have a picture of George Washington, such as on a coin or bill, or a picture of one of your ancestors, hold it over your heart, and say:

> O father of my soul, I
> thank you for your love,
> guidance, and wisdom.
> Guide me as I navigate
> through chaos. Show me
> how to be strong. Help
> me to be honest. Lead
> me to victory.

Resolve to be completely honest today.

Luci Sophia Zain

Notes:

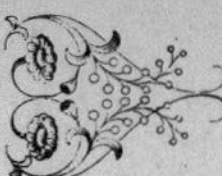

Holiday lore: We all know the lore about our first president—cherry tree, silver dollar, wooden teeth—but the truth behind this most legendary of American figures is sometimes more entertaining than the folklore. For instance, did you know that once, when young George went for a dip in the Rappahannock River, two Fredericksburg women stole his clothes? This story was recorded in the Spotsylvania County records. Picture then the young man scampering home flustered and naked, and the icon of the dollar bill becomes just a bit more real.

February 23
Thursday

4th ♐
☽ → ♑ 3:16 am

Color of the day: Turquoise
Incense of the day: Jasmine

Cash in Your Pocket Spell

Take out all of the cash in your wallet or all of the change in your pocket today. Set it on a table about a foot away from you. Rub a small amount of cedar or pine oil on your hands. Rub them quickly until you feel your hands warm up. Then say to yourself or chant:

> **Money, money, come to me.**
> **Riches and wealth,**
> **Increase by three times**
> **three times three.**

Count your money three times by pulling each bill or coin closer to you as you count it. Continue your chant as you count. When you are done, fold the bills toward you and return them to your wallet or pull the coins in to you before returning them to your pocket. Repeat this spell every three or nine days until you have what you want.

Kristin Madden

Notes:

February 24
Friday

4th ♑

Color of the day: Coral
Incense of the day: Nutmeg

Less Stress in Business Spell

As we work in a business, we interact with many different types of people and we may find relationships strained. There can be many reasons, ranging from personal

issues to business issues. Stress can be caused by overwork, poor business, irritating customers, product failures, or a combination of many issues. A piece of sodalite that you charge and carry in your pocket will serve as a reminder that we all can get stressed out from time to time, for whatever reason. Keep it in your pocket, and the stone is always there to remind you. Charge the stone occasionally by rubbing some calming lavender oil on the stone and place it in the moonlight, as a reminder that this is a reflection piece. The stone should cause you to pause, take a moment to calm down, and reflect on how we affect others with our moods, just as others affect us.

Boudica

Notes:

February 25

Saturday

4th ♑

☽ → ♒ 5:14 am

Color of the day: Indigo
Incense of the day: Lavender

Connection Mask Spell

Choose a deity or element you wish to honor and connect with today. You can make a mask to hang on a wall or place on an altar. Buy a bit of patterned fabric and an embroidery hoop. Loosen the hoop by turning the screw. Place the fabric within the two hoops. Tighten the hoop back up and pull the fabric tight. Decorate the fabric with anything that represents the deity or element you wish to connect with. Some items you can use include beads, ribbons, fabric paint, decals, thread, sequins, and natural items such as shells, feathers, bark, pine cones, and so on. Place some ribbon around the hoop screw and hang the mask up where you can see it. Put a candle in front and burn it. Use it to meditate daily on your deity or element.

Olivia O'Meir

Notes:

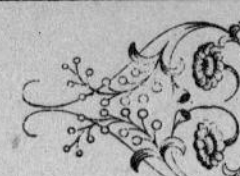

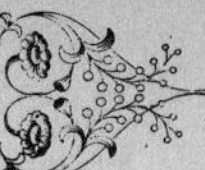

February 26
Sunday

4th ♒

Color of the day: Orange

Incense of the day: Peony

Compassion Meditation

To soften emotions and promote understanding of others on this day at the end of the shortest month of winter, take a piece of dry tree bark, break it into small pieces, and place them in a burning bowl. Next, write some harsh judgments you have made about yourself or others on small pieces of newspaper and tuck the paper around and under the tree bark. Be specific with what you write. Burn the paper and bark down to the ashes as you envision all of your harsh judgments, both present and future, transforming to ash. On top of the cooled ashes, light some myrrh incense to help promote compassion and openness to others. While the incense is burning, breathe deeply and feel your heart opening to more tender feelings. After the incense has burned away, take all of the ashes and place them in a small flowerpot filled with earth. On a windy day, put the dirt and ashes outdoors to be scattered and purified by the four winds.

Gail Wood

Notes:

February 27
Monday

4th ♒

☽ → ♓ 4:56 am

New Moon 7:31 pm

Color of the day: Ivory

Incense of the day: Gardenia

Wash Away Judgment Ritual

Pisces is the water sign of the compassionate and creative, the humanitarian who has opened his or her heart to befriend humanity and to feel empathy. Embrace this energy by looking at people around you in a new way—not just by placing yourself in their place, but by seeing them in you. Make a new beginning by looking at an old friend or enemy. Ask yourself what irritates you the most about them. Why does it bother you? Ask yourself if this trait or characteristic is not something that you work very hard not to do

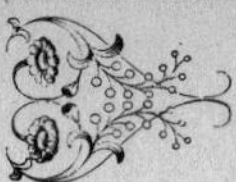

yourself? Is it something you do yourself and then deny; only allowing yourself to recognize it in others? Have you ever been where they are? See if you can let go of assumptions about how they got where they are or why they do what they do. If you feel that you can, ask them to tell you a story about their past and why they do a certain thing or are the way they are. Make a promise to yourself to listen with an open mind and compassionate heart. See yourself as human, and promise you will let the imperfect person in you see them as human too. Would you like to be judged as critically as you have been judging them? How would the world be different if you put the energy that you would use judging them into improving your own life and improving the world around you?

Lady MoonDance

Notes:

February 28

Tuesday

Mardi Gras

1st ♓

Color of the day: Scarlet
Incense of the day: Maple

Cure an Illness Spell

The epic poem, Kalevala, is celebrated by the Finns this day with parades and readings from the poem. The Kalevala recounts a battle of wits between three wizard brothers and the witch goddess, Louhi. It is a treasure trove of ancient shamanistic practices including the following healing spell. For this ritual, stand in the east and call in the element of air. Ask in all humility for assistance. Light a blue candle and a stick of sandalwood incense as an offering to the element. Now say:

> Sickness,
> Vanish into the sky!
> Pain, fly up into the air.
> Burning vapor,
> Rise up into the air!
> So that the wind may
> take thee away.
> So that the storm may
> chase thee to far places.
> Where neither Sun nor
> Moon gives light.
> Where no hot wind
> burns the flesh.

   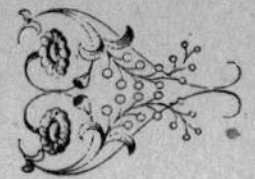 

Thank the element of air, and let the candle burn down. As with all magic, in addition to this spell, it is essential that you have done everything possible in the physical realm to aid the healing.

Lily Gardner-Butts

Notes:

March is the third month of the Gregorian calendar, and it was the first month of the Roman calendar. The month is named for the Roman god of agriculture and war, Mars. Its astrological sign is Pisces, the fish (February 18–March 20), a mutable water sign ruled by Neptune. March is a month of transition between winter and spring. Daffodils begin to brighten the early garden. The sap rises, and robins return. In the hardware stores, shelves are stocked with garden tools and packages of flower and vegetable seeds. Still, late-season snowstorms are not unusual in March. Ostara, the main holiday of the month, celebrates the lengthening hours of daylight and the awakening of the Goddess. Eggs, whether dyed or intricately decorated, are popular seasonal symbols of life and fertility. St. Patrick's Day, March 17, is rich with Pagan symbolism. For example, the shamrock was once used to depict the three aspects of the Goddess. Sunny, breezy days encourage kite-flying, another seasonal activity. Kites are magical because they soar toward the realm of spirit. The ancients used the March wind to carry their wishes to the divine. The winds of March bring the promise of a new season and a fresh start. March's Full Moon was called the Storm Moon, and it remains a potent time to work magic for change and renewal.

March 1

Wednesday

Ash Wednesday

1st ♓

☽ → ♈ 4:18 am

Color of the day: Brown
Incense of the day: Cedar

Gender Balance Ritual

March is Gender Equality Month. Throughout history, the war between the sexes has created a lot of casualties. Although some of the worst inequities have been addressed, domestic violence and sexual assault still haunt our society. Women often bump into a "glass ceiling" at work. Men often have trouble keeping custody of their children in a divorce. We all pay the price. In Paganism, we explicitly acknowledge the duality of nature and honor the balance between the divine feminine and the divine masculine. It's our responsibility to manifest that ideal in our own lives. Here is a prayer to help:

> Let each of us see
> Ourselves in the other,
> And the holy in the
> whole.
>
> Let us honor women's
> strength
> And men's compassion
> And children's promise.
>
> Let us build a world
> where gender
> Exists not as a barrier
> But as a bridge.

Elizabeth Barrette

Notes:

Holiday lore: On March 1, Roman matrons held a festival known as Matronalia in honor of Juno Lucina, an aspect of the goddess Juno associated with light and childbirth. Some records indicated that her name was derived from a grove on the Esquiline Hill where a temple was dedicated to her in 375 BC. Whenever a baby entered the world in Roman times, it was believed that the infant was "brought to light." Women who worshipped Juno Lucina untied knots and unbraided their hair to release any entanglements that might block safe delivery.

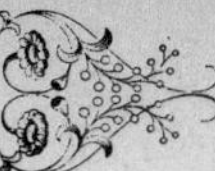

March 2
Thursday

1st ♈︎

Color of the day: White
Incense of the day: Jasmine

Right Your Debts Spell

This is a spell to make right any debts you have incurred. Place your bills and promissary notes on a table. Write the amounts on a small chalkboard and place it on top of the papers. Light four green candles around them. Say:

> By one month's end
> grant me the funds
> to see my debts come all undone.
> If not in total, at least in place
> The power to make
> these debts erased.

Take some salted water and wipe the debts from your chalkboard one by one. Imagine the relief of being debt free and your creditors happy with you. This spell honors the festival of atonement to Zeus Meilichios, a pre-Olympian form of Zeus who oft demanded propitiating. He took the form of a great serpent and was offered cakes in the shapes of animals this day. The wealthy also offered animals; the poor, incense. What will you offer?

Nancy Bennett

Notes:

March 3
Friday

1st ♈︎
☽ → ♉︎ 5:22 am

Color of the day: Pink
Incense of the day: Ginger

Goddess Spell of Three

The third day of the third month is a powerful day with the magical energies of the number three. This year, this day falls on a Friday, the day dedicated to Venus, making it an especially auspicious day for feminine energy. Dedicate a short ritual today to your unique Goddess energy. On your altar, place three candles—one white to represent the maiden, one red to represent the mother, and one black to represent the crone—and form a triangle. Ask yourself: What do you have that sets you apart from others? Think about how you respond to situations and how diverse your talents and emotions are. Your blend

   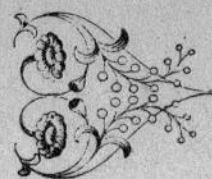 

of qualities is an outcome of your dark and light sides. Your Goddess make-up is a unique tapestry made up of several archetypes arranged in varying quantities and combinations. Dare to be different, because you are! Celebrate that unique combination that is you!

Emely Flak

Notes:

March 4
Saturday

1st ♉

Color of the day: Gray
Incense of the day: Patchouli

Sacred Hare Spell

The hare was a sacred animal in many cultures. It was both feared and venerated due to its nocturnal activities and its ability to "disappear" into the landscape. For these reasons, in later times the hare became associated with Witches. In March, when hares breed, their behavior becomes unpredictable. They appear in the daytime and in the moonlight, and their actions are erratic—hence the expression "mad as a March hare." Witches were said to be able to turn themselves into hares by reciting a certain charm. We can honor the hare now by learning to adopt its form spiritually and to learn its power and wisdom. Here is a modern revision of a Scottish Witch charm to use in a meditative journey. Repeat it three times:

> I shall go intill a hare
> With loyalty and honor
> there.
> I go in the name of the
> Old Ways
> Ay while I come home
> again.

Sharynne NicMhacha

Notes:

March 5
Sunday

1st ♉
☽ → ♊ 9:37 am

Color of the day: Gold
Incense of the day: Parsley

 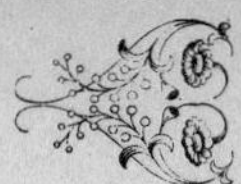  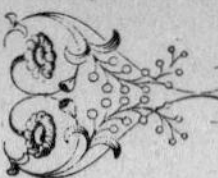 

Praise Isis Spell

To the ancient Greeks and Romans, Isis was queen of the stars, the seas, and sailing. This day was set aside to honor her because it was when the seas would begin to calm, and the sailing season would begin again. Keeping this in mind, let this be a day to celebrate the loosening of winter's grip. Place cut flowers around the home, light pastel candles, and place small mirrors nearby to reflect the candle flames. As you gaze at the flames, visualize winter's gloom being released and reflected from the mirrors. If you can get outdoors, place a small bouquet of flowers into a body of water as a gift to Isis. At night run a luxurious bath with your favorite oils, and bathe in the light of a vanilla-scented candle. As you bathe, say: "Isis, queen of sky and sea, let your spirit reside in me."

James Kambos

Notes:

March 6
Monday

1st ♊
2nd Quarter 3:16 pm

Color of the day: White
Incense of the day: Lilac

Isis Crystal Ball Divination

Today is a day of Isis, Moon mother and mother of the sea. Use her symbols respectfully to pay tribute to her and to conjure her spirit. Draw a bath. Add a half cup each of Epsom salt, coarse and fine Dead Sea salt. Wear on a piece of moonstone on a ring, necklace, anklet, or bracelet. Light a blue candle, and place it on a fireproof container near the bathtub. Bring a crystal ball with you into the bath. Gaze at the candle as you breathe deeply and very slowly until you are very relaxed. Realize that you are bathing in the incense of Isis. Call her name quietly and deliberately, drawing it out like a snake's hiss: "I-sis, I-sis, I-sis." Breathe in, and with the exhale whisper "I-sis" for about five minutes. Lift up the crystal ball once you feel the spirit of Isis with you in the room. Hold the ball in front of the candle flame and gaze for a few minutes. See what is in store as you divine by scrying both fire and crystal.

Stephanie Rose Bird

 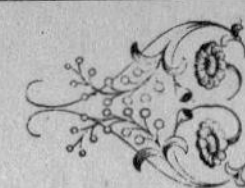  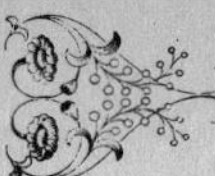 

Notes:

March 7
Tuesday

2nd ♊
☽ → ♋ 7:32 pm

Color of the day: Red
Incense of the day: Poplar

Energy and Protection Spell

For energy and protection, gather some sea salt and red chili powder. Set up sacred space in your usual manner and invite the spirits of the place to join you. Have a bowl of warm water on your altar and burn cedar incense. Add the sea salt and chili powder to the water. Stir it three times while asking the spirits to bless you and your home with renewed energy to create an honorable life and protection against any unwanted energies, thoughts, or foreign beings. Starting in the east, go around your home, sprinkling a small amount of water in each room. If possible, sprinkle a small amount of water around the outside of your home or at least around the front door.

Kristin Madden

Notes:

Holiday lore: Although the month of June is named for Juno, principal goddess of the Roman pantheon, major festivals dedicated to her are scattered throughout the year. For instance, today marks Junoalia, a festival in honor of Juno celebrated in solemnity by matrons. Two images of Juno made of cypress were borne in a procession of twenty-seven girls dressed in long robes, singing a hymn to the goddess composed by the poet Livius. Along the way, the procession would dance in the great field of Rome before proceeding ahead to the temple of Juno.

March 8
Wednesday

2nd ♊
Color of the day: Yellow
Incense of the day: Pine

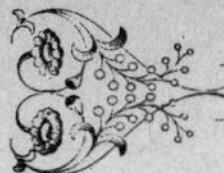

Key Ring of Protection

Let yourself dance to music as you weave today's spell. Pick a tune to suit your mood. Arrange to have it play over and over. As it plays, dance. Dance with your body, but dance also with your mind and heart, and soul. Dance until you feel as one with the music. Gradually, instead of being led by the music and just following along, begin to consciously weave a dancing spell of your own devising. Many legends tell of the gods dancing the world into creation. You can dance something into creation. Dance for love. Dance for prosperity. Dance for healing. Dance as you are led to dance, but dance proactively not just reactively. When your dance is complete, stop and place your hands on the floor to thank it for giving support for your dance.

Luci Sophia Zain

Notes:

Holiday lore: While most holidays across the world celebrate the lives and achievement of men, this is one day wholly dedicated to the achievement and work of women. Originally inspired by a pair of mid-nineteenth-century ladies' garment workers strikes, today the holiday is little known in its country of origin; though this day's legacy is clear in March's designation by the U.S. Congress as Women's History Month. Throughout the month, women's groups in American towns hold celebrations and events, concerts, exhibitions, and rituals that recall heroic and gifted women of every stripe.

March 9
Thursday

2nd ♋

Color of the day: Green
Incense of the day: Sandalwood

Flowing Money Spell

To bring yourself a flowing source of money, take a coin of silver or a silvery metal and toss it into a flowing body of water, such as a river or a stream. Reinforce this spell with a visualization of the coin floating away with the moving water, and in return visualize that dollar bills, in denominations of 10s, 20s, and 100s, are coming back toward you on the water's surface. Softly chant "abundance" as you work this visualization.

Boudica

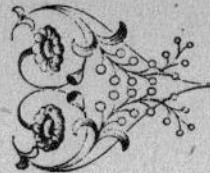

Notes:

March 10
Friday

2nd ♋
☽ → ♌ 4:42 am

Color of the day: Purple
Incense of the day: Rose

Personal Freedom Spell

Today is Harriet Tubman's birthday. She was born in slavery and escaped to freedom, then she helped others to freedom. She reminds us that no matter the circumstances of our birth we can find freedom through our own strength and determination. To find personal freedom, gather together a key and a rock. Hold the rock in your throwing hand. Lift it up and think hard of all the things that enslave you. Take the rock outside and throw it away from you, being careful that it does not land on or near your property. Turn around and walk away from it without looking back. Next, hold the key in your receptive hand. Lift it up and project into it of all the things you will do now that you are free. Hold the key close to your heart and breathe in that freedom energy. Place this key to freedom on your altar.

Gail Wood

Notes:

March 11
Saturday

2nd ♌

Color of the day: Brown
Incense of the day: Lilac

Neutralize Nasty Influences Spell

For revitalizing drained energies or deflecting any nasty negativity directed toward you, select nine smoky tumbled quartz stones to add to a cleansing bath. Place the smoky quartz in the bathtub along with some Epsom salts or bath oil. Scrub from head to foot while visualizing yourself being purified from all malefic influences, known and unknown. Before stepping out of the bath, take a quick full body dip, then stand up, letting the bathwater drip off your

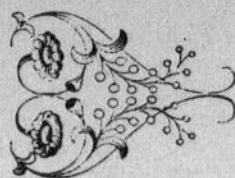

body for a few minutes before reaching for the towel. Put on some fresh clothing, and apply your favorite scent. Remove the smoky quartz crystals from the bathtub and let them dry in sunlight or moonlight. This particular crystal also has an ability to passively facilitate positive changes at a slow but steadfast level.

S. Y. Zenith

Notes:

March 12
Sunday

2nd ♌

☽ → ♍ 5:23 pm

Color of the day: Yellow
Incense of the day: Cinnamon

Reawakening to Nature's Beauty Ritual

As winter gives way to spring, we become more outwardly focused. This spell should be done outdoors on a clear day. Set up an altar to the four elements, using candles, incense, and natural items. Start at the east, with air, and say: "Spirit of air, who tickles our senses with sweet breeze, open my mind to the beauty of the earth." Turn to the south, and fire, saying: "Spirit of fire, who raises our senses with scorching flame, open my desire to the earth." Face the west, and water, and say: "Spirit of water, who soothes our senses with moist coolness, open my soul to the beauty of the earth." Finally, turn to the north, and earth, and say: "Spirit of earth, who heals us with mountainous compassion, open my body to the beauty of the earth." Meditate for a while and enjoy the environment around you. When you feel refreshed, put out the candles.

Olivia O'Meir

Notes:

March 13
Monday

2nd ♍

Color of the day: Silver
Incense of the day: Chrysanthemum

Seed Bead Fertility Charm

This spell makes use of the humble, yet aptly named, seed bead.

   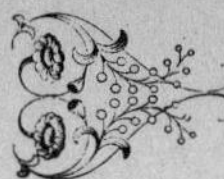 

You will need red, green, and brown seed beads. You will also need beading thread and needle. In your ritual space, rinse the beads and then pat them dry. You may need to let them rest for a moment or two to finish drying. After the beads have dried, begin stringing them on to the thread. This is meant to be a necklace with no obvious end, so make sure it is long enough to fit over your head. When you have finished stringing, tie it off and place the coiled necklace in a bowl of sand. Beach sand that still has little bits of shell in it would be ideal. Smudge the necklace with a fertility-type incense, and your charm is ready to wear.

Laurel Reufner

Notes:

March 14

Tuesday

Purim

2nd ♍

Full Moon 6:35 pm

Color of the day: Black

Incense of the day: Juniper

Pagan origins of Purim Ritual

Generally occurring on the Full Moon in March, Purim may have descended from the same origins as Ostara. On this day, Jews are required to read the story of Queen Esther, the Persian name given to a woman named Hadassah. "Esther" may be etymologically related to the goddess names Isthar, Astarte, and Ostare, after which Ostara and Easter are named. Some scholars also believe that Purim may have evolved from a Full Moon spring festival held during the Babylonian New Year, the land of the Jews' exile when the story of Purim begins. The story: A Babylonian ruler, Haman, was an arrogant man who required everyone to bow before him. Esther's uncle, Mordecai, refused because his beliefs forbade him to bow before anyone but God. In his rage, Haman convinced King Ahasuerus to issue an edict to destroy the Jews as a "strange" people with different customs. Esther, the king's new wife and secretly a Jew, invited him to a banquet. After preparing herself spiritually, she revealed herself to him there. The king refused to revoke the edict, but allowed the Jews to fight back so that they easily won. On this day, Jews celebrate because Esther was able to save her people by revealing the truth of her own heritage, even though it might have meant her own death. This is an important lesson for Witches of all faiths, as she also took the time to prepare herself while planning the right moment to speak, thereby choosing her battle rather than letting it choose her.

Lady MoonDance

Notes:

March 15
Wednesday

3rd ♍
☽ → ♎ 6:12 am

Color of the day: White
Incense of the day: Neroli

Anna Perenna Ritual

Shakespeare made famous this ancient Roman date—the Ides of March. At this time of the year the Romans celebrated the festival of Anna Perenna, Roman goddess of the New Year. From her name, we derive the words "annual" and "perennial." In ancient Rome, the meaning of New Year was twofold. It was a review of the year just passed and a time to plan for the year ahead. To harness today's energies from Anna Perenna's festival, identify one thing you would like to bring into your life. This could be a hobby, a new job, or more friends. Write your goal on a piece of paper, along with these words:

> This is what I wish to sow
> With this seed, my goal
> will grow.

Bury it with a seed to nurture the growth of your intention.

Emely Flak

Notes:

Holiday lore: Why is March 15 so notorious? On this date in 226 BC, an earthquake brought the Colossus of Rhodes—one of the Seven Wonders of the Ancient World—to its knees. But a more famous event likely accounts for the notoriety of the "Ides of March." Julius Caesar's rule, somewhere along the way, became tyrannical. In February of 44 BC, Caesar had himself named Dictator Perpetuus—Dictator for Life. Brutus assassinated him on March 15, 44 BC. Caesar's murder was foretold by soothsayers and even by his wife, Calpurnia, who had a nightmare in which Caesar was being butchered like an animal. Caesar chose to ignore these portents and the rest, of course, is history.

March 16
Thursday

3rd ♎

Color of the day: Purple
Incense of the day: Carnation

March Sowing Blessing

In Ireland and Scotland, the word for March (Mairt, Marta) came to mean "the appropriate time to perform agricultural work." Sowing was a magical act performed in a very ritualized manner. Here is a traditional Scottish sowing blessing you can use for planting seeds in the earth or in a spring ceremony for magical growth:

I go out to sow the seed
In the name of the gods
who give it growth.
I will put my face toward
the wind
And throw a goodly
handful on high.
The dew will come down
to welcome the seeds,
And every one will take root.
The power of the gods be
upon
Every thing that is in my
ground.

Sharynne NicMhacha

Notes:

March 17
Friday
St. Patrick's Day

3rd ♎
☽ → ♏ 5:59 pm

Color of the day: Coral
Incense of the day: Dill

Shamrock and Hazel Tree Lore

Two of the most common symbols associated with St. Patrick, the shamrock and hazel wood, have ancient links to magic. The three-leafed clover known as the shamrock was used by St. Patrick to teach the meaning of the Holy Trinity to the Celts. But it has even older associations with magic. It symbolized the Spring Equinox to the Druids, and the Celts used it in spring and summer magic. It also represents the Triple Goddess aspect. As for the hazel, this wood is thought to have been used for the magic rod, which aided St. Patrick in driving the snakes out of Ireland. Since this St. Patrick's Day falls on a Friday, try adding crushed hazel nuts to a love or fertility charm. It should yield powerful results.

James Kambos

Notes:

   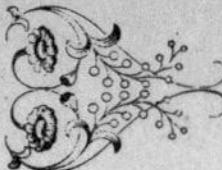 

Holiday lore: Much folklore surrounds St. Patrick's Day. Though originally a Catholic holy day, St. Patrick's Day has evolved into more of a secular holiday today. One traditional icon of the day is the shamrock. This stems from an Irish tale that tells how Patrick used the three-leafed shamrock to explain the Trinity of Christian dogma. His followers adopted the custom of wearing a shamrock on his feast day; though why we wear green on this day is less clear. St. Patrick's Day came to America in 1737, the date of the first public celebration of the holiday in Boston.

March 18
Saturday

3rd ♏

Color of the day: Blue

Incense of the day: Pine

Spring-Cleaning Spell

Make today a time for spring-cleaning, in your home and in your life. Before beginning, draw a rough outline of your home. Assign a part of your self or your life to each room. For example, your living room may be your social life, your bedroom your love life or private life, and so on. Remember to include those junk rooms or drawers. As you clean each room, visualize yourself cleansing and eliminating all the aspects of that part of you that no longer serve you. Be sure to clear out the cobwebs in the corners and other hidden places, like the junk drawer. Before moving on to the next room, stand in the center of the newly cleaned room and imagine it full of light. Feel the light transform the energy of the room and that particular part of your life. Be aware of any insights or messages you receive during the process.

Kristin Madden

Notes:

March 19
Sunday

3rd ♏

Color of the day: Orange

Incense of the day: Sage

Osayin Tea Party Ritual

Today is an excellent day to invoke the spirit of the orisha Osanyin. This is customary during this time in Africa. The story of Osanyin is telling. Osayin tried to hide all the herbal knowledge he possessed inside a gourd hung high in a tree so the other orisha

wouldn't be able to use it. The gourd fell, teaching us that herbal knowledge is not to be rarified but rather shared by all. Today, have an herbal tea party for your coven, friends, or family. Share some powerful healing herbal teas, choosing nature's best healers: peppermint, chamomile, rose hips, green tea, or rooibos. Boil a kettle of water over an open fire, if possible. Set out some nice earthenware cups, and pour a bit of water into each of the cups to heat it. Pour the water out, and add tea bags to each cup. Pour the water over the herbs. Shake a gourd rattle over your guest's heads as you sing praise to each person:

> I give you tea in good health.
> Blessings.
> Herbal knowledge is free.
> Blessings.
> Praise Osayin.
> Blessings.
> Praise Mother Earth.
> Blessings!

Sweeten the tea with honey if desired, and enjoy the fellowship of your circle.

Stephanie Rose Bird

Notes:

March 20

Monday

Ostara – Spring Equinox – International Astrology Day

3rd ♏
☽ → ♐ 3:43 am
☉ → ♈ 1:25 pm

Color of the day: Lavender
Incense of the day: Myrrh

Ostara Spell

Ostara, otherwise known as the Vernal Equinox, marks the date when day overcomes night. Plants re-emerge from the earth, the air is filled with birdsong, and animals mate and bear young. Humans feel an overpowering urge to build now, to plant and to fall in love. This powerful time is when winter dreams need to be acted upon. The most potent talisman we have this time of the year is the egg, symbol of rebirth, new beginnings, and growth. Here are some old and new ways to use eggs in your spellwork. For a new love, take a raw egg and dye it red. Poke holes on either end of the egg with a needle or a small nail. Make the hole on the small end of the egg large enough so that you can insert a crystal and herbs. Blow the contents of the egg out the holes and thoroughly clean out the inside. Insert into the egg a the small rose quartz

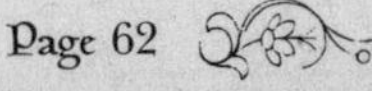

 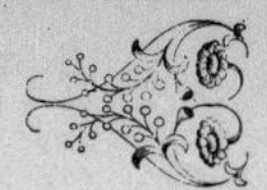  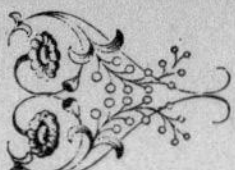 

crystal, rose petals, and a sprinkle of catnip. Visualize a new love entering your life. Glue over the hole with pink tissue paper. You can modify this spell for abundance or any new venture with a change of color, crystal, and herb. To keep a family together, the eldest member of the clan divides a hard-boiled egg so that each member gets a piece to eat. Throughout one's life, if any member of the family gets lost one must think about those he or she shared the egg with. This will cause the others to think of him or her. The combined physic energies will guide the lost one home. To ensure the safety and well-being of your household, bury a magically charged egg in each of the four directions. Charge an egg with visions of an abundant harvest and bury it in your garden before you plant. Hang decorated eggs from the trees around your property on Ostara to bring prosperity to your family for the year.

Lily Gardner-Butts

Notes:

March 21
Tuesday

3rd ♐

Color of the day: Gray

Incense of the day: Honeysuckle

Irish End of Day Ritual

Every day when you arrive home, start a daily ritual by leaving your work shoes at the door. As you take off your shoes, think about "taking off" all your work issues and problems along with your shoes, and leaving them at the door. This will allow you to leave any negativity that you may have brought home with you at the door and not into your home or family life. This will increase your personal energy as you focus on happy evenings at home with your family and friends.

Boudica

Notes:

 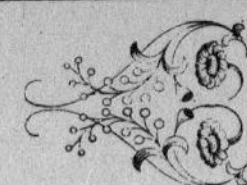  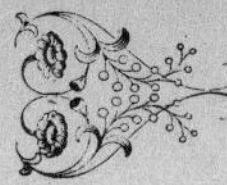 

March 22
Wednesday

3rd ♐

☽ → ♑ 10:36 am

4th Quarter 2:10 pm

Color of the day: Topaz
Incense of the day: Coriander

Travel Flow Spell

When traveling for business, pay attention to the flow of energy. You go and return; you exchange power with other people. It's all about building connections. This spell enhances positive energy flow. For it, you will need a pair of candles—one representing yourself and the other representing whomever you're going to meet—some gold yarn, and a lighter. First, name the candles for yourself and your business partner. Set them up and wrap the yarn around their bases in a figure-eight pattern. Light the candles. Now say:

> Golden thread and golden light,
> Spin a trail of truth and right.
> As we follow, let us see
> All the worth in you and me.
> As the shadows softly fall,
> Let this trip bring good for all.

Meditate for a while on your trip's purpose, then blow out the candles. Carry the string with you when you travel.

Elizabeth Barrette

Notes:

Holiday lore: Cybele was the Great Mother of the gods in Ida, and she was taken to Rome from Phrygia in 204 BC. She was also considered the Great Mother of all Asia Minor. Her festivals were known as *ludi*, or "games," and were solemnized with various mysterious rites. Along with Hecate and Demeter of Eleusis, Cybele was one of the leading deities of Rome when mystery cults were at their prime. Hila'aria, or "Hilaria," originally seemed to have been a name given to any day or season of rejoicing that was either private or public. Such days were devoted to general rejoicing and people were not allowed to show signs of grief or sorrow. The Hilaria actually falls on March 25 and is the last day of a festival of Cybele that commences today. However, the Hilaria was not mentioned in the Roman calendar or in Ovid's *Fasti*.

March 23
Thursday

4th ♑

Color of the day: Crimson
Incense of the day: Evergreen

Give Me Liberty Spell

Today is the anniversary of U.S. patriot Patrick Henry's famous "Give me liberty or give me death" speech. Where in your life do you need liberty? Set out a red candle and a pair of scissors. Light your candle, and pass the scissors through the candle's flame. Visualize yourself surrounded by colored strings of energy. Examine the strings closely, noting which strings seem positive and which seem negative. Say: "I cut the strings of all that keeps me imprisoned." Cut any strings that seem unhealthy or negative, leaving any that are healthy or positive. After cutting, run your fingers around your body to "finger comb" and "fluff" your aura. Shake yourself like a dog shaking off water. Take a broom and sweep the floor, saying: "I sweep away the remains of all that kept me from true liberty."

Luci Sophia Zain

Notes:

March 24
Friday

4th ♑
☽ → ♒ 2:21 pm

Color of the day: White
Incense of the day: Almond

Eyes of Love Spell

To turn the eyes of love of a mate who is looking at others or cheating on you, find a picture of the person who has caught your loved one's attention. Or, if this is impossible, write the name on a piece of flower-shaped paper. Place the photo or paper in a shallow bowl and stir it clockwise, saying:

> Gather you flowers while
> you may.
> Time brings only sorrow.
> For the flowers of the day,
> Will just be weeds
> tomorrow.

Place the paper or picture in with your compost or weed pile. Soon your partner's fascination with this new bloom will end, and its true rotten nature will be revealed. This day marks the festival of Eostre, a Teutonic lunar and fertility goddess. Her totem symbols were the hare and eggs. Hard-boil two eggs and then color them red. Eat them with someone you wish to associate with.

Nancy Bennett

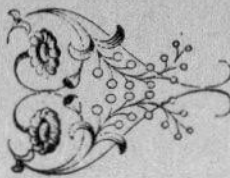

Notes:

face every time you hear the music of the Winds of Change.

Laurel Reufner

Notes:

March 25

Saturday

4th ♒

Color of the day: Indigo

Incense of the day: Lavender

Winds of Change Ritual

Chase out ennui and the remnants of winter's cooped-up energy with this tuneful spell. To perform the "Winds of Change" you will need a good set of wind chimes. They needn't be expensive, but make sure you enjoy the sound they make when they jingle in the wind. Also, try to buy chimes with hollow tubes. You're generating better energy and luck that way. Charge the chimes by forcing out stale, negative energy and raising up positive, happy energy everytime the wind blows through them. Then hang them outside somewhere where they will catch the wind on a regular basis. In no time at all you'll have a smile on your

March 26

Sunday

4th ♒

☽ → ♓ 3:33 pm

Color of the day: Amber

Incense of the day: Basil

Orange Carnelian Spell

When feeing uneasy at work, at home or about attending occasions you're not keen to attend, carry or wear a piece of orange carnelian. Cleanse the stone with spring water, lay it on the altar, and light an incense stick and votive candle. Sit comfortably and meditate with your eyes closed for half an hour. Open your eyes and then direct healthy and positive thoughts to the carnelian, requesting its assistance to get you out of ruts—whether physical, mental,

   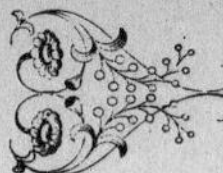 

or emotional. When ready, pick up the stone and use it right away. With its stimulating vibrations, carnelian also helps improve motivation for those prone to lethargy. Those who meditate regularly will find this stone grounding as it clears the mind of extraneous thoughts, thus enhancing healthy progress. At the same time, orange carnelian possesses a subtle guiding force that strengthens the ability to be unfazed by life's challenges.

S. Y. Zenith

Notes:

March 27
Monday

4th ♓

Color of the day: Ivory
Incense of the day: Daffodil

Throwing Troubles to the Wind Spell

Use the freeing powers of air to remove any obstacles in your path. You only need three things for this spell: a banishing herb, a windy spot, and a real desire to banish the obstacle. Gather a herb that represents what you want to banish. Garlic, rosemary, vervain, and sandalwood will all work well. Next, find a quiet, private, and somewhat windy spot. Place a pile of the herb in your cupped hands, and say:

> This herb symbolizes all
> that blocks me. I throw
> it to the winds. Take it
> far from me, with harm
> to none, so mote it be!

Feel your own desire to banish your obstacle grow. Once the desire becomes strong, throw the herb into the winds. Take a few deep breaths and think of the blessings that will take the place of the block you've banished. When you are ready, turn and walk away—refreshed and ready to start your new path.

Olivia O'Meir

Notes:

   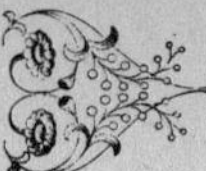 

March 28
Tuesday

4th ♓
☽ → ♈ 3:31 pm

Color of the day: White
Incense of the day: Musk

Mystic Vision Spell

Sometimes we lose the heart and soul of our magical selves in the midst of the living our daily lives. To regain a magical life, find a quiet time and space. Create beauty, peace, and pleasure in this space, surrounding yourself with images of stars, moons, and other magical symbols. Use frankincense scent for psychic development, and light a purple candle. Breathe deeply and fall into a meditative state, then say:

> Come, spirits, and join
> your mystery with mine.
> Show me the road and
> show me a sign.
> I seek the road to mystery
> divine.

Continue breathing deeply and watch the visions that unfold before you. When all is revealed to you, thank the spirits for their wisdom.

Gail Wood

Notes:

March 29
Wednesday

4th ♈
New Moon 5:15 am

Color of the day: Yellow
Incense of the day: Sandalwood

Start Something Now Spell

The New Moon in Aries, the first sign of the zodiac, means a new beginning in the home of new beginnings. This time is good for new ideas and getting things started, though Aries isn't always good on the follow-through. Ruled by Mars, Aries has a lot of straightforward, restless, and aggressive energy—best when channeled into simple projects that don't require patience or a long-term commitment. Now is the time to ask yourself what you have been putting off, and just do it. The energy now is all about what you can get done today. So pull out that mental list of tasks and projects that you have been dreading, and give your energy some direction. Write it down so you'll be able to find direction without thinking too much each time you finish a task. Light a red candle for Mars, and start with the shortest or easiest task, marking it off as you go. The inner Aries child will be glad to see how much you have done, and the more organized signs can tackle the rest later. When you are done work-

ing hard, remember to play hard with some hot, fast, and fiery fun. Just leave plenty of time to sleep hard as well.

Lady MoonDance

Notes:

March 30
Thursday

1st ♈
☽ → ♉ 3:31 pm

Color of the day: Turquoise
Incense of the day: Carnation

Shamrock Omen Ritual

The four-leafed clover, or shamrock (in Gaelic, *seamrag*), has long been considered a potent good-luck charm. It was also associated with good omens and blessings. Like other propitious plants, it was most powerful when found without searching or seeking. If you come across a four-leafed, or even better, five-leafed, clover you may ritually gather it and keep it as a powerful talisman for luck. To show the spirit of the plant that you are grateful for its power, repeat the following charm:

Thou shamrock of good
omens,
Thou shamrock of promise,
A bounty and blessing
thou art
At all times.

The seven joys are on thee,
Peerless one of the sun-
beams.

Joy of health.
Joy of friends.
Joy of cattle.
Joy of sheep.
Joy of sons,
And daughters fair.
Joy of peace,
And joy of the gods!

Sharynne NicMhacha

Notes:

March 31
Friday

1st ♐

Color of the day: Rose
Incense of the day: Thyme

Luna Sanctuary Spell

On this day, the ancient Romans celebrated the festival of Luna, virgin goddess of the Moon. This year the sacred day falls on a Friday, a day aligned with feminine energies and passion. Luna had a temple sanctuary that was believed to be located on Aventine Hill in Rome. Like Luna, you can create your own sanctuary. Set up an altar, even if it's only temporary. In a fast-paced lifestyle, your altar becomes your anchor. It's a place where you can relax and experience inner calm. It reminds you of your spiritual dimension and your relationship with the divine. Select altar items that are personal to you. These could be shells, affirmation cards, motivational quotations, special crystals, or photographs. Spend a few moments here each day to reflect and unwind, speaking an affirmation:

> **I invite the divine force**
> **within me every day.**

Emely Flak

Notes:

April is the fourth month of the year of the Gregorian calendar, and the first month of the astrological calendar. Its astrological sign is Aries, the ram (March 20–April 20), a cardinal fire sign ruled by Mars. The name of the month comes from the Latin *aprilis,* which derives from *aper,* or "boar," as April was thought to be the month of the boar. April delights the senses: the damp earth after an April rain and the sweet fragrance of flowering crab apple trees. Some of the most dramatic changes in nature occur in April. Buds swell and growth begins. Flowering trees such as dogwood, redbud, cherry, and apple are at the height of their beauty. Azaleas burst into bloom, bringing color to shady places. And, weather permitting, gardens and fields are tilled, ready to receive early crops of lettuce, spinach, and onion. Birds add to the beauty of April—not only are they busy building nests, but their songs now greet us on misty spring mornings. Holidays of the month are April Fools' Day, when we celebrate the Trickster, and Earth Day on the 22nd, which makes us aware of environmental issues. The beautiful flowering trees of the month gave April's Full Moon its charming old-fashioned name—the Pink Moon. Early herbalists and folk magicians used this period to enhance spells concerning health and general well-being.

April 1

Saturday

April Fools' Day

1st ♉

☽ → ♊ 6:49 pm

Color of the day: Black
Incense of the day: Jasmine

Journey of the Fool Spell

Today we honor the Joker, Fool, and various trickster characters. And what a perfect time to do so. Buds are swelling on branches. Seeds are sprouting, and the earthy scent of soil is in the air. The world is fresh and young, and the Fool begins his journey. The tarot depicts the Fool as an innocent traveling the path of life. He looks skyward without a care, even though he is near the edge of a cliff. Meditate on your own life's journey today. Start by looking closely at the Fool card from your favorite tarot deck. Imagine your life being as uncluttered and carefree as possible, then on your altar spread out a blue cloth. Place a crystal sphere on the cloth, and gaze at it without thought for a few moments. Let all images come and go freely, and simply be open to all possibilities. Naturally, you need not forge ahead foolishly. The best lesson the Fool can teach us is this: We are free to create our own opportunities.

James Kambos

Notes:

April 2

Sunday

Daylight Saving Time Begins 2 am

1st ♊

Color of the day: Yellow
Incense of the day: Coriander

Three Spells for Your Hair

Today on Saint Urban's Day, a sixteenth-century spell claims, if you hang a lock of your hair in front of an image of Saint Urban it will grow long and golden. A strand of hair can also serve as a divination tool. Just pluck a single strand of hair from your head. Hold the strand tightly between your thumbs and forefingers, then release it. The number of bends the hair takes are the number of spouses you will have. To see one's future mate, two unmarried people must sit before a blazing fire from midnight until one in the

   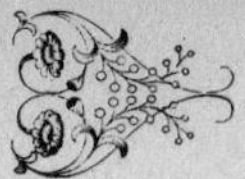 

morning. It is essential that they remain absolutely silent. At one o'clock, each person plucks as many hairs from their head as they are years old. Feeding each hair into the fire they say:

> I offer this my sacrifice
> To him most precious in
> my eyes
> I charge thee now come
> forth to me
> That I this minute may
> thee see.

Lily Gardner-Butts

Notes:

April 3
Monday

1st ♊

Color of the day: Gray

Incense of the day: Rose

Yield to Impulse Spell

During Aries, while Mars rules the Sun, you may feel energized and ready to begin new projects. Yield to the impulse! This is an excellent time for new beginnings. So ask yourself: What have you been putting off? Put it off no longer! Make sure that your plans are fairly well thought out, however. Try to temper your excitement with common sense. Today, get out any noisemakers that you have: drums, whistles, horns, or even a kitchen pot and a big spoon. Play your instrument. Move your body. Shout. Clap your hands. Stomp. As the Psalmist put it, make a joyful noise. Be energetic. You are making noise to birth your new project. Speak this affirmation:

> I am excited about all
> beginnings and possibili-
> ties. I take a step forward.
> I look carefully at my path,
> anticipating any problem.
> I see all clearly. I move
> toward my goals with
> energy and wisdom. I say
> it and make it so.

Luci Sophia Zain

Notes:

April 4
Tuesday

1st ♊
☽ → ♋ 2:15 am

Color of the day: White
Incense of the day: Gardenia

Protection of Ancestors Spell

Place pictures of your ancestors and those who have passed and are important to you in a circle on an altar table. Light a candle in the northern corner of the table. Light some incense, clear your mind, and say:

> Here I see the line of love,
> stretching down from above.
> Kinsmen whose love never
> leaves,
> Protect me in my time of need.

Place a photo of yourself in the middle of the table. See the circle of love around you and know you are blessed. Blow out the candle and imagine the smoke from this and the incense carrying your wishes to your kin. Today is tomb-sweeping day in Taiwan. Further honor your ancestors by tending their graves or keeping their memories alive by writing their stories for the generations to come.

Nancy Bennett

Notes:

April 5
Wednesday

1st ♋
2nd Quarter 8:01 am

Color of the day: Topaz
Incense of the day: Eucalyptus

Luck of the Draw Ritual

In ancient Rome, this day was sacred to Fortuna Publica. As such, it is a great day to work with the luck-of-the-draw. Using a blue pen or crayon and a yellow sheet of paper, draw a picture of something you wish would happen to you today. Make it a stick figure drawing if you like, but include as much detail as possible. Be sure in particular to put yourself in the picture. Next, holding the completed picture with both hands, bring it to your forehead. Visualize this scene in your mind as vividly as you can. Bring the image to your heart, and feel how you will feel when this wish actually comes true. Take care to truly grasp the emotions you will feel. Finally, bring the picture to your solar plexus, and send your will for the wish's fruition into the picture. From now on until your wish manifests, carry this drawing with you throughout the day and consciously feel its energy working for you.

Kristin Madden

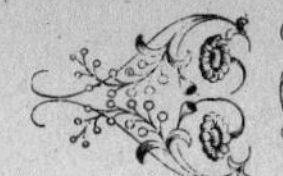

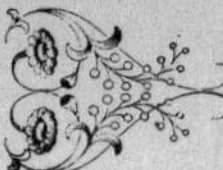

Notes:

April 6
Thursday

2nd ♋
☽ → ♌ 12:25 pm

Color of the day: Green
Incense of the day: Geranium

Seed Moon Magic

On this day of Jupiter, honor the Seed Moon by planting seeds for greater abundance. Go out under the light of the Seed Moon, dig a shallow hole, then bury all of your pocket change. Mark the spot with an X made from birdseed; in the morning plant sunflower seeds on this spot. A year later, if your intent was strong and true your change should have doubled.

Stephanie Rose Bird

Notes:

April 7
Friday

2nd ♌

Color of the day: Pink
Incense of the day: Ylang-ylang

Improve Your Difficult Relationships Spell

When relationships turn sour or reach a stagnant stage, or when you have to handle a difficult partner, family member, colleague, or friend, the use of pink smithsonite is beneficial. Smithsonite is named after James Smithson, the founder of the Smithsonian Institution. The stone can be found in various colors, but the pink variety can be applied in particular to relationship spells. Find a few pink smithsonites to keep around the home or at work, or to carry on your person when you are forced to deal with irritating or agitated people who carry strong negative vibes with them. The energies of this stone help promote a sense of security within the self and facilitate the gravitation toward a more balanced equilibrium. To further enhance the magic, write your wish on a piece of brown paper. Charge the stone at your altar, and read your wish before burning it in a ritual fire. Invoke the blessings of your personal deity for success in relationship matters.

S. Y. Zenith

  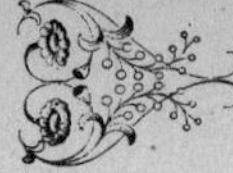 

Notes:

April 8

Saturday

2nd ♌

Color of the day: Brown

Incense of the day: Violet

Computer Protection Spell

To keep your computer running and in peak condition, once a week update your virus definitions for your virus protection program, check your computer for parasites (those nasty advertising hijackers), and optimize it once a month. For added protection, keep a piece of smoky quartz near your CPU and ask for the protection of the Great Mother Board against hijackers, hackers, and nasty virus e-mails. If you do not have virus protection software or parasite identifying software and you don't know how to optimize, please seek the counsel of the great search engine god (Google) and get this necessary protection for your machine or the Great Mother Board will soon crash!

Boudica

Notes:

April 9

Sunday

Palm Sunday

2nd ♌

☽ → ♍ 12:58 am

Color of the day: Amber

Incense of the day: Clove

Mindful Stretching Ritual

Stretching is a very healthy activity—for both body and mind. If you engage in mindful stretching, the benefits go to a whole new level. Mindful stretching, drawing on yoga and tai chi, is what happens when you are in the moment, fully aware of how your muscles feel, of how you breath in and out with each movement, and of how the motion helps clear your mind. The best way to enjoy mindful stretching is to develop a bit of

a routine composed of stretches that not only loosen and energize your muscles, but that you also enjoy. And then try to do them every day. If you are unsure of how to start, or you need to be careful with old injuries or sore joints, ask your doctor for help. Then, check out some of the wonderful books and videos available at your local library.

Laurel Reufner

Notes:

April 10
Monday

2nd ♍

Color of the day: Silver
Incense of the day: Frankincense

Safety Pin Spell

The safety pin was patented on this day in 1849 by Walter Hunt. Imagine being able to join two or more things together without being pricked or stuck with the sharp point. Baby diapers could be pinned at long last, rather than tied, holding in all sorts of unpleasantness until it could be cleaned up at a more appropriate time. In our lives, we often end up with unpleasantness that cannot be handled in the present, and we end up dwelling on the situation for no good purpose. To hold things out of your life until they can be dealt with, write the issue in one succinct word on a small scrap of fabric. Fold the fabric into fourths. Write the date on which you will handle this problem on the outside of the cloth. Pin a tiny gold safety pin into the fabric so it will not come unfolded. Set it aside for the appropriate date, but do not forget to deal with the problem on that day!

Gail Wood

Notes:

April 11
Tuesday

2nd ♍
☽ → ♎ 1:46 pm

Color of the day: Red
Incense of the day: Ginger

Feast of Anahit Ritual

Today is the Feast of Anahit, the Armenian goddess of love and of lunar mysteries. Known as the Golden Mother, she was worshipped in temples equipped with statues of pure gold. Her loyal followers left offerings of roses and doves to her. Meanwhile, Anahit bestowed her blessings on people by sprinkling them with rosewater. Honor Anahit today by decorating your altar with roses or by burning some rose-scented incense. Plan to cook Middle Eastern foods today—especially dishes such as *kheer,* a rice pudding flavored with rosewater and cardamom. Chocolate coins covered with gold foil are a whimsical modern touch beloved of many goddesses and their followers! Say this prayer today in the hopes you can attract Anahit's particular favor on her day:

Golden mother,
Woman of roses,
Shower me with petal-
soft blessings.

Let my heart open
Like a desert rose
To embrace the love
That comes my way.

May my hands overflow
with gold
And may I never forget
to share my bounty.

Elizabeth Barrette

Notes:

April 12
Wednesday

2nd ♎

Color of the day: Yellow
Incense of the day: Cedar

Moon Balance Spell

At this time we are in the Celtic Moon month of the Alder Moon. As a waxing Moon close to the Spring Equinox, this period is an ideal time to focus on balance and new beginnings. When an alder tree is cut, its wood turns from white to red, making it a strong symbol of fertility and rebirth. With tonight's Moon almost full, examine areas in your life that will benefit from balance or improvement. You can use this quick three-point checklist of questions to assess your condition now:

1. How is my bank balance, and how can I save a little more?

   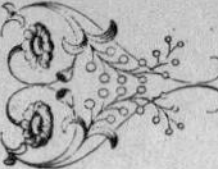 

2. How is my diet? Can I improve it by eating healthier food and by drinking more water?

3. How is my emotional state these days? Can I become more centered with an activity such as yoga or tai chi?

Emely Flak

Notes:

Historical note: On April 12, 1961, Yuri Gagarin piloted the first manned spaceship to leave the pull of our planet's gravity. This achievement is given much less attention than it deserves; part of it is politics, since Gagarin was a cosmonaut for the Soviet Union. Part of it, too, is time; today, space pilots live and work for months aboard space stations, so a simple space flight seems routine. Still, Yuri Gagarin's 108-minute flight in space represented not only a triumph of science and engineering, but it also broke a psychological barrier. It was literally a flight into the unknown. "Am I happy to be setting off on a cosmic flight?" said Yuri Gagarin in an interview before the start. "Of course. In all ages and epochs people have experienced the greatest happiness in embarking upon new voyages of discovery . . . I say 'until we meet again' to you, dear friends, as we always say to each other when setting off on a long journey."

April 13

Thursday

Passover begins

2nd ♎

Full Moon 12:40 pm

Color of the day: Purple
Incense of the day: Cedar

Sweep Away the Past Spell

During Passover, Jews are not allowed to eat *chametz,* or leavened bread, or to have any in their possession. Homes are traditionally cleaned from top to bottom, so as not to allow for the possibly of a single breadcrumb to remain. Likewise, this is the perfect time to do your own spring-cleaning, both of the physical and the spiritual sort. As you sweep, vacuum, and scrub, imagine removing any negativity that has built up right along with the dust and dirt. When you are done, set up a white cloth on a table or shelf near the

heart of the house and place a bell, sage or cedar incense, a lighter, salt, a chalice or cup filled with water, and a stirring device on this altar. Place a new broom nearby, then use the broom to symbolically sweep the house, beginning in the back rooms and always going toward the door. Open the door and sweep all of the negativity that you have gathered outside, saying: "I sweep out the old and gather in the new." Shut the door and return to the altar. Light the incense, saying: "By air and fire, I cleanse and bless my home. Let it be a place of wisdom and love." Go around the house in a clockwise circle, smudging, making sure to get into every nook and cranny. Finally, pour three spoonfuls of salt into the water and stir, saying, "By water and earth, I cleanse and bless my home. May it be a place of healing and sanctuary." Repeat the clockwise circle, carrying a chalice of salt water from which you carefully sprinkle. Return to the altar and ask for the blessings of your patron deities. "By my will, and with your blessings, this rite is done." Ring the bell.

Lady MoonDance

Notes:

April 14

Friday

Good Friday

3rd ♎

☽ → ♏ 1:08 am

Color of the day: Coral

Incense of the day: Nutmeg

Enjoying Your Body Spell

April is the month of Venus, goddess of self-love and beauty. By honoring your body, you honor her. Place pink candles around your bathroom and burn some rose incense. Stand in front of a mirror and ask Venus to help you see your beauty. Then, still in front of the mirror, take off your clothes. Enjoy the freedom of being naked. Draw a warm bath. Mix rose petals, lavender flowers, jasmine, rose hips, patchouli, and sea salt in cheesecloth bag and add it to the bath. Take some time to soak in the water and gently and lovingly wash yourself with a sponge. When you're ready, leave the tub. Take some rosewater and splash it over your body. Take time to get dressed, wearing something that you love and that makes you feel good. Thank Venus for her help in enjoying your body. You can call on her and perform this ritual anytime you need a boost in your self-esteem.

Olivia O'Meir

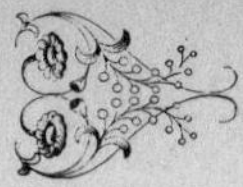

Notes:

April 15
Saturday

3rd ♏
Color of the day: Blue
Incense of the day: Patchouli

Serpent Stone Protection Spell

Egg-shaped magical objects have been used by Celtic people for thousands of years. Stones shaped like eggs were found in prehistoric ritual sites in Britain. In ancient Gaul, the Druids revered something called a Druid's Egg—a strange natural object that they believed was created by the hissing of intertwining serpents. Almost two thousand years later, a similar belief still existed in Scotland. People encountered strange gray-colored, egg-shaped objects among the heather which they believed were created by the hissing of serpents. These were called Serpent's Stones, and they were used for healing and protection. Find an egg-shaped stone and bathe it in springtime dew. Set it in a dish of spring water. Pick some springtime flowers and float these on the surface of the water for three days. Consecrate the stone and include this object in your ritual gear, especially when doing magical work for healing, protection, fertility, or growth.

Sharynne NicMhacha

Notes:

April 16
Sunday
Easter

3rd ♏
☽ → ♐ 10:19 am
Color of the day: Gold
Incense of the day: Poplar

Fresh Start Spell

Today is the Christian Easter. One modern Easter tradition is to wear something new. Wearing new clothing is an excellent way to express a commitment to a fresh start, a new direction, or simply a renewal of dedication. Do you have

a new or special garment that you could consecrate today? If so, make sure that the garment is clean and in good repair. Have a blooming flower, potted or cut, nearby. Say:

> O flower of spring, your
> fresh bloom symbolizes
> my spirit today. I conse-
> crate my garment to my
> new direction.

Lightly blow the flower's fragrance over your garment, top to bottom, front to back. Afterward, you may wish to take a ritual bath before you don the garment. Go out someplace special. Let others see you in your newly consecrated garment.

Luci Sophia Zain

Notes:

April 17
Monday

3rd ♐

Color of the day: Ivory

Incense of the day: Peony

Spring Creativity Spell

Water has been used in sacred rites since the ancient times. Water symbolizes all potential, and to immerse oneself in water is to gain strength from a vast source of potential. April 17 is the feast day of the Himalayan rain god Machendrana. Today, Poles celebrate Drenching Day and Hungarians celebrate Water Plunge Monday. In a vessel of holy water, add one teaspoon lavender flowers, five tablespoons of orange zest, one teaspoon rosemary, and one teaspoon of dried geranium flowers. Steep this mixture overnight. Add this to a sacred bath, visualizing yourself partaking in a vast source of possibility. It is very lucky if it rains today. By all means, walk outdoors and feel each raindrop as a blessing.

Lily Gardner-Butts

Notes:

April 18
Tuesday

3rd ♐

☽ → ♑ 5:13 pm

Color of the day: Black

Incense of the day: Pine

Fern Protection Spell

Millions of years before flowering plants appeared on our planet, ferns grew here. They are the ancient ones of the plant kingdom and are among the most magical of plants—used for centuries to repel evil. If you feel you are the subject of negative magic, start a fire in a heat-proof dish or fireplace. Scry into the flames to reveal the source of the harmful magic. Take three fern fronds that you've cut and dried, crush them, and begin sprinkling them over the flames, saying:

> Turn back the spell,
> Undo the deed
> Protect me
> In my time of need.
> Break the curse,
> Let the spell return.
> I am protected
> By fire and fern.

Let the fire die, and then sprinkle the cooled ashes around the outside of your home.

James Kambos

Notes:

April 19

Wednesday

Passover ends

3rd ♑

Color of the day: Brown

Incense of the day: Maple

Consecrated Cloth Divination

Divination provides an important glimpse of your path before it unfolds fully. Most divinatory tools, such as tarot cards, respond better if laid out upon a properly consecrated cloth rather than on a bare table. You may use a plain cloth or one with markings for a specific system. To consecrate your cloth, first spread it flat. Lay out all your cards on it in order. Now say:

> Tools of power,
> Tools of art,
> Tools that see the hidden
> heart,
> Tools that tell the path
> before
> Be you blessed by ancient
> lore.

Wrap the cloth around the deck, and continue:

> Now together be you bound
> Cards and cloth that
> wraps around
> One in two, and two in one,
> By these words my will
> be done!

The cloth is now consecrated. Keep it wrapped around your deck when not in use.

Elizabeth Barrette

Notes:

April 20

Thursday

3rd ♑

☉ → ♉ 1:26 am

☽ → ♒ 9:56 pm

4th Quarter 11:28 pm

Color of the day: Crimson
Incense of the day: Sage

Seafarer's Money Spell

On this day of Mercury, business, and travel, engage the herb of the seafarers, Irish moss, to assure prosperity and abundance in all of your work. Use dried Irish moss gracefully, knowing that it comes from the depths of our sea mothers. Crumble it into a bowl. Place this herb under your bed. Each night

visualize waves of prosperity coming toward you from the sea. Hold the thought steadily, think it frequently, and prosperity yours shall be.

Stephanie Rose Bird

Notes:

April 21

Friday

Orthodox Good Friday

4th ♒

Color of the day: Purple
Incense of the day: Ginger

Make New Friends Spell

Use this spell to bring some new friends into your life. Perform this spell by the light of a pink candle. Using a gold ink, write the names of your friends on a piece of paper. Don't worry if it's not a very long list. Many of us only have a few friends, but lots of acquaintances. Roll the paper up into a small scroll and keep it somewhere safe. That's your treasure. On another piece of

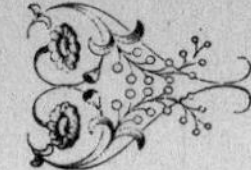

paper, in silver ink, write all the places you like to go where you might meet new friends. Post this piece of paper where you will see it often, helping remind you to get out and meet new people.

Laurel Reufner

Notes:

April 22

Saturday

Earth Day

4th ♒

Color of the day: Gray

Incense of the day: Lilac

Plant a Tree Spell

Balled and burlapped trees should never be carried by the trunk but always by the ball. Dig the hole three times as wide as the root ball but no deeper than the top of the root ball. Remember to remove twine or wires. Soil should be compacted around the ball but not overly tight so that it prevents water from seeping through the peat moss, compost, and topsoil. Water the tree after planting and repeat this spell:

Bless this tree I plant
today,
And for generations may
it stay
Always strong and
growing tall,
Providing beauty and
shade for all.

Water the tree once a week when there is no rain, and a bit more often during hot summer months, repeating the spell, substituting "water" for "plant" in the first line.

Boudica

Notes:

April 23

Sunday

Orthodox Easter

4th ♒

☽ → ♓ 12:43 am

Color of the day: Orange

Incense of the day: Cinnamon

Improve Your Appetite Ritual

To improve your appetite and your health, start with a clean

tablecloth spread on your table. Make an altar using your finest china and silver, as well as a goblet of wine. Encircle the plate with healthy foods such as apples, oranges, and spring flowers. Say:

> From this table shall I dine
> From foods of plenty, health
> be mine
> No more will my appetite
> be sour
> I will grow stronger,
> hour by hour.

Follow up this spell by making sure to serve yourself well at every meal. You are an honored guest at the table of the Goddess. Relish in her bounty and honor your host. This is a good spell to do after a lengthy illness. Today marked the ancient festival called Vinalia Priora. Wine from the previous year was drunk in honor of Jupiter and Venus.

Nancy Bennett

Notes:

April 24
Monday

4th ♓

Color of the day: Lavender
Incense of the day: Lavender

April Spring Lore

We all know that April showers bring May flowers, but what other gems of wisdom does folklore have to offer us in the spring? Well, in fact we can watch the world at this time to know what the rest of the year might be like.

> When April blows his
> horn, it's good for both
> the hay and corn.
>
> A wet spring means dry
> harvest weather.
>
> A rainy spring forecasts
> a hot, dry summer.
>
> If the spring is windy,
> the summer will be cool.
>
> If it is a dry spring, it
> will be a wet summer.
>
> A mild winter precedes
> a cool spring.
>
> When dandelions bloom
> late, summer will be dry.

Also, give this neat bit of folk wisdom a try: Listen to the sound of a cricket chirping. Count the number of chirps you hear in fourteen seconds and you

will know the temperature, in degrees Fahrenheit, where the cricket is.

Kristin Madden

Notes:

April 25
Tuesday

4th ♓
☽ → ♈ 2:12 am

Color of the day: Scarlet
Incense of the day: Juniper

Clear Away Mold Spell

Today is the Robigalia festival of ancient Rome. This agricultural festival gave offerings to Robiga, the spirit of mildew and dust, so she would stay away from the crops. Today, we are separated from the agricultural process, but can connect with it by growing our homes, families, and projects. Mold and mildew can affect these things in different forms, like jealousy, anger, hate, and prejudice. Let's light a black candle and leave an offering of ash, dust, dirt, or mulch for Robiga. Ask her to spare your projects, by saying:

> Robiga, please spare my
> projects from the mildew
> and mold known as hate,
> jealousy, and anger. I offer
> you an offering to gain
> your favor. Blessed be.

Make sure you live in accord. Don't manifest the very things you are trying to keep away.

Olivia O'Meir

Notes:

April 26
Wednesday

4th ♈

Color of the day: White
Incense of the day: Pine

Finding Courage Ritual

On your altar, place pictures of men and women that you admire, people that live their lives with courage and spirit. They may be leaders in public life, or they may be gods and goddesses from other cultures. Include those who have flaws as well as those who succeeded. Using crayons, colored pens, and pencils, create a courage card. Using symbols, sigils, and words, draw yourself as a courageous person, using symbols, sigils, and words. When you are done, introduce your card to

 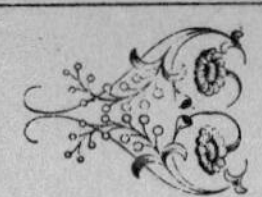   

the brave beings already on your altar. Place your courage card in the center, where the deity symbols reside. Light a red candle for courage and energy and a white candle for awareness and understanding. Sprinkle your card with dried rose, rosemary, and thyme, and chant:

> Strong and brave
> Now
> Keep resolve
> Now
> Craven fear
> Never
> Bless'd courage
> Forever.

Gail Wood

Notes:

April 27
Thursday

4th ♈

☽ → ♉ 3:44 am

New Moon 3:44 pm

Color of the day: Turquoise
Incense of the day: Jasmine

Sensual Grounding Spell

The New Moon in Taurus, a fixed earth sign ruled by Venus, brings groundedness, stability, and sensuality. Take some time to get grounded today by taking a walk in nature. Sit in a garden. Hug a tree. Take off your shoes and walk barefoot in the grass. Dig your hands into some mud. Repot some plants. Don't be afraid to get a little dirty today. You can always take a bath. In fact, that is next on the agenda. While you are outside, touch the plants and smell the flowers. Pick or buy several bunches of flowers or herbs that appeal to you. Roses, violets, or apple blossoms are the most appropriate, but look for ones that you find the most beautiful, fragrant, or otherwise attractive. When you get home, surround your bathtub with green candles. Draw a warm bath, adding a couple handfuls of Epsom salts. Light the candles and scatter small blossoms and flower petals in the bath. Undress slowly by candlelight. Lie back in the water, close your eyes, and feel the water on your skin until the water grows too cold.

Lady MoonDance

Notes:

 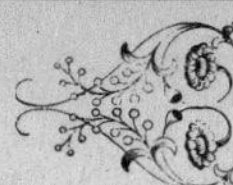   

April 28

Friday

1st ♉

Color of the day: Rose
Incense of the day: Rose

Water Feature Love Spell

Water features, such as fountains and birdbaths, help reinforce commitment, stability, mutual support, loyalty, and fidelity in relationships between two people. Purchase a water feature and place it outside your home. It must be placed on the left of the main door when viewed from indoors or when looking out. Decorate the fountain with some rose quartz and other pink crystals. Each time you make a wish regarding love matters, add a new crytal or pebble. Red, pink, and champagne-colored rose bushes can be planted near the fountain for an extra romantic touch. Be sure to add fresh water to the fountain at least once a week. Cleaning it once a month will prevent stagnation. As you perform these tasks, visualize love being strengthened. Water the rose bushes regularly and as they grow, so will your love.

S. Y. Zenith

Notes:

April 29

Saturday

1st ♉
☽ → ♊ 5:58 am

Color of the day: Indigo
Incense of the day: Juniper

Honoring Flora Spell

In ancient Rome, people celebrated Floralia today to honor Flora, the goddess of flowers. Activities on this day included theatrical performances and public games. Today is a good day to plant flowers that can withstand the spring weather. You can also work over your garden, raking away leaf litter to allow the soil to warm for planting. As you work, say:

> Flora,
> Hope of ancient Rome,
> Let my garden be your
> home.
> Bless the earth and
> make it warm.
> Shape the flowers to
> your form.

Save the empty seed packets from the flowers you plant today. Keep them on your altar and your plants will be magical and healthy.

Elizabeth Barrette

Notes:

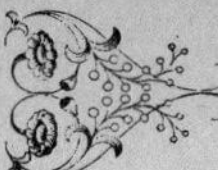

April 30

Sunday

1st ♊

Color of the day: Yellow

Incense of the day: Sage

Walpurgistide Spell

Together with Samhain, this night is the most powerful in the year for Witches. Walpurgistide is the dark twin of May Day. The purpose of rituals performed tonight is to drive the Hag of Winter back to her cave for the next six months. Go into the woods tonight and bring your worn-out bits of wood, clothing, brooms, and papers to build a Bel-fire. Your household items represent winter, with its dreariness, cold, and illness. Before you build a fire out of these objects, consider old thoughts and habits you wish to cast off. As you watch the flames dance above the cast-off bits of your life, visualize the old habits and thoughts consumed by the fire and going back into the earth, the womb of regeneration. Now dance around the fire. When the fire burns low enough to the ground for safety, jump it and make wishes for the summer.

Lily Gardner-Butts

Notes:

May is the fifth month of the year. Its astrological sign is Taurus, the bull (April 20–May 21), a fixed earth sign ruled by Venus. The month is named for Ma'a, a Roman goddess and mother of the god Hermes. May is known as the queen of months. It is a month of lushness and beauty. The main holiday is May Day, or Beltane. This sabbat celebrates the sacred union of the Goddess and God. It is a celebration of growth and fertility. A traditional part of this holiday is the maypole, usually a fir tree with the side branches removed—a symbol of fertility. Since growth is a theme of May, another central figure of the month is the Green Man, a male form covered with leaves and branches. He is an ancient nature spirit, who brings life to the fields and forests after the long winter. Flowers are popular during Beltane rites, which gives May's Full Moon its lovely name—the Flower Moon. Many flowers and trees that bloom this month are associated with magic. Lilacs were originally grown near the home to repel evil. Wild blue violets can be used in love magic. A steaming infusion made with dried dandelion root was used to contact spirits. The hawthorn tree is also associated with May folk magic. To make a wish come true, burn three hawthorn branches in a Beltane fire.

 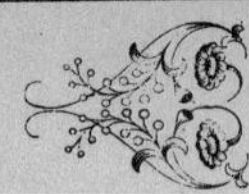  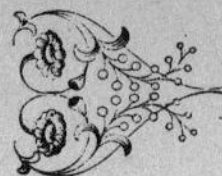 

May 1
Monday
May Day – Beltane

1st ♊
☽ → ♋ 11:17 am
Color of the day: White
Incense of the day: Coriander

A Fairy Spell for Beltane

In a woodland clearing, spread a clean green cloth. On it place small cakes and flowers, especially primroses, in a circle. Imagine the magic around you and say:

> O Fairy Queen,
> Upon your white steed,
> Within me plant
> A magic seed.
> From you may spring
> Many new beginnings.
> Great Queen,
> Accept these offerings.

Leave the items and walk around the altar three times, then slowly walk the path back to your home. Listen for the sound of laughter and bells and know you are blessed. Beltane is the time when fairies return from their winter rest, carefree and full of mischief and delight. On the night before Beltane, in times past, folks would place rowan branches at their windows and doors for protection. If you do not wish the fairies to visit, do the same! This is also a perfect time for night or predawn rituals to draw down power to promote fertility in body and mind. At Beltane, the Pleiades star cluster rises just before sunrise on the morning horizon. The Pleiades is known as the seven sisters, and resembles a tiny dipper-shaped pattern of six moderately bright stars in the constellation of Taurus, near the shoulder. Watch for it low in the east-northeast sky, just a few minutes before sunrise.

Nancy Bennett

Notes:

May 2
Tuesday

1st ♋
Color of the day: Black
Incense of the day: Honeysuckle

Morning Due Collection Spell

In Ireland, morning dew was collected during the month of May for health and beauty. It was considered especially potent if gathered on a May morning, but it was also col-

lected throughout the month and into June. The dew was either brushed off the grass into a dish, or it was collected with a clean linen cloth that was then wrung into a vessel. Sometimes it was placed in a glass bottle and set out in the sunshine for an entire day. Daring young women rolled naked in the dew for beauty. Dew was not to be wiped off but let dry in the air. Here is a traditional charm for collecting May dew, which alludes to its mysterious and otherworldly qualities:

> I wash my face in water
> That has neither rained
> nor run,
> And I dry it on a towel
> That was never woven
> or spun.

Sharynne NicMhacha

Notes:

May 3
Wednesday

1st ♋
☽ → ♌ 8:18 pm

Color of the day: Yellow
Incense of the day: Neroli

Bless Your Garden Spell

May 3 is the last day of the Floralia festival, which honors the Roman goddess Flora. Flora's domain includes flowers, herbs, and gardens. Go out to your garden, wearing brightly colored garments and flowers in your hair. Burn some floral incense in Flora's honor. Try rose, rosemary, vanilla, daisy, lavender, gardenia, and jasmine. The incense smoke will carry your desires to her. Sit by the garden for a while, and say:

> Flora, goddess of garden
> and flower. Bless my
> garden this very hour.
> Let it flourish and be
> fertile. Grace this space
> with your smile. Blessed
> be.

Know that Flora will honor your wish.

Olivia O'Meir

Notes:

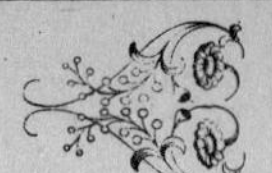

May 4

Thursday

1st ♌

Color of the day: Purple

Incense of the day: Vanilla

Celtic Fairy Day Spell

Today is Celtic Fairy Day. This is traditionally celebrated by leaving food and drink for the fairy folk on your doorstep or next to a tree to attract luck and protection. Celebrate Fairy Day by bringing out your inner child for some whimsical fun. Have a get-together with friends and eat some party food from your childhood, such as fairy bread and chips. Dress up as fairies or as your favorite gods and goddesses. Sprinkle fairy dust on the floor and on the tablecloth with small silver stars. Use food dye to create different colors of mineral water or sparkling wine. Indulge yourself in some fun games such as musical chairs or a board game. Make lolly bags for your guests to take home. Before you go to bed, don't forget to leave out some of the party food for your fairy friends!

Emely Flak

Notes:

May 5

Friday

Cinco de Mayo

1st ♌

2nd Quarter 1:13 am

Color of the day: Coral

Incense of the day: Dill

New Beginnings Meditation

Spring is a good time to meditate on beginnings. You will need a small seashell with a spiral pattern, such as a nautilus or a conch. If you can find one that is a necklace or keychain, so much the better. Seek out a quiet place and seat yourself comfortably. Study the seashell until you can clearly picture it in your mind. Trace its curves with your fingers. Now close your eyes and visualize the seashell in as much detail as you can imagine. See that it begins with a twist as tiny as a grain of sand. Every chamber builds on the one before it. If that first foundation is built crookedly, then everything built on it will be warped also. But if that tiny beginning is well formed, everything follows accordingly in a natural and graceful order. Finally, carry your seashell with you as you go through your day, and pay careful attention to any potential beginnings you make.

Elizabeth Barrette

 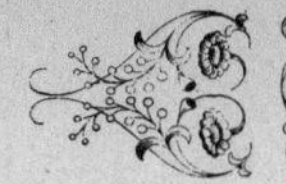  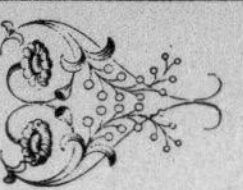 

Notes:

Holiday lore: Don't confuse Cinco de Mayo with Mexican Independence Day on September 16. Cinco de Mayo marks the victory of the brave Mexican army over the French at the Battle of Puebla. Although the Mexican army was eventually defeated, the *Batalla de Puebla* became a symbol of Mexican unity and patriotism. With this victory, Mexico demonstrated to the world that Mexico and all of Latin America were willing to defend themselves against any foreign or imperialist intervention.

May 6
Saturday

2nd ♌
☽ → ♍ 8:20 am

Color of the day: Brown
Incense of the day: Pine

Flower Moon Truth Divination

During this first quarter of the Flower Moon, blossoms fill the air with their potent fragrance. Today is the day to see who is good and who is true by using flowers as a diviner's tool. Start by taking a daisy in your dominant hand. Inhale its delicate aroma with one long, sustained breath. Exhale away from the flower. Repeat slowly and methodically seven times. By the seventh time you should feel light and clear. Now is time for the magic. Close your eyes, and stroke the flower. Speak the following incantation:

> Daisy delicate,
> Soft yet strong,
> Tell me the truth for
> which I yearn.
> Is this notion I hold close
> True or false?

Now begin removing the petals. Each time you pluck one, answer your own question, yes or no, until you have no more petals left. The last word, yes or no, is your answer. Thank the daisy for sharing its magic with you during this divination. Set it free on fresh water.

Stephanie Rose Bird

Notes:

May 7
Sunday

2nd ♍

Color of the day: Orange
Incense of the day: Basil

Invoking the Warriors Ritual

When you feel a cold or a flu coming on, in addition to what your doctor has suggested, you can focus—through meditation—on having your body produce little "warriors" that travel through your body attacking the nasty little germs or viruses. The meditation is based on using your body's own antibody system, but encouraging it to produce more and directing it to attack the invading germs or viruses at this time. Do this meditation as early in your illness as you can to help lessen the impact of the cold or flu. This is a good companion therapy to any herbal or medical treatments you may be undertaking.

Boudica

Notes:

May 8
Monday

2nd ♍
☽ → ♎ 9:10 pm

Color of the day: Lavender
Incense of the day: Chrysanthemum

Pet Protection Bottle Spell

To many of us, our pets are like our children and considered close family members. Here is a spell bottle to help keep your four-legged friends from straying too far and getting lost when they explore the outdoors. On a small piece of paper, draw the outline of a house. Inside the outline, write your pet's name and your address. Roll the paper up, scroll-fashion, and place it inside the bottle along with a small amount of dirt from your home. If you live in an apartment, soil from around a houseplant will do. Add nail clippings and strands of fur, plus a garlic clove or two. Close the bottle and seal it with red candle wax. Place this in a safe place, perhaps near where your pet supplies are kept.

Laurel Reufner

Notes:

May 9
Tuesday

2nd ♎

Color of the day: Scarlet
Incense of the day: Evergreen

Banishing Past Sorrows Spell

There are times when our past mistakes and fractured hopes impinge on our present and make us feel low and depressed. This occasional feeling keeps us from realizing our full joy and happiness. We return again and again to the memories of broken promises and our various disappointments. Instead of greeting each new day as a moment of opportunity, our hearts remain stuck in the past. Not to worry, we can banish these sorrows. Gather together paper, a pen, and string. After centering yourself, write your sorrows and broken hopes on to the paper, using precise language. Roll the paper in a tube and tie it with the string, knotting it tighly. Place the tied paper into a burning bowl. Light the paper and chant:

> The ties of the past
> must vanish.
> With fire and knot I do
> banish.

Chant until the paper and string are burned entirely to ash. Gather up all the ashes and bury them in the earth.

Gail Wood

Notes:

May 10
Wednesday

2nd ♎

Color of the day: Brown
Incense of the day: Eucalyptus

Business Presentation Spell

This spell is especially useful for those whose work requires making presentations or attending meetings but they are afflicted by anxiety, nervousness, "stage-fright," or a lack of confidence. It is also beneficial for persons attending job interviews. One hour before the stressful occasion, take several deep breaths while holding a blue crystal of your choice. Visualize the stirring of inner strength and confidence stimulating your entire psyche. Breathe in deeply, and hold the breath for three to five seconds. When ready, breathe out in short but strong spurts. Repeat this process

nine times while still holding the blue crystal. Feel the crystal emitting positive energies, giving guidance, insight, and calm. Dab on some light cologne, tidy up your appearance, have a glass of water or mild fruit juice, and line your tummy with a slice of bread for grounding. The blue crystal can be carried in a pouch, or tucked into a pocket, bag, or briefcase.

S. Y. Zenith

Notes:

May 11
Thursday

2nd ♎
☽ → ♏ 8:24 am

Color of the day: White
Incense of the day: Sandalwood

Corn Prosperity Spell

Traditionally this was the time of year to plant corn. The farmers would walk the newly planted fields with members of the clergy, blessing the fields for abundance. Since this is the Thursday before May's Full Moon, today would be excellent for casting a prosperity spell. For this, will need a pinch of cornmeal, three blue violets you have picked, and a cup of water to which you've added a bit of sea salt. In the evening, as the Moon rises above the eastern horizon, go outside where you won't be disturbed. Sprinkle the cornmeal on the ground and scatter the violet petals over the cornmeal. Pour the salt water over all and say:

Grain of gold,
Give me wealth to hold.
Flowers from the earth,
Water from the sea,
Favor me with prosperity.
So mote it be.

James Kambos

Notes:

May 12
Friday

2nd ♏

Color of the day: Pink
Incense of the day: Thyme

Lovable You Spell

Celebrate the wonderful, lovable you today! Buy yourself one perfect red rose. As you breathe in the delightful fragrance, feel yourself filling with love and joy. Breathe deeply and close your eyes, visualizing a bubble of happy, loving energy surrounding you. Imagine everyone you meet treating you with love. Tell yourself that you are loved and that you love yourself. Keep breathing the aroma until you really feel it. Carry the rose with you throughout the day and evening. When someone asks you who gave it to you, smile mysteriously. Before going to sleep tonight, write yourself a love note. Write down all the wonderful and great things about you. Take one more deep breath of the beautiful rose, and carry these loving feelings into sleep with you.

Kristin Madden

Notes:

May 13
Saturday

2nd ♏

Full Moon 2:51 am

☽ → ♐ 4:56 pm

Color of the day: Blue
Incense of the day: Lavender

Sex Magic Spell

The Full Moon in Scorpio is a time of deep of magic and heightened sexuality. Passions run high and desires run dark. Instead of feeling frustrated, decide to channel this energy into your highest desires. When you next make love, put intention into your pleasure. One of the easiest ways to do this is to develop a simple sigil symbolizing your intention. Place the symbol on your altar, carve it into a candle of the appropriate color, or paint it on your body or on a poster to hang over your bed. Put it everywhere around you. Then make love, periodically concentrating on the symbol, and making sure to visualize it as you reach the climax of your passions. If you are celibate, you can do the same work, by breathing energy up through your chakras one at a time, starting with the root chakra. Take time to go through each chakra, slowly working your way up until you feel the energy in your root, belly, solar plexus, heart, throat, and third eye. Keep going until the energy goes out the crown

   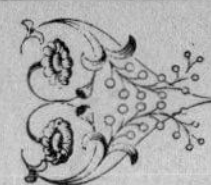 

of your head. Know that this is an advanced working, which takes a great deal of practice. Do only as much of this as you are comfortable with. At any time, you can stop and either send the energy out of your hands or back down into the earth.

Lady MoonDance

Notes:

May 14
Sunday

Mother's Day

3rd ♐

Color of the day: Amber

Incense of the day: Coriander

Honoring Your Mother and Your Mother Earth Ritual

Mother's Day is one holiday that reminds us to honor our mothers. The mothers I am referring to are our biological and spiritual mothers—good old Mom and good old Mother Earth. Set up an altar to your mothers, including pictures, mementos, and natural items like feathers, stones, and nuts. Place a green candle in the center of the altar. Light some "earthy" incense like sandalwood, patchouli, or sage. Think fondly about your mothers, and of any special events or feelings you've shared. Light the green candle, and say:

> I honor my mothers, who
> gave birth to me. They
> comfort, console, bless, teach,
> and love me. May they be
> blessed with love, honor,
> and prosperity. Blessed be.

Leave the altar up the whole day. Take time today to express your love and admiration for them.

Olivia O'Meir

Notes:

May 15
Monday

3rd ♐

☽ → ♑ 10:59 pm

Color of the day: Gray

Incense of the day: Myrrh

 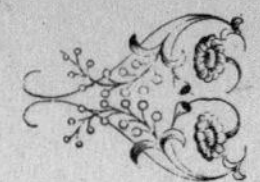  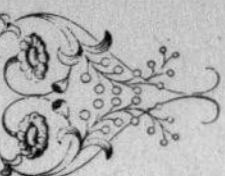 

Listen to Teacher Ritual

Today, listen to your teacher. Put school implements on your altar: book, paper, pencils, book bag, and so on. If you have an apple, put it on the altar as your gift to your teacher. Ring a bell or sound a buzzer to represent the beginning of the school day. Then sit quietly with your pencil and paper. Think on a favorite teacher, either carnate or incarnate. What lessons have you learned from this teacher? There is a lesson still to be learned. Focus on the mental image of your teacher, and say: "Teacher, I am ready to learn." If your mind wanders, gently bring it back. Record any message that you receive. When done, give thanks to your teacher, lifting up the apple, and put away your school implements. School is over for now. Ring your bell or buzzer for the end of school.

Luci Sophia Zain

Notes:

May 16

Tuesday

3rd ♑

Color of the day: Red

Incense of the day: Sage

Genie Lamp Spell

Arabic legend tells of magic lamp that, when rubbed, produced a genie who granted wishes. Modern lamps, of course, are constructed differently from those of olden times. Still, we use the image of a lightbulb over someone's head to represent an idea. This spell unites the two concepts. You will need a small desk lamp, preferably with a brass base and a fancy shade that looks magical to you. Hold the lamp and charge it with power, saying: "Spirits of inspiration, genies of wind and flame, I invite you to dwell in this lamp." Keep the lamp on your desk. When you need inspiration, rub it, and say: "Lamp that burns bright, grant me graceful words that soar like birds, as I write this night.

Elizabeth Barrette

Notes:

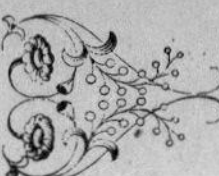

May 17
Wednesday

3rd ♑

Color of the day: White
Incense of the day: Cedar

Prayer for Lost Luggage

If you lost something important like your luggage during a recent trip, don't despair. Instead offer up a prayer to Osiris. Find a quiet space and think of the item that is missing. Imagine it making its way to you. See honest and caring people speeding it on its way. Then say:

> Osiris,
> God of resurrection,
> For my lost item
> Please offer protection.
>
> Help clear its way back
> to me
> By honorable hands,
> So mote it be!

Osiris is god of resurrection and new beginnings, but also a judge of the dead and good deeds. Before you begin a trip it is wise to ask his blessings so your roads will be free of lost luggage.

Nancy Bennett

Notes:

May 18
Thursday

3rd ♑
☽ → ♒ 3:19 am

Color of the day: Topaz
Incense of the day: Cedar

Cusp of Optimism Spell

As we currently pass time between the start of spring and the longest day of the year, we are already enjoying the extra hours of sunlight in the Northern Hemisphere. This cusp of spring and summer is a time when we feel optimistic and abundant. It's a time that we often spend more hours in the garden or spring-cleaning our homes. Today, make a start to remove stagnant energy that has accumulated over the winter months, and take care now to cleanse the space in your home. Don't despair if you cannot complete your spring-cleaning in the space of one day; just keep plugging away a little at a time. Take your unwanted clothing and other items to a charity shop. Clean your windowsills and bench tops with diluted white vinegar or eucalyptus. Clearing space makes way for new opportunities to enter your life. When your are finished, ring a bell in each corner of each room to mobilize energy, and say:

> With each bell ring,
> As I scrub and clean,

   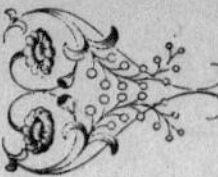 

No more staleness,
Can be felt or seen.

Emely Flak

Notes:

May 19
Friday

3rd ♒

Color of the day: Purple
Incense of the day: Ylang-ylang

Organize Your Grimoire Spell

Every Witch should have his or her own Book of Shadows and a complete grimoire. What's a grimoire? It's a personal book of spell craft. If you're like me, you probably have a folder of notes, some perhaps clipped out from the past years of this very *Spell-A-Day Almanac,* and you've been meaning to organize and copy them into one complete and comprehensive spell book. So why not make May 19, the feast day of Saint Peter Celestine, patron saint of books, the day to work on your grimoire? To start this process, clean off your work area. Place a pentagram on the top of your desk, burn a black candle and a stick of vanilla incense, and begin work. If you are one of those highly organized individuals whose grimoire is current, then try some research on the web to get new ideas, or buy a new book on spell work.

Lily Gardner-Butts

Notes:

May 20
Saturday

3rd ♒

4th Quarter 5:20 am

☽ → ♓ 6:39 am

Color of the day: Indigo
Incense of the day: Jasmine

Goddess Burn-It Spell

With the large hard drives on today's computers, we tend to store a lot of data on our computers: music, pictures, articles, diaries,

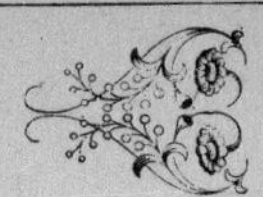

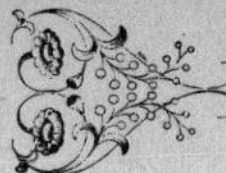

letters, checkbooks, even bank accounts. You name it, we store it—our computers have become "gigabyte closets." But what happens when we have a computer crash? We lose the family pictures of Aunt Ruth and Uncle Bob's fiftieth wedding anniversary. We lose our bank balance. To help avoid this situation, as your collect your precious memories and essential data, remember the goddess Burn-It. She is matron of CD burners. Whenever you download the pictures, or come to the end of the month and have to balance your checking account, or store any sort of correspondence on your computer, remember to say a prayer to Burn-It. You can't simply take for granted that the information will always be there simply because it's in a computer. Always remember Burn-It and you will not lose the really important memories and information in your life.

Boudica

Notes:

May 21

Sunday

4th ♓
☉ → ♊ 12:31 pm

Color of the day: Yellow
Incense of the day: Parsley

Sun Spirit Floor Wash Ritual

What better day than this day of rest to prepare for the brand new week? Lemon grass oil has a bright, sunny, energizing effect on the spirit. Add sixteen drops of lemongrass essential oil to a cauldron of water, followed by a teaspoon of unscented Castille soap. Stir with your magic wand, or a wooden spoon if you don't have a wand. Use a natural sea sponge to wash your floors, imbuing your living space with energy, inspiration, zest, and bright energy for the entire week!

Stephanie Rose Bird

Notes:

 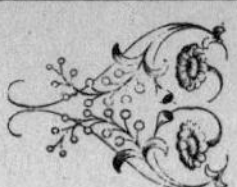  

May 22
Monday

4th ♓
☽ → ♈ 9:24 am

Color of the day: Silver
Incense of the day: Daffodil

Apple Branch Spell

The apple tree was very sacred in Celtic tradition. Its fruit and its branches were considered to tokens of passage to the otherworld. In the story, "The Voyage of Bran," a fairy woman appears and hands Bran a beautiful apple branch of silver and crystal. This is meant as an invitation to the sacred Realms of Faerie. Here is a May-time spell for connecting with the otherworld. Find a fallen apple branch (crabapple is fine), peel off the bark, and sand it. Paint the branch silver, and attach small bells or crystals. Ask the spirit of the apple tree for its blessing and assistance in deepening your connection with the Realms of Faerie:

O apple tree,
Apple branch,
Tree of sweetest fruit,
Roots growing and top
bending,
O apple tree,
May every bounty and
desire be with you.

May every passion and
sacred thing be with you!

Sharynne NicMhacha

Notes:

May 23
Tuesday

4th ♈

Color of the day: Gray
Incense of the day: Musk

Tubilustrium Sanctity Ritual

For the ancient Romans, today was Tubilustrium—one of two days when ceremonial trumpets were purified and sanctified. Whether you work with a drum, bell, harp, or tuba, this is a wonderful time to bless and reconsecrate your ritual instruments. Light a cedar and sage smudge or some incense. Holding the instrument in the smoke, ask that the smoke of the sacred plants purify this instrument and release any lingering unwanted energies. Then sit with the instrument for a few

  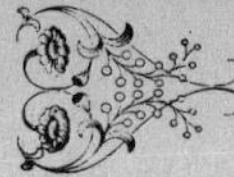 

moments. Thank it for being your partner in ritual and for the blessings it has brought your work. Ask if it holds any messages for you at this time. When ready, sprinkle a very small amount of cornmeal on the instrument. Hold it up and dedicate it to your path. Ask that your gods and goddesses bless and consecrate this instrument for the highest good of all. Then play it freely and joyfully.

Kristin Madden

Notes:

May 24
Wednesday

4th ♈

☽ → ♉ 12:00 pm

Color of the day: Topaz
Incense of the day: Maple

Salt Decision Ritual

Do you ever have trouble making up your mind? Here's a spell to help you with decision making. Set out a small bowl full of salt. Let your hands flow through the salt until you are calm. Say: "By the crystals of salt, I crystallize my thoughts, making them clear and concrete." Think of a decision that you need to make now. Take a pinch of salt, and think carefully on your choice, weighing all of the pros and cons. When you are ready to make a decision, say: "I make a firm decision now." Toss the salt into the air. Wipe your hands together, and say: "It is so." Put the leftover salt aside in a dark cupboard, and bury a crystal in the salt for recharging.

Luci Sophia Zain

Notes:

May 25
Thursday

4th ♉

Color of the day: Crimson
Incense of the day: Carnation

 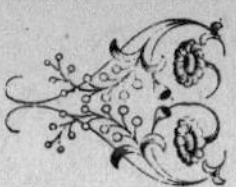  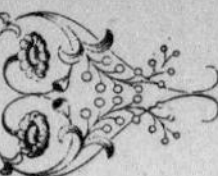 

Wise Abundance Spell

Until one can personally identify the level of success, abundance, and prosperity one requires to live, the psyche will remain blocked—at least in terms of considering which affirmations and psychic work to undertake for these wishes. To make a start along the path of success and abundance, write one sentence on a piece of paper clarifying the level of prosperity you think you desire. Be rational, reasonable, and concise in stating these goals. Tell yourself that you want abundance with a passion but you are not obsessed. On the same paper, mention your immediate needs, such as paying an unexpectedly hefty bill, or revamping an old wardrobe, or working toward a new set of wheels. Use what money you now make wisely and seek to conserve any extra for rainy days, future security, or any particular wishes you have. Wanton and profligate spending on things that are not essential necessities in daily life will dissipate your psychic abundance energies—so put yourself in the right mindset and try to stay there. When ready, place the piece of "wish-paper" on your altar. Put a small handful of coins and several dollar bills around the paper. Light some incense and a votive candle. Sit before your altar and petition Jupiter for granting your wish for abundance and prosperity for the foreseeable future.

S. Y. Zenith

Notes:

May 26
Friday

4th ♉
☽ → ♊ 3:19 pm

Color of the day: White
Incense of the day: Almond

Connect with Animal Spirits Spell

There are many animal spirits and totems that want to work with us, help us, and build relationships with us. To connect with the animal spirit that would be most pertinent and useful to you in your life now, find a quiet sacred space and settle yourself there. If there are animal images that are important to you, bring them into the space, but let go of any expectations at the same time. In your space, have a bowl of earth from a place that is special

   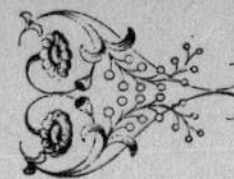 

to you, and bring a rattle. Light a brown candle that is scented, if possible, with musk and rose or juniper. Breathe deeply and go into a meditative state. As you breathe, begin to rattle gently and softly ask the animal to come to you. Be patient and continue your efforts with a focused mind. As an animal approaches, ask if it is your spirit guide. Listen to the answer and the messages that follow. When you have an answer, or if the animal seems ready to leave, stop rattling. Breathe deeply and thankfully. Extinguish the candle and clear your space.

Gail Wood

Notes:

May 27

Saturday

4th ♊

New Moon 1:25 am

Color of the day: Black

Incense of the day: Violet

Launch Your Ideas Spell

The New Moon in Gemini is a time for novel ideas, increased communication, and new connections. Harness this energy by focusing on making new friends and networking to support a new project or business idea. Plan to go to a new event or venue, preferably one with an opportunity for plenty of socializing. Before you leave, dab a bit of clary sage oil to clear your mind and lavender oil for relaxation on a yellow candle. Carve the symbol of Gemini into the candles, and think of two minds coming together on common ground. Carry an agate in your pocket to help you see the truth, improve your memory and concentration, and encourage honesty. If you are nervous, add a tiger's-eye for courage. As you leave for your meeting or event, hold the stones in your hand and say:

Open my heart and mind
To new connections
And new ideas.

May my words be heard
And visions remembered,
As I remember
The important words
Spoken around me.

So mote it be.

Lady MoonDance

   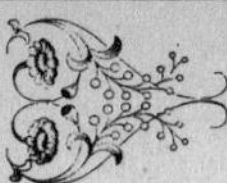 

Notes:

May 28
Sunday

1st ♊

☽ → ♋ 8:33 pm

Color of the day: Gold
Incense of the day: Clove

Health Bundle Ritual

Begin this ritual at noon during a waxing Moon. Place a pine cone on a square of white cotton cloth. Over the pine cone sprinkle a pinch each of cinnamon, nutmeg, and rosemary. Light an orange candle on your altar, and wrap the pine cone and herbs tightly in the cloth. Tie the bundle with orange ribbon or yarn, wrapping it around three times. As you wrap, say these, or similar, words:

> With pine and herbs
> My good health will stay.
> Let no ailment come my way.

Snuff out the candle and leave your bundle alone for one hour. During this time prepare and take a hot and relaxing bath. After one hour, hide your secret bundle. Renew this spell at each New Moon by holding your magic bundle and speaking the same charm.

James Kambos

Notes:

May 29
Monday

Memorial Day (observed)

1st ♋

Color of the day: Ivory
Incense of the day: Rose

Playful Wishes Spell Bottle

A home where people know how to be playful, and where they have a sense of humor, is a welcoming place where you want to spend time. Use this spell bottle to help counterbalance the sometimes harmful effects a busy life can have on

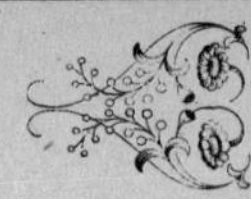

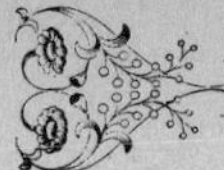

our psyche and family dynamics—effects that overshadow the natural humor and lightheartedness in a household. To start, you'll need a small, wide-mouthed jar to serve as a container. Into the bottle go the following goodies, in order: beach sand, small shells, hemlock or other small cones and seed pods, and one butterfly wing. As you place them in the jar, remember the fun you had while gathering your items and imagine this playful energy infusing your home, making it more and more welcoming. Remember: Please don't harm a live butterfly in order to get its wing. Be patient and ask nature—in time, you will be provided with one.

Laurel Reufner

Notes:

May 30
Tuesday

1st ♋

Color of the day: White
Incense of the day: Gardenia

Good Health Apple Spell

The end of May brings the popular British festival of Oak Apple Day. The festival celebrates the end of Oliver Cromwell's dictatorship and the return of the reign of King Charles II in 1660, making England whole again. You can use the powers of oak and apple to heal you completely. Buy a red or green square of cloth and place a crushed oak leaf and a bit of apple peel in it. Tie the bundle shut with contrasting red and green threads. As you tie, say:

> I call upon the strength
> of oak. I call upon the
> energy of apple. May I be
> healed of illness, disease,
> and injury. May I grow
> healthier and wiser
> every day.
>
> With harm to none,
> So mote it be.

Carry the bundle with you for as long as you need it. When you are finished, untie the bag and bury the leaf and peel. Thank oak and apple for their help.

Olivia O'Meir

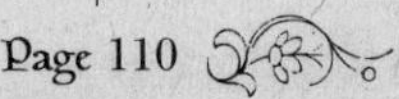

Notes:

Holiday lore: Opinions are divided concerning the origins of the holiday of Memorial Day in the United States. This is a day set aside for honoring the graves of American war dead. While most historians credit the origins of the custom to Southern women, there is also a rumor, historically speaking, of an anonymous German who fought in the American Civil War (no one is sure on which side). At the end of the war, this soldier was allegedly overheard commenting that in the Old World people scattered flowers on the graves of dead soldiers. In May of 1868, a Union army general suggested to Commander John A. Logan that a day be set aside each year to decorate Union graves. Logan was game, and he set aside May 30 for this ritual. His proclamation acknowledged those "who died in defense of their country" and "whose bodies now lie in almost every city, village, or hamlet churchyard in the land." This patriotic holiday was later amended to include all the dead from all the wars, and its date was shifted to a convenient Monday late in May.

May 31

Wednesday

1st ♋

☽ → ♌ 4:51 am

Color of the day: Yellow
Incense of the day: Pine

Triple Goddess Womanhood Ritual

Today is the Old European feast of the Triple Goddess. This holiday marks her transformation from virgin to mother. It is an auspicious time now to hold rites of passage, such as womanhood ceremonies for girls becoming women or baby showers for expectant mothers. Honor the mother Goddess by decorating the table with big red candles, the color of womanhood. Serve a feast of comfort foods such as homemade fresh-baked bread, stewed chicken, and apple pie. Before people start eating, offer this toast:

> **Virgin to mother she passes,**

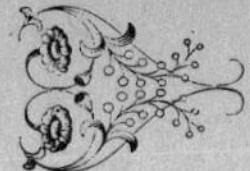

Good Pagan folk raise
glasses.

Make a toast to the
newcomer,
Goddess of birth and of
summer.
From her breasts flow
milk and honey;
She makes life sweet
and days sunny.

Hail,
Hail to the divine
Mother!
Before her stands no
other!

Clink glasses together, drink, and commence the feasting.

Elizabeth Barrette

Notes:

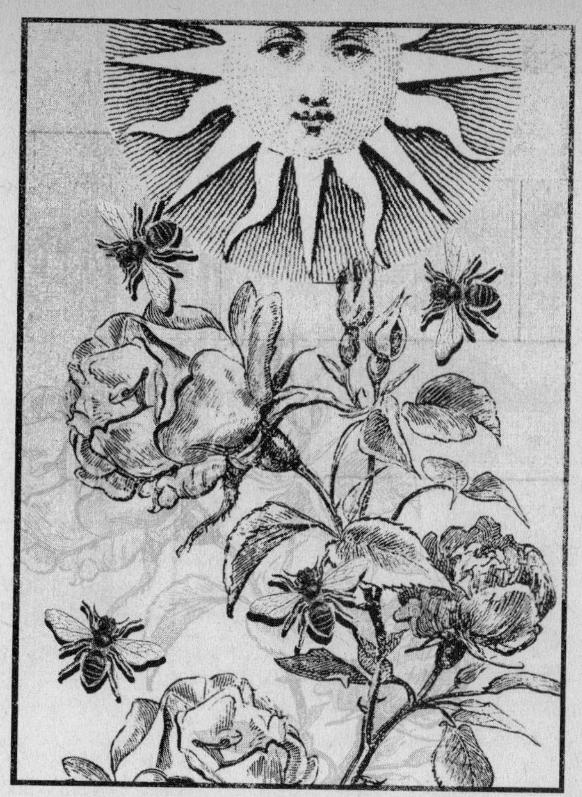

June is the sixth month of the year. Its astrological sign is Gemini, the twins (May 21–June 21), a mutable air sign ruled by Mercury. It is named for Juno, the principal goddess of the Roman pantheon and wife of Jupiter. She is the patroness of marriage and the well-being of women. June is a month of plenty. Mother Earth is young and fresh. The air is sweet with the age-old scent of freshly cut hay. Honeysuckle covers old fences and fills June afternoons with its perfume. In the fields, corn and wheat reach for the Sun. In the garden, bees dance among the roses and larkspur. In June, the ancients prepared for the return of the Sun on the main holiday of the month, the Summer Solstice, or Midsummer. Wooden hoops were set ablaze, through which livestock and humans would pass as an act of purification. Herbs such as vervain and rue were cut on Midsummer and hung over doors and barn stalls to provide protection. The wild white daisies that bloom now along country lanes and in meadows were considered magic, for they represented the Sun. By mid-month the heat of summer begins, which gives June's Full Moon its name: the Strong Sun Moon. The beauty of summer's first Full Moon is rivaled only by another glowing token of June, the twinkling firefly.

   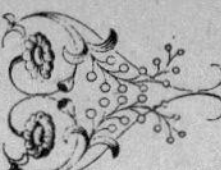 

June 1
Thursday

1st ♌

Color of the day: Green
Incense of the day: Geranium

Dream of Blue Almonds Spell

For this success and divination spell, carry an almond with you for one full day before proceeding. Light a dark blue candle and sprinkle a pinch of cinnamon over the flame, visualizing the success you seek. See yourself waking up each day with new ideas and spirit guidance. Feel creativity flowing through you. Holding the almond with tweezers or tongs, warm it in the flame, chanting three times:

> As I lay me down to sleep,
> Spirit guidance I do seek.
> Success and vision, come
> to me—
> Bless me with creativity.

Place the almond under your side of the bed. Each night as you lie down to sleep, hold the intent to remember dreams that will show you the answers you need for success.

Kristin Madden

Notes:

June 2
Friday
Shavuot

1st ♌
☽ → ♍ 4:17 pm

Color of the day: Pink
Incense of the day: Nutmeg

Shavuot Bread Offering

Take two pieces of unleavened bread, such as pita bread, and on one carve something that you wish for yourself, such as the words "good luck." On the other carve something that you wish to change, like a bad habit. Spread the first piece with honey and say:

> Sweet is the future,
> My future renewed.
> I harvest this wish.
> My wish will come true.

Eat this piece of bread. Spread the second piece with salt and water and say:

> By salt I cleanse myself
> of thee,
> Saltwater wash this
> (bad habit) from me.

Break the bread, and toss it out. Shavuot, the Feast of the Weeks, is the Jewish holiday celebrating the harvest season in Israel. The name of the holiday refers to the timing of the festival, which is held exactly

seven days after Passover. It also celebrates the giving of the Ten Commandments to Moses. To further this spell consider ten things you wish to do in the coming year. Carve images and words describing your goals in clay, and keep the clay in a special place to dry out. Shavuot is also the time known as the day of first fruits. Bring an offering from your garden to someone you respect and love. Alternatively, give a gift of something handmade. This is a time for remembrance. On the second day of Shavuot, a candle is lit to honor the ancestors who have passed before.

Nancy Bennett

Notes:

June 3
Saturday

1st ♍

2nd Quarter 7:06 am

Color of the day: White
Incense of the day: Pine

Give Up Past hurts Spell

Holding on to grudges and vengeful thoughts only drain positive emotional energy. Feelings of anger or past hurts should be released in constructive ways. Forgiveness creates a sense of self-acceptance, improves well-being, and brings liberation. If you unleash those suppressed feelings forgiving, you thus release yourself of blockages. Take a piece of black obsidian or jet crystal with you on a walk to the nearest river. Find a quiet spot and sit comfortably. Hold the crystal with both hands. Reflect upon events that had upset you and find the true source of anger. Cry and silently rant and rave your feelings, releasing them into the crytal. Recite a relevant affirmation to free yourself of anger. Repeat the affirmation seven times. Throw the crystal into the river with all your strength. Walk home and do not look back.

S. Y. Zenith

Notes:

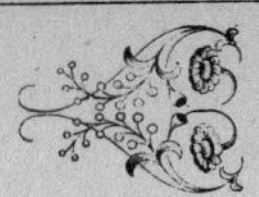

June 4
Sunday

2nd ♍

Color of the day: Orange
Incense of the day: Cinnamon

Pick Me Spell

There are times when we wish to remain unnoticed. But there are other times when we really want to stand out in a crowd. This happens in particular when we are competing with other candidates for a job or a promotion, or are trying out for that special part in a play, or are striving for anything else that demands that attention be placed on us. The ideal time for a "pick me" spell is during a waxing Moon, such as today. Anoint a red candle with clove oil and gaze into the flame. While gazing, imagine yourself in your new desired position. See the candle flame warm and illuminate you, making you stand out, and say:

> Only for the good of all
> If this is meant to be
> Forces work together
> To help pick me!

When you face the time of selection, imagine yourself surrounded in the same red candle glow as when you spoke the charm. Work to project the electrifying energy of the flickering flame.

Emely Flak

Notes:

June 5
Monday

2nd ♍

☽ → ♎ 5:08 am

Color of the day: Black
Incense of the day: Lavender

Find a Sacred Stone Spell

The Celts celebrate the feast day of Saint Gobnatt, a Christianized version of the earth goddess Domna, by going on a long walk today. This goddess rules the mountains, the land of rock and crystal. Try taking a hike today, but before you begin turn clockwise three times. Say:

> May all evil sleep,
> May all good awake.
> May the hills lie low,
> May the sacred stones
> come up to greet me.

Leave a crystal as a gift to Domna and be on the lookout for a stone in return. The luckiest find would be an agate, the stone associated with June.

Lily Gardner-Butts

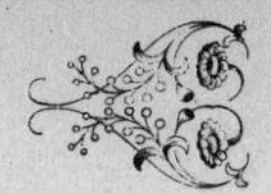

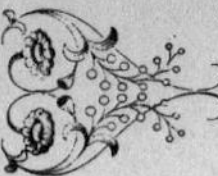

Notes:

June 6
Tuesday

2nd ♎

Color of the day: Red
Incense of the day: Ginger

Witches' Bottles Spell

Witches' bottles are jugs, bottles, or jars filled with items directed toward a specific magical purpose, usually protection. These bottles can sometimes still be found in the ruins of old houses. This spell will help you create a magically charged bottle to protect your home and property. You'll need a small jar about the size of a jelly jar. Fill the jar halfway with vinegar. Add some salt, a generous dash of pepper, and a rusty nail. Concentrate on your purpose as you fill the jar. Take the jar outside after night has fallen and bury it. As you cover the bottle with soil, whisper these words: "Vinegar cleanses, salt purifies, pepper stings, and the rusty nail protects. Let friends be welcome here, and let foes retreat." Walk away and tell no one about your bottle. The bottle may remain undisturbed for years, or you may repeat the spell occasionally if you wish.

James Kambos

Notes:

June 7
Wednesday

2nd ♎
☽ → ♏ 4:41 pm

Color of the day: Topaz
Incense of the day: Neroli

Fire and Water Spell

Fire and water were sacred to the Druids, who venerated and respected the power of each. Fire ignited and intensified ritual workings, while water blessed, purified, and healed. Fire was connected with inspiration, and water with wisdom. "Fire in water" referred to the illumination of poets, and to the power

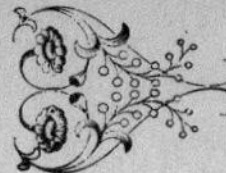

of the Sun which was present in warm, healing springs. One of the most famous goddesses of a hot spring was Sulis, who presided over the ancient spring at modern Bath, England. Her name means "eye," alluding to the Sun, the "eye of the sky." Here is a prayer to the Sun or to the sun goddesses (for the Sun is feminine in Celtic tradition):

> Hail to you,
> Sun of the seasons,
> Glorious mother of the stars.
> You lie down in the ocean without fear
> And rise up on the wave crest
> Like a queenly maiden in bloom.

Sharynne NicMhacha

Notes:

June 8

Thursday

2nd ♏

Color of the day: Purple
Incense of the day: Musk

Never Be Broke Spells

Keep a piece of malachite in your purse to assure you will never be broke. A piece of peridot in your pocket will do the same. A silver coin is also a good talisman to keep so you will never be without cash. A piece of devil's shoestring in your pocket at a job interview helps to increase your chances of landing the job. It is also good to keep in your pocket when you ask for that raise at work! Burning patchouli during a money spell adds to the spell's abundance energies. Set a piece of bryony (*bryonia alba*) root on your money to increase prosperity. Burn chamomile or add some to a spell bag to increase money. Sprinkle Irish moss in your wallet for gaining and keeping a steady income of money.

Boudica

Notes:

June 9

Friday

2nd ♏

Color of the day: White
Incense of the day: Rose

Love Stick to You Spell

In today's hectic world, finding and keeping other people in your life can pose quite a challenge. This spell helps love "stick to you." You will need a ball of craft foam, a package of tiny rosebuds (preferably dried, but silk will also work), some glue, and ribbon. Begin by imbuing the ball with your personal energy and the rosebuds with loving energy. Now glue the rosebuds to the ball, one at a time, packing them tightly together over the sphere until the whole surface is covered. Visualize yourself surrounded by love. Allow the glue to set completely, then wrap ribbon around the ball, and tie a bow. Hang the love globe in your bathroom or bedroom. Whenever you need extra assurance, speak these words:

> Loving thoughts, come
> to me.
> Loving hearts, come to me.
> Loving deeds, come from me.
> Loving ways, come from me.
> As I will, so mote it be!

Elizabeth Barrette

Notes:

June 10

Saturday

2nd ♏
☽ → ♐ 1:05 am

Color of the day: Gray
Incense of the day: Sandalwood

Rose Moon Love Spell

It is soon the Rose Moon, a time to reflect on the patron goddess of the month, Juno. Juno is goddess of love. Rose quartz, stone of friendship, warmth, and love, symbolizes Juno and this month's Moon. Take a piece of rose quartz that you find attractive and put it inside a crystal bowl. Set this out under the light of the Rose Moon on Sunday. Dance around the bowl chanting:

> Rose of Juno,
> Named for this Moon,
> Bring me love
> And bring it soon!

Say this with passion until you can't say it anymore. Leave this bowl out-

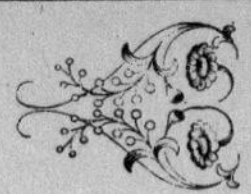

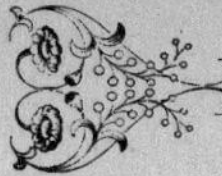

side until it has rained. The night after the rain bring the stone inside. Wrap it in a piece of white fabric. Tie it with a pink ribbon. Give it to your intended. If love is meant to be, the next Full Moon will reciprocate your gift of the heart.

Stephanie Rose Bird

Notes:

June 11
Sunday

2nd ♐

Full Moon 2:03 pm

Color of the day: Gold
Incense of the day: Basil

Expand Partnerships Spell

With the Full Moon in Sagittarius, the fire sign of expansion and friendship, now is the time to revel in new communications and new ideas that came at the New Moon. Follow your ideas as far as they will go. Don't confine yourself to just one approach. Explore boundaries and try new angles. Don't be afraid to think outside the box. On this night, dab a bit of sweet orange oil on a purple candle and decorate it with the symbol for Sagittarius, which looks like an arrow being drawn back and made ready to take flight. Place a turquoise stone on your altar. An all-around beneficial stone, this Sagittarian gem is said to attract money, success, love, luck, health, and friendship. Hold the stone in your hands, saying:

May creative inspiration
for synthesis and for
manifestation flow into
my spirit.

May the energy and
courage to realize these
ideas enliven my spirit.

May the wisdom and
support of others sustain
my will, until the work
is done.

So mote it be.

Lady MoonDance

Notes:

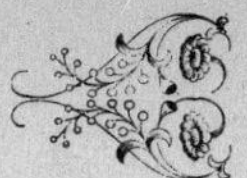

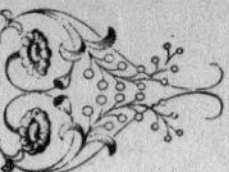

June 12
Monday

3rd ♐
☽ → ♑ 6:19 am

Color of the day: Silver
Incense of the day: Peony

Safe Perimeter Spell

Place a protective perimeter around your yard or play area to help keep everyone safe this summer. The kids can even help with this spell. You will need lavender or sandalwood stick incense, water with a pinch of salt added to it, and, if you don't mind making some noise, drums, rattles, bells, or some other music maker. Pick a starting point and slowly make your way around the yard infusing the boundary with incense smoke and sprinkled water. As you walk, visualize a barrier of white light forming, keeping out violence, accidents, and other unwanted incidents. When you return to the starting point, take a moment to "see" the energy swirling about the lawn, protecting all within.

Laurel Reufner

Notes:

June 13
Tuesday

3rd ♑

Color of the day: Black
Incense of the day: Poplar

Find Something Green Spell

Summer has definitely arrived. Today, find something green and growing. It can be a meadow of grass, a tree, or a potted plant. Scientific studies have proven that plants do respond to our words. Praise the plant or group of plants excessively. Tell it how beautiful it is and how grateful you are for it with words such as these:

> O spirit of green summer,
> I praise thee. Thy beauty
> lightens my heart and
> gives me joy. Thy oxygen
> gives me clean breaths.
> Thy presence improves
> my planet and my life.
> Existence would diminish
> without thee and thy kin.
>
> Thou are magnificent. I
> thank thee. I praise thee.
> I love thee.

Gift the plant with a hug, a kiss, or a song. Gift someone else with a growing plant in order to share your love of the natural beauty and energy of life-giving plants.

Luci Sophia Zain

Notes:

June 14
Wednesday

Flag Day

3rd ♑

☽ → ♒ 9:32 am

Color of the day: Brown
Incense of the day: Coriander

Honoring Finished Projects Ritual

Whenever we finish a project, there is always a loss or death involved. As a result, we often feel a sense of depression and sadness when it's over. These feelings should be honored. One way to do this is to create a sacred collage celebrating your achievement. Use pictures, words, and objects that symbolize the project and its meaning to you. It can be as big and bold or small and detailed as you desire. While making the collage, burn some candles and incense to create a sacred space. Use white candles with sandalwood, nag champa, or frankincense and myrrh. After you make the collage, place it on your altar, in a scrapbook, or somewhere in your office so it will frequently remind you of your pride of finishing your project.

Olivia O'Meir

Notes:

June 15
Thursday

3rd ♒

Color of the day: White
Incense of the day: Sage

Willpower Spell

To know, to will, to dare, to be silent are the four corners of the Witch's pyramid. Fire is the element that summons will and summer is its corresponding season. A fire spell is especially fortuitous now, as this is the feast day of Vesta, the hearth flame. To begin this spell you need to spend time reflecting on what you wish to manifest. Ask yourself

   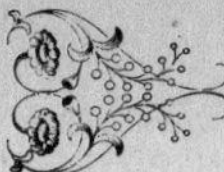 

what you need to do in the physical world to accomplish your aim. When you feel certain of what you need to do, build a sacred fire. Give an offering to the spirits of fire. Any of the following will do: allspice, basil, clove, dill, ginger, or frankincense. When the offering is burnt away, say:

> **Fiery spirits of the south**
> **lands, burn away my**
> **lazy ways. Light my will**
> **with your sure flames.**

Visualize the fire's flames burning away your excuses and lack of energy. Then visualize the flames lighting the fire in your belly that won't allow you to quit until you've achieved your aims. Thank the fire spirits for their aid.

Lily Gardner-Butts

Notes:

June 16

Friday

3rd ♒

☽ → ♓ 12:05 pm

Color of the day: Rose
Incense of the day: Dill

Find Your True Vocation Spell

A vocation is often thought of as just work. One's true vocation reveals the origins of the word—it is a "calling." It calls to our spirits, our hearts, and our passions. A vocation may be where we earn our money, but it should also be where we devote our waking moments and thoughts. True vocation should really be both—work that absorbs us and makes us passionate while giving us a living and paying our bills. To find your true vocation, spend some time now thinking about what excites you and what ignites your passions. Think about the times in your life where every fiber of your being was alive with excitement. Fill a dark-colored bowl or pan with water. In a darkened room, settle yourself into a meditative state. Swirl the water in the bowl until it is moving in a deosil direction. Hold it before your eyes and meditate on the movement of the water. Allow the images to come to you and the messages to speak to your heart.

Gail Wood

Notes:

June 17
Saturday

3rd ♓

Color of the day: Blue
Incense of the day: Maple

Rutile Spell for Neutralizing Dark Feelings

Rutile is a black, prismatic crystal that can be found in igneous and metamorphic rocks worldwide. In rutilated quartz, rutile appears as tiny needle-like inclusions. Although it can come in other colors—such as blue, red, gray, and brown—the black variety is useful for filtering out past unpleasant memories that impact subconsciously upon the soul in a negative way. It is a gentle mediator and guides its owner whenever self-confrontation is required for clearing away old cobwebs and for achieving clarity regarding one's direction in life. For those with low self-esteem, rutile dispels feelings of self-contempt. When going through stages of what some would term the "dark nights of the soul," obtain a few small rutiles for placing around the home, bedroom, workplace, and for carrying on the person.

S. Y. Zenith

Notes:

June 18
Sunday

Father's Day

3rd ♓

4th Quarter 10:08 am

☽ → ♈ 2:54 pm

Color of the day: Amber
Incense of the day: Parsley

Spell to Protect a Special Man

Purchase or make a tie. Before presenting it as a gift, find a quiet space. Make a ritual circle using a golden cord or ribbon with a picture of your special man inside it. Place the tie in the center and say:

> Amaneut,
> heed my request.
> Imprint your will,
> This man protect.

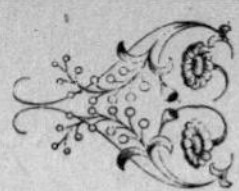

O shadowed one,
Please hear my wish.
Protect the one
Who wears this gift.

Place the tie in a box and tie it thrice round with the golden cord, making a knot at each turn. Imagine all your protection and love being sealed in the knots. When the gift is given, the energy will be released to the one who opens the knots. Amaneut is an Egyptian goddess of protection. Her name means "hidden one," and if her shadow falls on you she will protect you from harm.

Nancy Bennett

Notes:

June 19
Monday

4th ♈

Color of the day: Gray
Incense of the day: Lavender

House Hunting Spell

It can be tricky to find the right combination of price, solid structure, and features that you want when you are shopping for a home. Look at as many houses as possible and spend as much time as you can looking. Do not jump at the first house you see. Always seek advice from experts when there are contracts to sign, offers to make, and questions to ask on the structure of the house. Before you start viewing each day, say this spell:

Hestia,
Guide my search today.
Help me find a home I
pray.
Show me problems before
I sign
So I can choose the right
home to be mine.

Again, I can not emphasize enough the importance of seeking professional advice on issues that you have questions about. Half the work of a spell is doing the prep work and sweating just a little.

Boudica

Notes:

June 20
Tuesday

4th ♈
☽ → ♉ 6:23 pm

Color of the day: White
Incense of the day: Frankincense

Midsummer Herb-fire Ritual

In Scotland, many sacred herbs were gathered in preparation for Midsummer rites. These included yarrow, vervain, elderberry, St. John's wort, and the seed from night-seeding ferns. Such fern seed had the property of making people invisible, and elderberries gathered at this time conferred magical powers. St. John's wort was widely used for protection, abundance, and healing magic. It was believed to protect against thunder (thunderstorms being frequent at this time of year), and it was sometimes burned in the Midsummer fires. St. John's wort was effective only if accidentally found. Here is a Scottish charm for gathering St. John's wort at Midsummer for luck, protection, abundance, and prosperity.

> St. John's wort,
> St. John's wort,
> I envy whoever has you.
> I will pluck you with my
> right hand
> And preserve you with
> my left.
> Whoever finds you,
> Will never be without
> abundance.

Sharynne NicMhacha

Notes:

June 21
Wednesday

Summer Solstice – Litha

4th ♉
☉ → ♋ 8:26 am

Color of the day: Yellow
Incense of the day: Sandalwood

Longest Day Spell

Since the Summer Solstice is the longest day of the year, this magical day may be observed with activities throughout the day. In the morning, before sunrise, light a tall orange candle, and from its flame light four smaller white candles to represent the four seasons, saying: "Father Sun, you illuminate the year." Then, fashion a small hoop from a thin branch. Ignite the hoop and let it burn out in a heat-proof dish. As the Sun rises, snuff out the candles. At noon, the solar hour,

 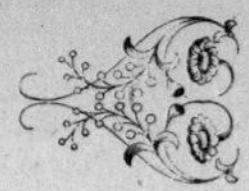  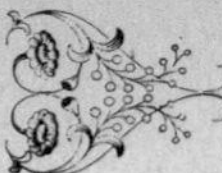 

go into a garden or wooded area and select a tree to honor. Trees are living beings who, although connected to Mother Earth, reach toward Father Sun to complete their growth cycle. Honor your chosen tree with a gift of compost or water. At sunset, light your candles again, and thank the Sun for returning. You may seek visions by sprinkling the area with larkspur, or you can simply meditate. When done, snuff out the candles. After dark, near midnight if possible, harvest any herbs for future magical use. As a final gesture on this longest day, sprinkle the ashes from the hoop you burned near your front door.

James Kambos

Notes:

June 22
Thursday

4th ♉
☽ → ♊ 10:49 pm

Color of the day: Crimson
Incense of the day: Carnation

Abundance Floor Wash Spell

Ah, the wonderful fields of summer green—symbolic of verdant earth, abundance, the fecundity of Gaia. Try this green-scented floor wash to harvest the abundance of the season. Add two cups fresh basil to a large cauldron of boiling water. Remove the cauldron from heat. Add one ounce of pyrite chips to the cauldron and cover. Set it outside overnight, then strain the liquid. Be careful to remove and save the pyrite for other spells. Add eight drops holy basil essential oil to the liquid. Put a bowl of fine sea salt in the center of the room you are blessing. Clean all surfaces with the abundance floor wash using a natural sea sponge, concentrating on your desires the entire time. Sprinkle some of the fine sea salt on stains as you work. Open the doors and windows if possible so the spirits can aid your work. Good fortune should flow your way.

Stephanie Rose Bird

Notes:

June 23

Friday

4th ♊

Color of the day: Purple
Incense of the day: Thyme

Desert Protection Spell

During summer, any place can seem like a desert. Take advantage of this hot, fierce energy to work a spell for protection. Just as cacti grow sharp spines to defend their moist, succulent parts from hungry animals, you can protect yourself in such a manner now. For this spell, you need a potted cactus and one or more stones that add to the protective, desert mood. Crushed lava rock can be used to cover the soil all around the plant. Smoky quartz crystals, flint arrowheads, and tumbled carnelians make good accents. Set the stone in the Sun for at least an hour to charge it. Then place the stone in the pot next to the cactus. Visualize your home protected by a layer of thorns projecting outward, just as with the cactus. Connect this image to the stone, which will provide power. Conversely to welcome someone inside that you'd like to have visit, visualize a cactus flower projecting beyond the thorns. Keep the cactus in a sunny window in your home.

Elizabeth Barrette

Notes:

June 24

Saturday

4th ♊

Color of the day: Black
Incense of the day: Lilac

Your Inner Storyteller Spell

We all have stories to tell that make others laugh, cry, and learn. We may not know that we have the ability to communicate these stories with joy and love. Find a quiet place sacred to you and settle into a meditative state. Breathe deeply and cast your awareness inside your body. As you walk around, go into the rooms of your heart. In one room, see the storyteller in a rocking chair. Go and sit there and listen to the stories. When the stories are done, the storyteller holds your hands, looks deep into your eyes, and then kisses you, saying: "Welcome, bard." You feel the power of stories fill you. With your hands and voice, you are now able to tell vibrant, beautiful stories.

With a long breath, open your eyes, now back in your sacred place.

Gail Wood

Notes:

June 25
Sunday

4th ♊
☽ → ♋ 4:48 am

New Moon 12:05 pm

Color of the day: Yellow
Incense of the day: Cinnamon

Finding Your Home Spell

The New Moon in Cancer, the sign of the crab, speaks of emotions, home, and the need for security. Real crabs carry their home wherever they go. Likewise, the members of this sign are sometimes oversensitive and grow a thick psychic shell for protection. This is a good time to work on your own inner home or temple, a safe place that you carry with you. Sometimes sudden changes in the world around us cause us to forget that we have this place. Even if you know it well, it is a good idea to go back and visit your safe place from time to time. For this working, place a silver candle in a bowl of water. The water is the world around you, ever changing. The candle is the light of your own spirit and the safe harbor it provides. Light the candle, put out the rest of the lights in the room, and concentrate on the flame. Breathe slowly, grounding and centering. Then close your eyes and ask yourself what your safe place looks like. If you don't know, ask to be taken to it. Soon, you will see some mode of transportation to take you there. It may be a special secluded spot in nature, a special room you knew as a child, or even an imaginary spot from a favorite book that captured your heart. Once you are there, look around, making a note of what it looks like. Tidy it up, add a few comfortable touches, whatever it takes to really make this space "home" for you. As you are getting ready to leave, know that this place is always waiting for you whenever you need to return. You don't even have to remember the way, because your heart and soul will remember for you.

Lady MoonDance

Notes:

June 26
Monday

1st ♋

Color of the day: Ivory

Incense of the day: Chrysanthemum

Home of Legos Spell

Need a new place to dwell? Dig out some small toy building blocks, such as Legos, and start building your dream home, or at least some semblance thereof. Build a good strong foundation. And don't forget to include some windows—we all need a little sunshine. As you build with your hands, also build in your mind, creating a mental representation of the type of home you would like to have. Picture yourself living there, with your things scattered about. Everything is in its place. Once, your LegoLand home is finished, find a spot for it on your altar. Place a brown candle nearby to help the magic along. Leave it in its place until your move is a reality, then discharge the energy and put your toys away.

Laurel Reufner

Notes:

June 27
Tuesday

1st ♋

☽ → ♌ 1:09 pm

Color of the day: Scarlet

Incense of the day: Honeysuckle

Do It Differently Spell

We've all experienced challenging moments when we've wished that we hadn't said or done what we had. If only we had someone with us to help guide to avoid such mistakes! You can appoint a spiritual guardian to help you. Today, mentally prepare this assistance so it's ready to invoke when you need it. Select a god or goddess who possesses qualities you admire. Create a symbol that you associate with your chosen deity. Place the symbol on your altar and say:

When I feel the need
I will summon you
For protection and confidence
And strength to shine
through.

Thank your guardian and call it when you need to gather confidence.

Emely Flak

Notes:

June 28
Wednesday

1st ♌

Color of the day: White
Incense of the day: Eucalyptus

Build Confidence Spell

Confidence is important. A confident person inspires trust from others. We all could use a bit more self-assurance at work and school. To build confidence today, brew some black tea. As you add honey to it, whisper: "The sweetness of life is mine to savor." Before drinking, say: "Black tea, evoke confidence within me." While you drink your confidence tea, visualize yourself confident and self-assured in every situation. Imagine the people you may encounter and the places you may go today. See and feel those around you reacting in a positive way to your calm confidence. To add potency to this spell, carry one black tea bag with you all day, then place black tea leaves in your pillow or under your mattress while you sleep.

Kristin Madden

Notes:

June 29
Thursday

1st ♌

Color of the day: Turquoise
Incense of the day: Geranium

Dream Getaway Spell

Do you have a place that calls to you, a place you long to travel to? If you can't travel there in person, plan a trip in imagination. Get out maps. Plan an itinerary. Cook foods that you would eat at your special getaway. Wear the clothes that you would wear at your special place. Put on the music of your favorite place. Light a candle, saying:

> As I have plotted my
> journey, dressed for my
> special place, eaten the
> foods of my special land,
> and listened to the songs
> of my heart home, let my
> heart rise up as it would
> if I were there. I will now
> be there in spirit. I cele-
> brate my love for another
> place. Blessed be.

Luci Sophia Zain

Notes:

June 30

Friday

1st ♌
☽ → ♍ 12:15 am

Color of the day: Coral
Incense of the day: Sandalwood

Gypsy Journey Spell

Aestas, goddess of summer, is honored today with flowers and sheaves of corn. This spell using the magical traits of corn and the waning of the Moon offers protection from accident and injury as we go off on summer holidays now. Light a new white candle and make a pan of cornbread as follows:

1 1/2 cup flour
2/3 cup sugar
1/2 cup cornmeal
1 tbl. baking powder
1/2 tsp. salt
1 1/2 cups milk
2 eggs, beaten
1/3 cup oil
3 tbls. melted butter

Mix together ingredients, visualizing the blessings of Aestas. Bake in a greased eight-by-eight-inch pan in a 350 degree oven for eighteen to twenty minutes. Gypsies carry a piece of cornbread in their pockets to ensure safe journeys.

Lily Gardner-Butts

July is the seventh month of the year. Its astrological sign is Cancer, the crab (June 21–July 22), a cardinal water sign ruled by the Moon. July is the month of the ripening. In orchards, fields, and gardens, nature moves toward the miracle of the harvest. In July heat, the Goddess fulfills her promise and oversees maturing crops. The Summer Solstice has passed, but nature pulses with life. Hummingbirds flash among the bee balm, and mint varieties spread like wildfire. Water is an important magical element in July. Birds refresh themselves in birdbaths. Thunder rumbles on hot afternoons, bringing a promise of rain. Dragonflies skim the surface of ponds, and vacationers head to the shore. Salt water and seashells are good ways to include the element of water in any rituals now. Independence Day, July 4, is the major holiday of high summer. Not only can we celebrate our nation's independence, we can also use give thanks for July's abundance, which will sustain us during the coming months. We are blessed with richness in July, perhaps the reason the old ones referred to July's Full Moon as the Blessing Moon. Magic during this Moon may include all forms of prosperity charms. When you cast a spell now, you will feel the vitality of the earth.

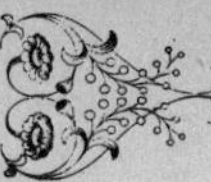

July 1
Saturday

1st ♍

Color of the day: Brown
Incense of the day: Juniper

True Blue Heart Spell

Sometimes we need courage and patience when intereacting with our families. Self-doubt and second-guessing need to be banished so we can feel safe in revealing who we really are, remembering that these people should love us best. This little talisman will go with you anywhere for a little extra courage from the heart, just when you need it most. You'll need red and blue crayons or colored pencils and a standard piece of paper. Work by the light of red candles, and wear your favorite scent. In the middle of the paper draw a heart and color it with the red crayon. Fill in the rest of the page with the blue crayon. Put the drawing on a bulletin board, or fold and carry it with you.

Laurel Reufner

Notes:

Holiday lore: Today is the first day of the season for climbing Mt. Fuji in Yamabiraki, Japan. Mt. Fuji is the highest peak in Japan and is revered in Japanese culture. Considered the foremother or grandmother of Japan, Fuji is an ancient fire goddess of the indigenous Ainu people. In modern times, the Ainu mostly resided on the northern island of Hokkaido. The name *Fuji* was derived from an Ainu word that means "fire," or "deity of fire." Each year since the Meiji era, a summer festival has been held to proclaim the beginning of the climbing season and to pray for the safety of local inhabitants and visitors or pilgrims to the sacred mountain. The two-month climbing season begins today, and ends on August 30.

July 2
Sunday

1st ♍

☽ → ♎ 1:06 pm

Color of the day: Orange
Incense of the day: Sage

Feast of the Charities Ritual

Today is the Feast of the Charites. These old Greek goddesses of beneficence were known to the Romans as the *Gratiae,* or "Graces." They are Aglaea, whose name means "splendor," Euphrosyne, or "joy," and Thalia, or "mirth." The Charites bestow charm,

   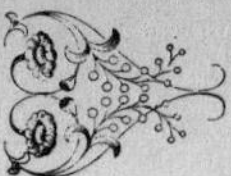 

beauty, and creativity on their worshippers. In this regard they serve a similar purpose to the nine Muses. Generosity and festive activities please these goddesses. Get some friends together and dress up. Arrange each other's hair. Dance and sing, or perform some sacred theatre. Visit an art gallery or walk through a street fair. Alternatively, do something nice for the less fortunate. Bundle up old clothes you never wear anymore to recycle for the less fortunate, or hold a food drive and donate the results to a local charity. (Yes, the term comes from the name of these goddesses, "Charites.") You could also donate your money or time. Give of yourself, and you shall receive "grace" from the Charites in return. Be kind and giving, and your creativity will overflow!

Elizabeth Barrette

Notes:

July 3
Monday

1st ♎

2nd Quarter 12:37 pm

Color of the day: Lavender
Incense of the day: Myrrh

House Renovation Spell

Before you begin with the house contractors—and all the dust, the noise and mess, the late deliveries, missed deadlines, and the headaches—gather the following: a black candle for protection, a green candle for money, and a yellow candle for success. Anoint the candles with a dab of patchouli oil. Burn the candles and say:

To change this house
and make it mine,
To get the job done in
reasonable time,
For weather fair and no
cost overrun,
May it be as I envision
when it's finally done!

Boudica

Notes:

   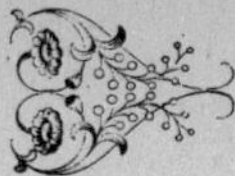 

July 4
Tuesday
Independence Day

2nd ♎

Color of the day: Red
Incense of the day: Evergreen

Freedom from the Chains that Bind Mojo

This is the date in 1776 when the Declaration of Independence was set forward. One of the more compelling portions of the declaration, particularly in relation to Pagans and Witches is: "all men are created equal, that they are endowed by their Creator with certain unalienable Rights, that among these are Life, Liberty and the pursuit of Happiness." Clearly though, this beautiful sentiment did not apply to all as it was not until 1863 that the Emancipation Proclamation was written, stating: "all persons held as slaves within any State or designated part of a State . . . shall be then, thenceforward, and forever free; and the Executive Government of the United States . . . will recognize and maintain the freedom of such persons." Later, the 19th Amendment gave women the right to vote. All the while there has been a humble root that Hoodoos of various faiths, colors, and creeds have placed in their mojo bags as emblematic of personal freedom and the promise of happiness. High John the Conqueror *(Ipomoea jalapa)* is more than a simple tuber, but is a symbolic representation of breaking free of the chains of slavery. High John, a relative of both the morning glory and sweet potato, represents the slave who fights against enslavement until freedom is obtained. We all suffer from one type of slavery or another. Today create a mojo, utilizing the power of the natural amulet, High John, along with the stone hematite to strengthen the system and help one break free of addiction. Find a red flannel bag with a drawstring closure, and place High John the Conqueror inside. Add a clear, charged hematite stone and a pinch of kosher salt. If you've got a few devil's shoe strings, add them in to keep evil at bay. Slippery elm, lemongrass, and eucalyptus are also known to aid in freedom, so add a pinch of each. Roll the bag on the ground a few times so the herbs crumble and are well mixed. Finally, add a few drops of rose oil to add extra power. Now, you've got yourself a Freedom from the Chains that Bind mojo bag.

Stephanie Rose Bird

Notes:

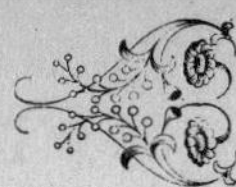

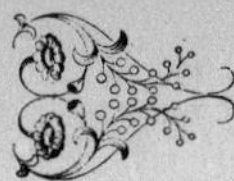

Holiday notes: On July 4, 1776, the Second Continental Congress adopted the Declaration of Independence. Philadelphians were first to mark the anniversary of American independence with a celebration, but Independence Day became commonplace only after the War of 1812. By the 1870s, the Fourth of July was the most important secular holiday in the country, celebrated even in far-flung communities on the western frontier of the country.

July 5
Wednesday

2nd ♎
☽ → ♏ 1:13 am

Color of the day: Yellow
Incense of the day: Cedar

Two Fairy Spells

The summer months are a great time to penetrate the veil between our world and the fairy realm. These spells, tried and true, were adapted from seventeenth-century manuscripts. To see fairies: Rinse a glass vial with a tea of rose and marigolds, then pour a pint of salad oil into the vial and warm it until the oil turns white. Add buds of hollyhock and hazel and blossoms of marigold and thyme. Add to this mixture blades of grass from a fairy throne, which are those grassy spots in the shade of an elder tree ringed by toadstools. Let this mixture steep for three days in the Sun, then keep it for your use. To break a fairy spell, wear your clothes inside out and turn round three times in a windershins direction.

Lily Gardner-Butts

Notes:

July 6
Thursday

2nd ♏

Color of the day: Green
Incense of the day: Musk

Spell for Spiritual Devotion

Today is the Dalai Lama's birthday. He is an inspiring and compassionate leader for people of all faiths. Each one of us can attain a high level of devotion to our spiritual paths. We find strength, honor, and devotion within ourselves all the time, and we can renew our intention and our devotion at any time. Find a quiet place and settle yourself into it. Light a pink candle

   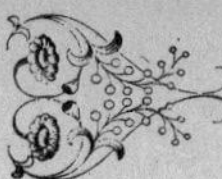 

for the affection and love you have for yourself, and a white candle for the purity of your love for the divine that guides you. Breathe deeply and fully. As you breathe out, expel everything that pulls your attention away from your spiritual devotion. As you breathe in, take in peace and compassion. When you have expelled all distraction, simply breathe for a few moments. Breathe in pink and breathe out white. Continue to breathe in the sweetness and peace for at least twenty minutes. When you are finished, thank all the spirits that guide you, then extinguish the candles.

Gail Wood

Notes:

July 7

Friday

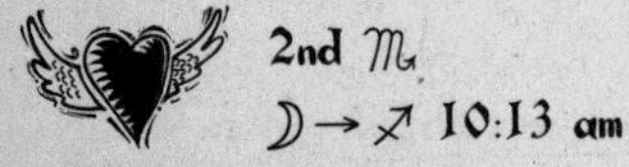

2nd ♏
☽ → ♐ 10:13 am

Color of the day: White
Incense of the day: Ylang-ylang

Find Love Spell

The seventh day of the seventh month is a potent time to perform magic. Seven is the number of the mysteries—powerful but secretive. Since it is also a Friday, this would be a good day to draw a romance into your life. Spread out a cloth of deep maroon, and place a maroon candle, a piece of white paper, and an envelope on it. Also assemble a teaspoon each of orange peel, rose geranium leaves, and rosemary. Pour a glass of sweet red wine. Light the candle, sip the wine, and say:

I am warmed by love's
sweet fire.
Bring me the love I desire.
I taste the sweetness of
love's wine,
For the love I want is
mine.

Wrap the herbs in the paper and seal them in the envelope. Hide the envelope among your clothes. Love will come.

James Kambos

Notes:

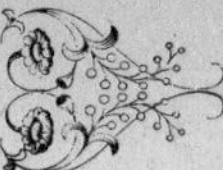

July 8
Saturday

2nd ♐

Color of the day: Gray
Incense of the day: Pine

Foxglove Healing Spell

Foxglove, a plant long associated with the fairies, blooms at this time of year. It is sometimes also called "fairy's thimbles" or in Scottish Gaelic *Lus-nam-ban-sith*, the "plant of the fairy women." Certain parts of the foxglove can be used for healing remedies, but they must be used very carefully. The plant was also associated with Witches and with a variety of magical spells for love, protection, and success. Use this charm when gathering foxgloves:

> I will pluck the fairy wort
> from the fairy bower with
> expectation to overcome
> every oppression.
>
> Fairy wort, fairy wort, I
> envy the one who has you.
> There is nothing the Sun
> encircles, but to her is a
> certain victory.

Sharynne NicMhacha

Notes:

July 9
Sunday

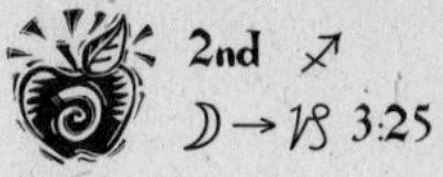

2nd ♐
☽ → ♑ 3:25 pm

Color of the day: Amber
Incense of the day: Pine

Kam-Kwat Health Spell

Kam-kwat, a Cantonese-Chinese word, is a species of the mandarin and orange botanical family, known in English as kumquat. Some kumquat varieties are a cross between orange and lime. They can be found in Chinatowns all over the world if you enquire with Chinese grocers and florists. In many affluent and feng shui-conscious Chinese homes and businesses, two pots of kumquat are placed on each side of a home's front entrace, just outside the main door. Kumquat signifies gold and auspiciousness and symbolizes health, prosperity, and good fortune. An alternative to a pot of kumquats is having a small orange tree sprouting ripening fruit in your living space. According to the Chinese and feng shui, the fruit can be used as one of the ingredients in spells for health concerns. An example is to squeeze the juice from the fruit, which is sour, bitter, and tangy, and mix it with honey as a preparation for colds and influenza. In purification baths, add seven or seventeen kumquats to the water and visualize the toxins being

 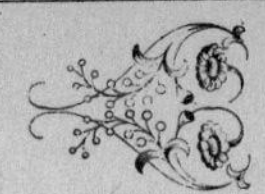  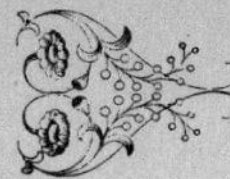 

removed from your body. Dispose of the fruit after the bath or bury it in the ground away from your home.

S. Y. Zenith

Notes:

July 10
Monday

2nd ♑

Full Moon 11:02 pm

Color of the day: Amber
Incense of the day: Clove

Bare Your Soul for a Goal Spell

On July 10, 1040, Lady Godiva rode naked through the streets of Coventry, England, in order to force her husband, the Earl of Mercia, to have a bit of mercy and lower taxes on his subjects. She asked that he reduce his overspending on elaborate public works, or to at least spend some of the money on art that the peasants might also be able to enjoy. He argued in return that the Greeks and Romans believed the nude body to be one of the greatest works of art and an expression of the purity and beauty of nature. He pledged to grant her request if she rode bare through the streets, and so the brave countess did just that. She rode clothed in nothing but her long, full hair, as the crowds turned away their eyes in respect. The Capricorn Full Moon, meanwhile, is about stability and a strong foundation: Reserved and unemotional, proper and yet not without some inner sensuality. Take time to ask yourself now what are you disciplined and determined enough to take on and achieve. For what goals are you are willing to strip away all your outer layers of comfort and armor? On a piece of parchment, write and sign a pledge to yourself to do something that will better your life or the life of those around you. Read the parchment every evening until your goals have been accomplished.

Lady MoonDance

Notes:

July 11
Tuesday

3rd ♑

☽ → ♒ 5:45 pm

Color of the day: Black
Incense of the day: Sage

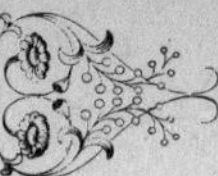

Seeing Synchronicity Spell

Is something that happens just coincidence or is it meant to happen? According to Carl Jung, the Swiss psychoanalyst, a coincidence is meaningful and occurs for a purpose. This also known as synchronicity. Pay close attention to events in your life that you might dismiss as mere coincidences. These could be important steps in your personal and spiritual development. An event that appears to be coincidental, or events that appear random and isolated, are connected to your subconscious and individual purpose. Synchronicity is a sign of magic happening, designed to deliver a message to you. As you become aware of these "meaningful coincidences," you will begin to notice synchronicity at work around you. Here are some tips to help you develop synchronicity awareness. Keep a journal so you can review events and identify connections. Take notice of apparent coincidences and ask: What does this mean to me?

Emely Flak

Notes:

July 12
Wednesday

3rd ♒

Color of the day: Brown
Incense of the day: Maple

Job Jolt Spell

Buy yourself some exotic coffee beans today, and take them home. Prepare a clean work space, and spread a green cloth on it. Grind the beans in a grinder while saying: "I'll break away from the daily grind. A new opportunity I'll soon find." Brew a cup of coffee and visualize the type of job you want. Make this coffee for yourself at work and at home until your wish is fulfilled. Gather the remaining beans in the green cloth and use them when needed. Today is known as a good-luck day in many parts of the world. Historically, it was considered among the most fortunate for traveling, finding a new home, or starting a new job. If you're content with your present situation, use this day to plan an adventure or vacation.

Nancy Bennett

Notes:

  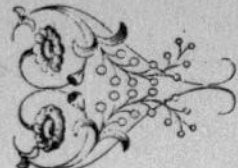 

July 13
Thursday

3rd ♒

☽ → ♓ 6:59 pm

Color of the day: Turquoise
Incense of the day: Jasmine

Money Tree Spell

Who says money doesn't grow on trees? Use this money tree spell to help grow your own wealth. Find a downed tree branch with several small twigs attached to it, and carve "Jupiter" into its base. Go over the carving with gold ink and add money symbols or other words associated with money to the rest of the branch. Then plant your branch in a pot of dirt. Make it stable enough to stand up unsupported. Tape three dollar bills to three separate twigs and give your tree a small offering of water. Visualize your tree growing more and more dollars until it is flush with money. Imagine that your bank account grows along with your money tree. Each time you receive unexpected money, place one more dollar on the tree, give thanks, and repeat your visualization.

Kristin Madden

Notes:

July 14
Friday

3rd ♓

Color of the day: Pink
Incense of the day: Nutmeg

Summer Storm Clear-Your-Head Spell

Summer thunderstorms provide a great opportunity for you to clear your head. You're caught up, no doubt, in the midst of a busy social schedule now, and perhaps looking for a way out of the whirlwind. The Chinese goddess Tien Mu creates lighting by reaching into the earth with one arm and reaching into a thundercloud with the other. She uses two huge mirrors, turning the reflective sides to face one another, to create the flashing bolt. This "enlightening" bolt can be used to clear your mind during a summer storm. See the storm clouds as your mental confusion and the earth as a grounding source. Each time the lightning strikes, imagine the clouds in your mind becoming illuminated, while your feet remain on the ground. When you are finished, thank Tien Mu for her gift.

Olivia O'Meir

Notes:

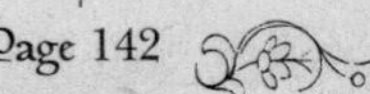

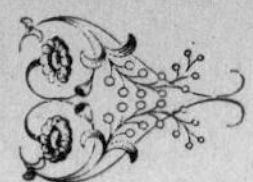

July 15
Saturday

3rd ♓

☽ → ♈ 8:39 pm

Color of the day: Blue
Incense of the day: Lavender

Midsummer Attraction Spell

We are approaching Midsummer now. This is a time when we are bound to become a little more frisky and romantically inclined. Pagans male and female know just what to do to attract others when their natures call. But in case you need a few reminders, here are a few herbs sure to do the trick. Dab pure sandalwood oil on pulse points to attract people of the opposite sex. Sandalwood also calms and relaxes nerves and eases sexual inhibitions. Men, especially in the Middle East and North Africa, find gulhina, the perfume oil of henna plant, a surefire way to become more attractive. It is used the same way as sandalwood oil. In Hoodoo and some other paths, folks who want to attract those of the same sex adore lavender. If this is your desire, dab some onto a few of your charkas. Southerners have taught us that the plants that grow so readily in their region can add a touch of magic to the love life. Slip a dried magnolia leaf or two between your mattress and box spring or under your futon to keep your lover close and faithful.

Stephanie Rose Bird

Notes:

July 16
Sunday

3rd ♈

Color of the day: Gold
Incense of the day: Basil

Safe Haven Spell

Home is a haven, a sanctuary. To keep our homes safe, sometimes we need to set up or reinforce our wards. Get out a small tray. On it, assemble a lit candle, some burning incense, and a dish of salt water. Decorate the tray with fresh flowers, crystals, or other talismans. This will be a portable altar. Carry the tray around each room of your home. Wave the incense, walking clockwise around each room, then carry the candle around the room. On your third circle around the room, sprinkle the salt water. As you walk, say:

   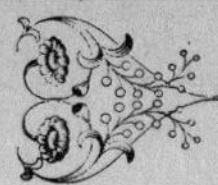 

I bless my home with love and light. Only these may enter. I bless my home by the four elements, and make it a safe haven for me and my family.

Luci Sophia Zain

Notes:

July 17
Monday

3rd ♈

4th Quarter 3:12 pm

☽ → ♉ 11:44 pm

Color of the day: Ivory
Incense of the day: Poplar

Butterfly Whispers Spell

In this day and age of global markets and global conflicts, our homes are often missing loved ones who may be half the world away. It is said that butterflies are the carriers of the soul to heaven. They were earthly representatives of the Greek goddess Psyche, who possessed the wings of a butterfly. These winged beauties also serve as messengers, carrying our thoughts and desires to those we love. Visit a place where the butterflies roam and can easily be found. Calmly and carefully try to get close to one of them so you can whisper your message to it. When its wings once again take flight, your message will be delivered.

Laurel Reufner

Notes:

July 18
Tuesday

4th ♉

Color of the day: Gray
Incense of the day: Musk

Deer Power Invocation

The deer is a very sacred animal in many cultures. In Celtic tradition, deer symbolized the abundance of the wilderness, fertility, speed, grace, and the magic of the otherworld. Supernatural deer sometimes appeared to lure or entice people deeper into the forest where they might experience an important spiritual test or adventure. Often these deer were gods

 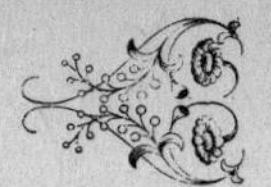  

or goddesses in the shape of deer. The milk of deer was also believed to have special properties, and various supernatural females were associated with deer's milk. Recite this spell for strength and success which invokes the powers of the deer:

> On milk of deer I was
> reared,
> On milk of deer I was
> nurtured,
> On milk of deer beneath
> the ridge of storms,
> On crest of hill and
> mountain.
> In likeness of deer, in
> strength and in power
> I move between the
> worlds in the name of
> the gods.

Sharynne NicMhacha

Notes:

July 19
Wednesday

4th ♉

Color of the day: White

Incense of the day: Pine

Hermes the Traveler Spell

To protect someone traveling to you, burn a red candle to promote strength, good health, and protection. Anoint the candle with sandalwood oil for focus and protection and clove oil for extra protection each day they are on the road. Say: "As my loved one travels night and day, Hermes protect him (or her) on the way!"

Boudica

Notes:

July 20
Thursday

4th ♉

☽ → ♊ 4:38 am

Color of the day: Crimson

Incense of the day: Chrysanthemum

Summer Prosperity Spell

In July, the countryside throbs with life. Bees and hummingbirds are busy, and the air is scented with herbs and honeysuckle. This spell combines money-attracting herbs of the summer season to draw in abundance. Combine one part each of basil,

   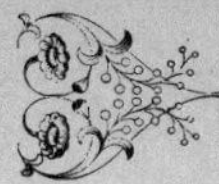 

dill, and mint. Finely chop the leaves and dry them on a paper towel, or heat them in the microwave for a few seconds on medium. Crumble together the herbs on a piece of cheesecloth and tie it all up with green ribbon. Anoint three green candles with olive oil and light them. Holding the charm bag before the flames announce in a clear voice:

> Herbs of protection,
> herbs of healing,
> herbs of wealth,
> Bring me just enough
> prosperity.
> With harm to none,
> So mote it be.

James Kambos

Notes:

July 21
Friday

4th ♊

Color of the day: Rose
Incense of the day: Ginger

Peony Love Spell

Many Chinese consider the peony flower a symbol of good fortune. Since ancient times, peonies have been associated with romance, beauty, and the female gender. It is believed that peonies keep romance and love alive. Ancient Chinese texts mention an emperor's concubine named Yang Kuai Fei who was considered the most beautiful woman in all of China. The emperor was enthralled by her throughout her life and decreed that her chambers be filled with peonies each day. While some cultures associate peonies with death, this flower is a potent ingredient in spells for love or attracting a soulmate. When gathering materials for a love ritual, add fresh or dried peony petals or use them as decoration during a candlelit dinner for two. Peonies can also be burnt in the censer when performing a spell that requires the burning of gum resins.

S. Y. Zenith

Notes:

July 22
Saturday

4th ♊
☽ → ♋ 11:28 am
☉ → ♌ 7:18 pm

Color of the day: Indigo
Incense of the day: Violet

Pester Me No More Spell

No one likes unpleasant people and few Witches like to be pestered while doing their magic. But there always seems to be someone disrupting our space. So to get rid of the door-to-door salesman, religious door knockers, or an unwanted guest, find a footprint the person has left behind. Hammer a nail into the footprint, and say:

> As I hammer in this nail
> My sacred privacy prevails.
> No more will I allow your
> pace
> To intrude upon my space.

Strike the nail into the footprint with three determined blows. Imagine the person's foot itching or burning if he or she returns. The person will not come back unless the nail is removed.

Nancy Bennett

Notes:

July 23
Sunday

4th ♋
Color of the day: Yellow
Incense of the day: Coriander

Neptunalia Water Spell

The ancient Romans celebrated Neptunalia, the festival of their god of the sea, Neptune, on this day. To honor the gifts of the ocean, they feasted and drank wine and spring water. Water held a special value at this time of the year because the weather was warm and dry. Honoring Neptune on this day was thought to ensure rain for the crops. Modern Italian Witches celebrate the ancient festival of Neptune by lighting blue candles. Decorate your altar with sea salt and seashells and light a blue candle. If you can treat yourself to a day spa today, do it as a way to relax your body with water. Take a long walk by a beach or river. Or, take a luxurious bath and pamper yourself with the healing and calming properties of water. Use bath salts to cleanse and refresh you.

Emely Flak

Notes:

July 24
Monday

4th ♋
☽ → ♌ 8:24 pm

Color of the day: Silver
Incense of the day: Peony

Spell to Enhance Psychic Abilities

To a cup of just-brewed hot tea, add a teaspoon of sugar along with a dash of nutmeg and cinnamon. These spices will enhance your psychic awareness. As you drink, chant: "Spiced tea, magic tea. Magic please speak to me." Light some sandalwood incense, an orange candle to promote psychic awareness, and a purple candle to open your mind to messages. Hold the tea to your nose and breathe. Open your senses. As you breathe deeply, your hands begin to tingle. Drink the tea, savoring its flavor and sensation as it moves through your body. Feel its magical energies fill you. When you are finished drinking, put your cup down and listen. When the incense is done burning, breathe deeply. Extinguish the candles and thank the spirits for their magic.

Gail Wood

Notes:

July 25
Tuesday

4th ♌
New Moon 12:31 am

Color of the day: Maroon
Incense of the day: Gardenia

Warmth of the Sun Spell for the New Moon

Leo is the sign of the lion, proud and strong, but even the king of the beasts starts out life as a small and playful cub. Get out and honor the power of this solar sign by basking like a lion cub in the warmth of the Sun. Think of what it is to be a kitten and to spend your days mostly resting, the calm monotony broken up only by the occasional playful game.

Lady MoonDance

Notes:

July 26
Wednesday

1st ♌

Color of the day: Topaz
Incense of the day: Neroli

Basil Security Spell

Basil is not just for cooking! Use it today for protection everywhere you may venture. Pour some basil into a glass or stoneware bowl. Holding your hands open over the bowl, visualize the protective energies of the plant surrounding you as you chant:

> **Spirit of this plant I pray,**
> **Keep me safe throughout**
> **this day.**
> **Bless me with security.**
> **Protected, I feel safe and**
> **free.**

Sprinkle a small amount of basil in each room of your house, visualizing the energy changing as the protective properties of the plant spread. Place a bit of basil in your purse or pocket for protection all day. Leaving some basil in your car will protect it both on the road and in the parking lot.

Kristin Madden

Notes:

July 27
Thursday

1st ♌

☽ → ♍ 7:36 am

Color of the day: Purple
Incense of the day: Evergreen

Water Restoration Spell

The ancient Roman gods Neptunus and Furrina govern over springs and wells, which are known for bringing healing and rest. The watery gifts of Neptunus and Furrina can to help you de-stress and renew today. This spell is great during or after a long day at work or running errands. It can be done in the car, bathroom, or in public. First, ground and center. After grounding, splash or spray rosewater, lavender water, or sandalwood water over your face, arms, and legs. Breathe deeply to inhale the scent and enjoy the water's coolness on your skin. Enjoy this for a few moments. When you are ready, return to your task.

Olivia O'Meir

Notes:

July 28
Friday

1st ♍

Color of the day: Coral
Incense of the day: Parsley

Remember Justice Spell

This is the day the Fourteenth Amendment was enacted. This amendment promises equal protection and due process of the law. Sometimes equal protection and justice, though promised, is not granted, so we need extra help from the domain of the spirit. This is a great time to engage the herb beloved by Hoodoos called Little John. Little John (*Alpina galanga*), also called galangal, is the herbal friend to fairness and justice in legal proceedings. Here are a few ways Little John can be used as a chew or charm in spell work. Put a cleaned piece of Little John into your mouth. Chew it until soft. Try not to swallow. If you are supporting a court case or are on trial, spit the Little John fluid outside the courthouse. If you want good outcomes to legal proceedings by mail, spit the Little John juice near your post box. If you want a lawsuit you've been informed of by mail to end peacefully, spit on the envelope and bury it at the crossroads or on your personal property. To influence the court in a generally positive way, keep Little John on your person inside a red mojo bag, along with some calendula flowers, deer's tongue, and oregano.

Stephanie Rose Bird

Notes:

July 29
Saturday

1st ♍
☽ → ♎ 8:27 pm

Color of the day: Black
Incense of the day: Cedar

Honor the Pantheon Spell

The old Greek calendar set aside certain times to honor all gods and goddesses together. This festival was called Metageitnion Noumenia. People said prayers and played music, especially flutes. They made offerings to their patron deities of barley, olive oil, incense, and libations of wine. Today is the perfect day to make a candle garden. You will need a large fireproof platter and a selection of candles. Mix and match different colors, shapes, and sizes. Name each for a different deity. You might choose a pink lady for Aphrodite or

blue pillar with seashells for Poseidon. Light the candles, saying:

> As I light these flames,
> Let them bless me.
> Each one is a different charm,
> Keeps me well and safe from harm.

Snuff the candles respectfully after you finish. Whenever you light them, you're praying to the whole pantheon.

Elizabeth Barrette

Notes:

July 30
Sunday

1st ♎

Color of the day: Amber

Incense of the day: Poplar

Fertility Glass Ritual

If you walk the beach during the summer months, collect any smooth bits of glass you find among the rocks. In ancient times, this sea-glass was known as "mermaids' mirror bits," and was considered good luck for the beachcomber. Often mermaids were depicted holding a mirror and a comb, symbols of Venus, the goddess of beauty and fertility. Venus was said to have sprung fully grown from the sea. Her Greek name, Aphrodite, literally means "foam-risen." Place the sea-glass you find in a little green bag with a piece of red silk cut in the shape of a heart. As you sew the bag closed, say:

> This bag I sew, fertility,
> A child will come from me.
> Fecund Venus, I pray,
> Abundant life come my way.

This spell will work equally well if you seek fertility of another sort. Just change the word "child" above to "creativity," or "abundant garden," or whatever it is you seek.

Lily Gardner-Butts

Notes:

   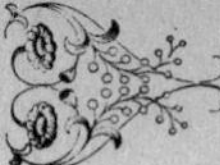 

July 31
Monday

1st ♎

Color of the day: Gray
Incense of the day: Lavender

Celebrate Your Divinity Spell

Put yourself at center stage and glory in your own divine nature today. The expression says "As above, so below." Recognize then that you are divine. Claim it and celebrate it. Prepare a simple altar with photographs of yourself. Place mementos and awards on the altar as well. In the center, place a large candle, preferably gold, and a mirror. Dress in your most celebratory costume. Light the candle, saying: "I am a star of the galaxy, golden and divine. I am beautiful and glorious, wise, wonderful, and talented." Hold the mirror to your face, saying: "I am the divine expression of the universe. I give thanks for my divinity." Call up someone, and tell him or her how special both of you are.

Luci Sophia Zain

Notes:

August is the eighth month of the year and named for Augustus Caesar. Its astrological sign is Leo the lion (July 22–August 23), a fixed fire sign ruled by the Sun. In August we are surrounded by the power and glory of the Goddess. The fields of August bring forth bounty. In nature, yellow and gold dominate with corn, sunflowers, black-eyed Susans, and goldenrod brightening the landscape. The month begins with Lammas, or Lughnasadh, the first of the harvest sabbats. Brains are honored now, and breads are always found on the Lammas table. Nowadays, attending a county fair is a pleasant way to observe the harvest season. Produce, canned foods, and baked goods are proudly displayed along with prize ribbons. In August you can occasionally feel the breath of autumn. There's a coolness in the breeze, and a change in the angle of the sunlight, which reminds us summer is not endless. At twilight, the katydid begins scratching its late summer song. The ancient Romans held Diana's feast day on August 13. It was a time of feasting and enjoying the farmer's bounty. Many Native Americans celebrated the corn harvest in August. This festival eventually gave August's Full Moon its name, the Corn Moon. Magic for the Corn Moon may focus on health, fertility, or abundance.

August 1

Tuesday

Lammas

1st ♎

☽ → ♏ 9:08 am

Color of the day: White
Incense of the day: Ginger

Sacred Feast of Lughnasadh

Lughnasadh was one of the four sacred feast days of the Celts. It marked the beginning of the harvest and was instituted by the god Lugh to honor his fostermother Tailtiu, who cleared the land for agriculture. *Nasadh* means an "assembly." Huge Lugnasad assemblies took place in ancient Ireland, including one called the Feast of Carmun, in honor of a supernatural but ill-fated sorceress and warrior. Music, poetry, and the recitation of sacred lore took place, perhaps under the patronage of Lugh, a skilled harper, poet, and magician. Recite these lines from an ancient Irish poem to bring a harvest of abundance, creativity, and wisdom into your life:

> Grain, milk, peace, and happiness,
> Full nets, ocean's plenty.
> Feasts and fairs,
> Knowledge and music,
> Truthful teachings,
> Books of lore.
> May there ever be given to us from the gods
> The pleasant fruits of the earth!

Sharynne NicMhacha

Notes:

Holiday lore: Lammas is a bittersweet holiday, mingling joy at the current high season's harvest with the knowledge that summer is soon at an end. Many cultures have "first fruit" rituals on this day—the Celt's version is called Lughnasadh; the Anglo-Saxon version called Hlaf-masse. In the Middle Ages, the holiday settled on August 1, taking its current form for the most part, with sheaves of wheat and corn blessed on this day.

August 2

Wednesday

1st ♏

2nd Quarter 4:46 am

Color of the day: Yellow
Incense of the day: Coriander

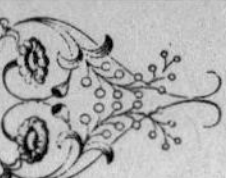

Carnelian Travel Spell

Carnelian reminds me of the fiery masculine energy of a lion. It is perfect for watching over yourself or a loved one while traveling. Charge a carnelian with health and protection while traveling. Place it in a small cloth drawstring bag. Add in a bit of comfrey, lavender, cedar, and some rose petals for good measure. Leave the amulet out where the Sun's rays can rest upon it, warming and charging the contents with health, safety, and enjoyable travel. After a short time in the Sun, the amulet will be ready. A good idea for its use is to place it somewhere safe in your car. If you travel by train or plane, try tucking it into your suitcase. It can easily be placed in your briefcase or backpack for that daily trek to work or school.

Laurel Reufner

Notes:

August 3

Thursday

2nd ♏
☽ → ♐ 7:13 pm

Color of the day: Crimson
Incense of the day: Dill

Aquarium Prosperity Spell

When sales are slow in your work, install an aquarium in the northeast or southeast corner of the business premises. Keep some goldfish or other brightly colored fish and decorations in the aquarium. Feed the fish daily and change the water regularly. Murky water denotes stagnation and stunted growth and is unhygienic. Aquariums attract prosperity and reduce stress levels in any environment. For an extra touch, place a bright light so it shines directly into the aquarium. When correctly placed, fish shadows will be seen moving on the ceiling. According to feng shui, this activates chi and generates stimulation, motivation, and enthusiasm in business. Each day light some incense and recite a prosperity chant for attracting money luck.

S. Y. Zenith

Notes:

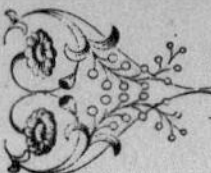

August 4
Friday

2nd ♐

Color of the day: Pink
Incense of the day: Rose

Goddess Selene Love Spell

Today was an ancient holy day of Selene, goddess of the Moon. What better time to attract love than under a waxing Moon on a day sacred to Selene? Take a silver cloth and place it on the ground where the Moon can shine on it. Place a silver goblet with liquid in it on the center of the cloth. Write the name of someone you desire, or the qualities you want in a mate, on a round mirror, and say:

> O goddess Selene,
> hear my request
> Shine on the one
> I love the best.
>
> My Moon's true love
> By me be seen
> Tonight within
> My sacred dreams.

Drink the liquid, then go to bed to dream of your love. If Selene grants, by the turning of one month, you will meet your love.

Nancy Bennett

Notes:

August 5
Saturday

2nd ♐

Color of the day: Brown
Incense of the day: Patchouli

Sleep of Morpheus Spell

In ancient Greek myth, Morpheus' help was invoked for dreaming. Morpheus, the Greek god of dreams, was believed to be able to bring us special messages from the gods through our nocturnal images. Morpheus was called upon for dreams about future lovers, happy occasions, and solutions to problems. For a solution to come to you in your dreams tonight, try this ritual. Think of a question or issue that needs a fresh insight or answer. Write your concern on a piece of white fabric and wrap it around some fresh lavender or an olive branch. Place this under your pillow. As you drift off to sleep, say:

> Morpheus in my dreams
> tonight,
> Offer me answers and
> insight.

Keep a notepad and pen by your bed to record your dreams when you wake.

Emely Flak

Notes:

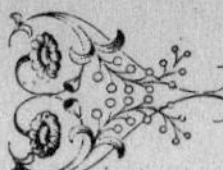

August 6
Sunday

2nd ♐
☽ → ♑ 1:19 am

Color of the day: Orange
Incense of the day: Cinnamon

A Spell for Peace

On this day in 1945, the United States dropped the atomic bomb on Hiroshima, Japan. 75,000 people were killed in the blast and tens of thousands died subsequently from radiation poisoning and cancers. Now, instead of building a case for war let us join together and build a case for peace. One way to contribute to the peace movement would be to cast this spell today. On a small American flag, place an almond, a rose quartz heart, and an amethyst. Visualize your family living in harmony, then extend the ring of harmony out to all your relatives. They might not think as you do, but fundamentally they want the same things as you. Extend this ring out further to encompass your city, then your state, your country, your hemisphere, and finally the planet. All of us, around the world, wish to be safe and loved and respected. Tie the flag with blue and white cords, saying:

> By knot of one, this
> spell's begun.
> By knot of two, it
> cometh true.
> By knot of three, so shall
> it be.
> By knot of four, the open
> door.
> By knot of five, the spell's
> alive.
> By knot of six, the spell
> is fixed.
> By knot of seven, the
> stars in heaven.
> By knot of eight, the
> hand of fate.
> By knot of nine, the spell
> is mine.

Lily Gardner-Butts

Notes:

August 7
Monday

2nd ♑

Color of the day: Ivory
Incense of the day: Maple

Threshold Protection Spell

The noble herbs goldenrod and yarrow should be combined to

protect your entryway from negativity. Gather three sprigs of goldenrod and yarrow. Hang them together and let them dry. This should take just a few days, as they dry quickly. Then obtain a small grapevine wreath from a craft store. Insert the stems of your herbs around the wreath. Fill the spaces with other herbs such as dried lady's mantle and thyme. These will create loving vibrations. Pass your power hand above the wreath three times, and charge it with these words:

> Herbs of Venus,
> Herbs of love,
> Protect this threshold
> And those who live here.

Hang the wreath on your porch or other protected area, where it will remind you of summer.

James Kambos

Notes:

August 8

Tuesday

2nd ♑
☽ → ♒ 3:47 am

Color of the day: Red
Incense of the day: Juniper

Stand in the Fields Spell

One of the most important steps to civilization was the invention of agriculture, especially the cultivation of grain. Over time, our ancestors changed the plants they grew. Corn and barley shaped the new world. Here is a song in praise of grain, at a time when it stands tall in fields yet is still vulnerable to all sorts of hazards before the harvest.

> Standing in the fields
> Blue corn and green,
> Mother and maid—
> Standing in the meadow
> Awaiting the blade.
>
> Sing of the old ones,
> Who were before we
> were born.
> Sing of the scarecrow
> And John Barleycorn.
>
> Bow to the east wind,
> And feed from the Sun.
> Bow to the west wind;
> The rain has begun.
>
> Bow to the north wind,
> Which brings winter's
> cold.
> Bow to the south wind,
> As green turns to gold.
>
> Honor ancestors,
> The proud and the plain.
> Pray for the farmers
> Who bring in the grain.

Elizabeth Barrette

Notes:

August 9
Wednesday

2nd ♒

Full Moon 6:54 am

Color of the day: Brown
Incense of the day: Sandalwood

Change the World Ritual

Intelligent and eccentric, the Full Moon in Aquarius is the height of change and innovation on a global level. This is a time to think not only of yourself, but to work to change the world in humanitarian ways. For example, working for world peace is the perfect example of an Aquarian goal. However, many spells of this sort are undeveloped, unfocused, and rather shortsighted. What is peace? How does it work? What about the technical, personal, and spiritual advances that come from facing up to conflicts and contentious issues? So, what is your real intention? Be specific. Try focusing your energy on one small building block that will make the world a bettter place, rather than trying to do it all at once. Instead of trying to change the lives of everyone across the globe, whose needs and wants you may not even understand, start with your home, your family, your neighbors, your community—*your* world. What one thing can you do to affect the world around you for the better? It's not just about doing a pretty, fluffy ritual and then feeling better about yourself. If you really want to create change, you have to be able to look at the dark details, see the whole truth of the situation, and then roll up your sleeves and get your hands dirty. Today, don't just light a candle. Donate some of your physical energy to a cause or idea that you want to further or help grow. As you do the work, ask the universe to to foster this cause, until your goals become reality.

Lady MoonDance

Notes:

August 10
Thursday

3rd ♒
☽ → ♓ 4:10 am

Color of the day: Green
Incense of the day: Carnation

Tulsi Protection Rituals

Today is ideal to work powerful green magic in honor of Jupiter's energy. So why not use one of India's sacred herbs now? Tulsi, (*Ocimum sanctum*), also called sacred basil, holy basil, or bhutagni ("destroyer of demons") is a benign-looking herb that is thought of as a divine incarnation of the Goddess. Worshippers of Vishnu perceive the plant as the goddess Lakshmi, goddess of prosperity, abundance, and fertility. Here are two ways to utilize tulsi in your magical workings today. To usher in prosperity and abundance, welcome Lakshmi to your life using tulsi. Lakshmi is embodied in basil, rice, coins, and other symbols of prosperity and fertility. To invoke Lakshmi's blessings, infuse cup basil leaves in four cups of water. Strain and add half teaspoons of peppermint and basil essential oil. Wash your altar, ritual space, or hearth with this tulsi spiritual wash. Place raw grains basmati rice in a small dish on your tulsi-scented altar along with an array of shiny coins. Also, you can try what many Indians do to assure a pleasant night of sleep. Place a tulsi leaf on your chest at bedtime. Tulsi on the chest promises pleasant dreams and protects against evil.

Stephanie Rose Bird

Notes:

August 11
Friday

3rd ♓

Color of the day: Purple
Incense of the day: Thyme

Sparkle and Shine Date Ritual

To prepare for a big date, start by taking a ritual bath with your favorite soap or bath oil. Indulge your hair with a conditioning shampoo. Meditate on possible conversations you might have on your date, to be sure you don't run out of things to discuss. Press your clean clothes with a touch of your favorite fragrance or oil by adding some to a spray bottle. Brush your hair till it shines, and brush your teeth till they sparkle. Polish

 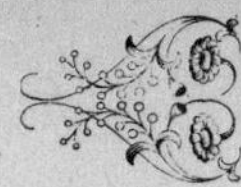  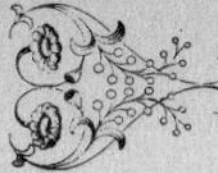 

your shoes until they gleam. Discuss with your date about going to dinner and a movie that you will both be comfortable with. And make sure you have plenty of cash in your pocket for whatever you agreed to be responsible for. Always make sure you have enough left over for transportation home. Keep a smile on your face and good thoughts in your head, and you both will have a great time.

Boudica

Notes:

August 12

Saturday

3rd ♓

☽ → ♈ 4:22 am

Color of the day: Gray
Incense of the day: Lilac

Protection of Isis Spell

August 12 is the birthday of the goddess Isis. Isis rules many aspects of life and the universe, such as magic and protection. Honor Isis and ask for her protection. To do this you will need an image of Isis, two white candles with holders, two garnets, and musk incense. Place the images of Isis on your altar. Put the candles near the center of the altar, one on each side, with the incense between them. Place one garnet before each candle. Light the candles and incense. While holding the crystals, petition Isis for her protection:

> Isis, I call to you. Lend
> your energy for this spell.
> Your protection is what
> I desire. Hear my prayer
> sent up by fire. Bless these
> stones offered as tokens
> of your protection.

Place the garnets back on the altar. Keep one stone with you at all times. Keep the other on your altar, kitchen, or by the front door.

Olivia O'Meir

Notes:

August 13

Sunday

3rd ♈

Color of the day: Yellow
Incense of the day: Sage

   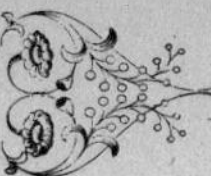 

Finding Luck Spell

We all have luck. Some days the luck is bad and some days the luck is extraordinary. The cycle of luck moves up and down, and we can ride it like a roller coaster. To do so, empty the coins from your wallet or your pocket. If you are in a cycle of bad or indifferent luck, take the largest coin and chant: "Bad luck change. Bad luck change. Bad luck change." Place the coin in a small bowl of salt to purify overnight. The next day remove the coin and keep it in a safe place for good luck. If you happen to be in a cycle of good luck, take the smallest coin and chant: "Good luck to spare, good luck to share." Give the coin away.

Gail Wood

Notes:

August 14

Monday

3rd ♈

☽ → ♉ 6:00 am

Color of the day: Silver

Incense of the day: Chrysanthemum

Moon Bath Ritual

Imagine you are lying down in an empty pool or tub outside on a clear, moonlit night. Or, if you can actually go out in the moonlight for this visualization, it will be even more powerful. Start by feeling the coolness of the Moon on your body and its light on your closed eyelids. Imagine moonbeams pouring down over you, bathing your body and spirit in cool light. The light fills the pool, covering you completely. It sinks in through your pores, your eyes, your mouth. The light relaxes your body and mind as it washes away all tension, illness, stress, or discomfort. Visualize these spiraling away from you as they wash away down the drain. As you rise from the bath, the light lingers in your skin and hair. You will carry this cool, relaxing experience with you throughout the week.

Kristin Madden

Notes:

August 15
Tuesday

3rd ♉
4th Quarter 9:51 pm

Color of the day: Red
Incense of the day: Honeysuckle

Tame Your Best Spell

Like the Strength card in tarot, tame your inner beast, but do not break your beast's spirit. Don't let your beast run amok, but tame your beast with love and gentleness. To encourage this balancing, place the Strength card from your favorite tarot deck on your altar. Light a yellow candle. Visualize yourself standing strong, proud, and free. You are a noble beast, courageous and generous. Say:

> I am the ruler of my inner
> beast. I honor my beast
> by feeding it and giving
> it exercise. I do not subdue
> it by force. I work with
> my beast for our mutual
> benefit. I love my beast
> and respect it. We are one.

Snuff out the candle but not your beast.

Luci Sophia Zain

Notes:

August 16
Wednesday

4th ♉
☽ → ♊ 10:07 am

Color of the day: White
Incense of the day: Eucalyptus

Lleu Llaw Gyffes Invocation

The Welsh counterpart to the Irish god Lugh was Lleu Llaw Gyffes, the "Bright One of the Skillful Hand." This name was similar to Lugh's titles—Samildanach, "the Many Skilled," and Lamfada, "of the Long Arm." Lleu is the son of the Moon goddess Arianrhod who, dishonored, angrily denied her son a name, arms, and a mortal bride, though his uncle Gwydion helped him obtain these. Lleu's wife Blodeuwedd was made of flowers and lacked both soul and divinity. In the end, she betrayed Lleu and tried to cause his death. But he underwent a shamanic illness and healing and was finally restored to health and power again after the betrayal. Here is an invocation of true path and power for daily use:

> Power of Sun be mine,
> Power of Moon.
> Power of storm,
> Power of earth,
> Power of sea,
> Power of land,
> Power of fire,
> And power of element.

Each day be joyous,
In honor and compassion.

Sharynne NicMhacha

Notes:

August 17
Thursday

4th ♊

Color of the day: Purple
Incense of the day: Geranium

Make a Wish Ritual

Find a picture of something you desire but can't afford, and place it on an orange cloth. Add four coins—each minted on the year you were born. Light a white candle, and focus on your desire, saying:

East force, west force,
South and north,
Find me the means to
soon bring forth
the extra funds I need to
acquire
to make come true my
heart's desire.

Use the wax and drip a little on each corner of the picture and fix to each a coin. When the wax has dried, wrap it in the cloth and place it in a safe place that you pass each day. Visualize yourself enjoying your new luxury. Today's spell honors the god Portunalia—the god of harbors. He assures safe passage for those who honor him. Eat fish or other seafood and make a wish for protection next time you travel.

Nancy Bennett

Notes:

August 18
Friday

4th ♊
☽ → ♋ 5:03 pm

Color of the day: Rose
Incense of the day: Sandalwood

Yummy Massage Oil

To make a yummy massage oil, mix together eight ounces of sweet almond oil with 35 drops of eucalyptus oil, 25 drops of lavender oil, 20 drops of jasmine fragrance oil, 20 drops of ylang-ylang fragrance oil, 15 drops of peppermint oil, 15 drops of rosemary oil, and 10 drops of tea tree oil in a glass or plastic bottle.

   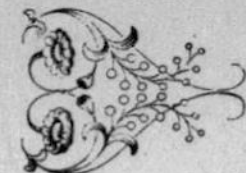 

Allow the mixture sit overnight for the scents to mingle. Remember to warm the oil before use either with your hands or in an oil warmer. This wonderful massage oil has been proven to satisfy the massager and the massaged, and it is wonderful for soothing tense, sore muscles as well as promoting other, amorous uses.

Laurel Reufner

Notes:

August 19

Saturday

4th ♋

Color of the day: Blue

Incense of the day: Juniper

Overcome Self-Doubt Spell

Negative thoughts create patterns that form part of your regular thinking. Make time on this waning Moon for a spell to break this pattern and overcome any self-doubt that is preventing you from reaching your full potential. You will need to gather three black candles, some paper and a black pen, and a quartz crystal.

On your altar light the candles. Hold the crystal in your hand and imagine the rock absorbing your negative thoughts while you download them. Write the same fears using the black pen. Now that you have now carried out a double disposal of your restricting thought patterns, say these words:

On this paper
And on this stone,
I have discharged my
worries,
And they will be gone.

Imagine yourself empowered, happy and free of fear. Throw out or burn the paper. Rinse your crystal under running water or in a river, and watch that negative energy wash away.

Emely Flak

Notes:

August 20

Sunday

4th ♋

Color of the day: Gold

Incense of the day: Clove

Fresh Air Good Health Ritual

Allergy season can be hard on you with all the ragweed and pollen streaming in our open windows or air conditioners on these late summer days. Start this ritual by closing the windows and checking and cleaning the filters in the air conditioners. Take allergy medications as your doctor prescribes. Keep the dust under control in your home and office, and don't use a lot of flowery air fresheners nor keep fresh flowers around to add to the already pollen-saturated air. Always check with your doctor about medications and shots for the prevention or control of allergy symptoms. And finally, make a personal prayer to Asklepios and his daughters Hygeia and Panakeia for good health.

Boudica

Notes:

August 21

Monday

4th ♋

☽ → ♌ 2:33 am

Color of the day: Lavender
Incense of the day: Frankincense

Home Harmony Mirror Spell

If you live in cramped surroundings, placing a wall mirror in a strategic position will enhance the flow of healthy vibrations that bring harmony to the home. The reflection of a mirror enlarges tiny rooms and deflects negativity. Mirror tiles are not advisable according to feng shui principles. Select a wall space that does not face the door, window, staircase, or lavatory. After fixing the mirror in place, decorate it with crystals, sea-shells, flowers, and other meaningful objects. Think positive thoughts, light an incense cone, and put on soothing music. Hold a clear glass of rosewater or other floral infusion and sit in front of the mirror. Take a sip, close your eyes, and meditate on harmony, relief from worldly burdens, and attainment of peace of mind for yourself and all who live in your house. As you meditate, with each sip of floral water direct thoughts of harmony to the mirror. This encourages the reflecting and spreading of positive thought-waves around the home.

S. Y. Zenith

Notes:

August 22
Tuesday

4th ♌

Color of the day: Maroon
Incense of the day: Evergreen

Discover Dishonesty Spell

If you suspect that others are lying to you, gather a clear bowl, some water, and a small piece of dark-patterned fabric that is long and wide, along with a small black candle in a clear holder. Place the black candle and its holder in the bowl and light it. Pour water into the bowl so that the candle is surrounded. Take the fabric in hand and chant three times: "Dark patterns reveal truth, and no longer conceal." Soak the fabric and place it in the bowl so that it surrounds the candle holder but does not cover it. When the candle has burned completely, tie the remaining wax in the fabric in several knots. Bury the fabric in the ground, and pour the water over it. Go about your life and watch the truth begin.

Gail Wood

Notes:

August 23
Wednesday

4th ♌
☉ → ♍ 2:22 am
☽ → ♍ 2:08 pm
New Moon 3:10 pm

Color of the day: Topaz
Incense of the day: Cedar

A Space for Learning Spell

Virgos are great at organizing—especially at organizing everyone else's stuff. Virgos also love thought, learning, and beauty. Whether you are going back to school or have long since graduated, you never really stop learning. This is the perfect time to design and organize a comfortable personal space where you can read, study, and learn. Set aside time and space for mental growth. Remove any unnecessary distractions, including TVs, but if music is not too distracting to you add a small stereo or CD player. Buy bookshelves, a comfy couch, and a sturdy desk. Organize your space so that you can more easily organize your mind, while giving it plenty of free space to expand. Light a yellow candle in the center of your space, and smudge with sage or cedar, clearing it of negativity. Alternately, place a few drops of clary sage oil into the candle as it burns in order to spread the scent throughout the space. Say:

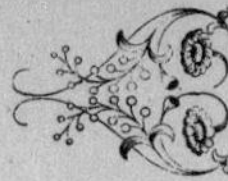

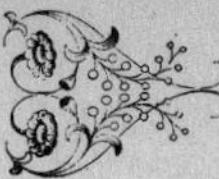

Athena, Sophia, Gnosis,
Knowledge and wisdom,
in all your many guises.
I dedicate this space to
learning.
Bring your words to my
ears and your ideas to
my mind so that I may
learn and grow in your
presence.
So mote it be.

Lady MoonDance

Notes:

August 24
Thursday

1st ♍

Color of the day: Turquoise

Incense of the day: Musk

Connect to Earth and Sky Spell

There must be a balance of earth and sky energy in each of us. Both are essential to our lives. Attuning to earth keeps us grounded and secure. Connecting to sky reminds us to dream and wish. Go outside on a bright, sunny day. Choose a firm spot to stand on. Make sure you can see the sky. Stand with your legs spread apart in a V shape. Make sure your footing is secure. Raise your arms outstretched in a V toward the sky. The V shape is symbolic of opening up to receive energy. When ready, say:

I am balanced between
earth and sky. I walk with
my feet on the ground.
(Look at your feet planted
on the earth.)
I walk with my head in
the clouds.
(Look above at the joyful
clouds.)
I am balanced between
earth and sky. So mote
it be!

Enjoy this balanced feeling.

Olivia O'Meir

Notes:

August 25
Friday

1st ♍

Color of the day: Coral

Incense of the day: Ylang-ylang

Honoring the Earth Goddess Spell

Among the oldest rituals observed by the ancients were those that

 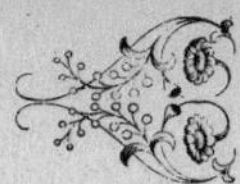  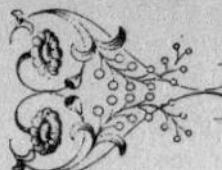 

honored earth goddesses. Known by various names, like the Roman Ops and the Greek Rhea, these goddesses guarded the harvested crops. Today was set aside in ancient Rome to give thanks to their earth deity, Ops. Little is known about these sacred rites, as they were very secret. It is known the ritual was simple. The earth itself was her altar. Her followers touched the soil with their hands. With the harvest season upon us, we can honor the earth goddess in many ways. Visit a county fair and observe the produce. Shop at your local farmer's market. Donate to a food bank. Press a coin into the earth. Take time to crumble the garden soil in your hands and breathe its earthy scent. Let any small, earth-oriented task be a ritual in her honor.

James Kambos

Notes:

August 26

Saturday

1st ♍

☽ → ♎ 3:30 pm

Color of the day: Indigo
Incense of the day: Pine

Chaos of Set Spell

Today is the birthday of Set, the Egyptian god of chaos and of destruction. Set rules over the red desert land, the borderlands, and the extension of existence. He sometimes appears as a fennec, the huge-eared Egyptian fox, in keeping with the tricksters and troublesome gods of other pantheons. This clever animal can survive in the worst terrain—just like Set. This time of year hovers between summer and fall. It's a good time to get rid of things you don't need. On papyrus paper, write something you want to banish from your life. Then go to a borderland away from open water, and say:

> Clever fox, red fox
> Hear me as I pray.
> Little fox, swift fox
> Take this thing away!
> Run to your master
> Set, merry and grim.
> Lord of destruction
> I give it to him.

Wad up the papyrus, throw it over your shoulder, and walk away without looking back.

Elizabeth Barrette

Notes:

August 27
Sunday

1st ♎

Color of the day: Amber
Incense of the day: Basil

Small Details Spell

Sometimes by paying attention to the small details, we can, with time, achieve great things. Today, pay attention to details, saying: "Today, I pay homage to all things small. I note the unseen and unnoticed. I am grateful for the unrecognized and forgotten." Today, as you go about your usual activities, notice the stitching in your clothing. Notice the hands you shake, the faces that greet, and the postage stamps on the mail you receive. Say: "I celebrate life by taking care of myself and my home." Perform any small grooming or health practices that you have been neglecting. Clean out a drawer or cabinet or closet. What forgotten treasures do you find? Place some on display and give others away. Clear out any rubbish. Consecrate your newly cleaned and organized space when you are done.

Luci Sophia Zain

Notes:

August 28
Monday

1st ♎
☽ → ♏ 3:56 pm

Color of the day: White
Incense of the day: Myrrh

Harmonious Times Spell

With Sun and Mercury in Virgo now, communications may tend toward the critical. But the Moon is in peacekeeping Libra. This energy can smooth the way for a harmonious time with loved ones. Begin the day with a visualization. See yourself surrounded by a beautiful pink bubble. All energy going in and coming out is filled with loving pink light. Ask that you may communicate with love and find the light in every encounter this day. As you inhale, you fill with love and light. As you exhale, you send out love and light. See yourself happily interacting with friends, family, and coworkers. Throughout the day, repeat this visualization, particularly before any potentially stressful encounters. If you find you feel you are becoming upset, breathe the pink light until you have restored harmony.

Kristin Madden

Notes:

August 29
Tuesday

1st ♏

Color of the day: Black

Incense of the day: Sage

Gopher's Dust Protection Magic

Take advantage of the protective energy of the planet of the day, Mars. To do so, you should borrow a traditional formula from the Hoodoos to add to your repertoire of home and hearth protective potions. This is, make and use some fierce Gopher's Dust today. Gopher's Dust is designed to protect your space from *hants*, or disruptive spirits, and any negative human energy. Mix equal parts sulfur (brimstone), sea salt, cayenne powder and black pepper (powdered), and you'll have homemade Gopher's Dust. Be sure to make enough of the powder for the job at hand. You'll want to spread it in a protective ring around your property. If it is an apartment, loft, or condo, make enough to spread out in front of your door. This dust protects the home, blowing toward intruders with malicious intentions.

Stephanie Rose Bird

Notes:

August 30
Wednesday

1st ♏

Color of the day: Yellow

Incense of the day: Maple

Yarrow Love Divination

Yarrow is the herb of Virgo the Virgin. It is a favorite of Witches and is often used in women's medicine. Yarrow tea is said to encourage menstrual bleeding, and help in treating inflammation of the ovaries and fibroid tumors. Yarrow, sometimes known as "nosebleed," has been used in magic for centuries to determine if your lover has been faithful. A leaf is placed in the nose and the following charm recited:

> Green yarrow, green
> yarrow,
> You wear a white bow.
> If my lover loves me,
> My nose will bleed now.
>
> If my lover doesn't love me,
> It won't bleed a drop;
> If my lover does love me,
> 'Twill bleed every drop.

To dream of a future love, you must put yarrow in your right stocking, tie it around your left leg, and get into bed backward chanting thrice: "Goodnight to thee, yarrow." And again say three times: "Goodnight, pretty yarrow. I pray thee tell me

   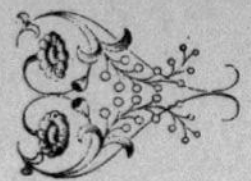 

by the morrow who shall my true love be."

Lily Gardner-Butts

Notes:

August 31
Thursday

1st ♏
☽ → ♐ 3:00 am
2nd Quarter 6:56 pm

Color of the day: Green
Incense of the day: Jasmine

Ancient Ones Harvest Spell

Harvest was a time for families, communities, and friends to come together. During harvest, special cakes were made in a ritual manner, and each person in the family or group would partake of this sacred meal. Mix together one cup oat flour, one pinch baking soda, two pinches of salt, and one teaspoon of melted butter. Add hot water to form a dough, roll it on a board, and cut it into shapes. Cook the bread in the oven at 375 degrees until it is nicely toasted. Share it with your tribe or family, reciting these words:

Consecrate the produce
of our land.
Bestow prosperity and
peace
In the names of the gods
and goddesses,
And in the names of the
ancient ones.

Sharynne NicMhacha

Notes:

September is the ninth month of the year. Its name is derived from the Latin word *septum,* which means "seventh," as it was the seventh month of the Roman calendar. Its astrological sign is Virgo, the maiden (August 23–September 23), a mutable earth sign ruled by Mercury. September is a month of fulfillment. Kitchens are busy, as the garden's last produce is canned and preserved. The air is filled with the cidery tang of harvest time. Squirrels hide their nuts, and chipmunks line their nests with grain. Asters raise their purple heads, and monarch butterflies add their black-and-orange hues to autumn's palette. The sacred beverages of the season—cider and wine—echo the colors of nature now. The Fall Equinox, or Mabon, is the major holiday of September. At Mabon we celebrate the second harvest, say farewell to summer, and enter the dark season. Days grow shorter as the Great Son, Mabon, returns to Mother Earth. For the sabbat, altar decorations include pumpkins, squash, and grapes. September's Full Moon is the Harvest Moon, perhaps the most well-known of the year. It rises above the horizon and glows in solitary splendor. She is queen of the September night. The night belongs to her, and to her alone. Honor her by raising a glass of cider or wine, then respectfully pour it onto the earth.

   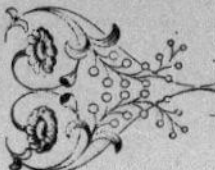 

September 1

Friday

2nd ♐

Color of the day: Pink

Incense of the day: Almond

Add Fun to Romance Spell

The combination of the reserved exterior of Virgo sun and the hidden playful exuberance of a Sagittarian Moon makes this a good time to add some fun to romance. You will need two candles—one pink and one red. You'll also need a vial of sensuous fragrance oil such as ylang-ylang or jasmine for women, or patchouli or sandalwood for men. Finally, get a moonstone chip small enough to fit in the vial. When it gets quiet tonight, light the candles and sit quietly, reflecting on being more playful with your mate. Charge the energy into the vial. Hold the moonstone in your hands and imagine frolicking in the moonlight with your lover—dancing, chasing fireflies, whatever works for you. Pour that frolicsome energy into the moonstone with all of your psychic intent. Finally, drop the moonstone into the oil and make this your special, playful, romantic oil that you wear only for your partner whenever you want to have "fun."

Laurel Reufner

Notes:

Holiday lore: Many Greeks consider this their New Year's Day. This day marks the beginning of the sowing season, a time of promise and hope. On this day, people fashion wreaths of pomegranates, quinces, grapes, and garlic bulbs—all traditional symbols of abundance. Just before dawn on September 1, children submerge the wreaths in the ocean waters for luck. They carry seawater and pebbles home with them in small jars to serve as protection in the coming year. Tradition calls for exactly forty pebbles and water from exactly forty waves.

September 2

Saturday

2nd ♐

☽ → ♑ 10:34 am

Color of the day: Black

Incense of the day: Carnation

Increasing Willpower Ritual

This quick spell will help you get the boost you need when working on a challenging project or goal. You will need a red taper candle and some oil—of cinnamon, clove, ginger, High John the Conqueror, or dragon's blood. Take the candle and mark your name across it. You may also want to add a symbol that represents your goal, such as a dollar sign for money or a heart for love. Take the oil and anoint the candle in the manner that seems most logical to you—for instance, in dabs or using a cloth, etc. Take your time and make sure to cover every part of it with oil. Light the candle and say:

> God and Goddess, increase
> my willpower, so that I
> may achieve my goal. Give
> me the power to resist
> anything that may block
> my path. So mote it be!

Olivia O'Meir

Notes:

September 3
Sunday

2nd ♐

Color of the day: Black

Incense of the day: Carnation

Relieving Mental Strain Spell

Those vulnerable to mental strain due to massive workloads, emotional issues, and family demands will find this spell useful. It also helps take away the blues and other anxiety, and it dissipates mental lethargy. Ingredients required are one ounce each of rosemary, fennel seed, and cardamom pods, and a quarter pint of vodka and of spring water. Crush the herbs with a mortar and pestle, then put them into a sterilized glass jar. Pour the vodka and spring water into the jar. Seal it and let it stand in a cool, dry cupboard for at least two weeks, shaking the jar every two days or so. After a fortnight, strain the concoction into a clean bottle, then label and refrigerate. It should keep for quite awhile if kept cool. This mixture can also be used in rituals for other health problems by mixing two teaspoonfuls of the liquid with water or orange juice and offering it to deities. If your ritual work is done outdoors on a sunny day, pour some on the ground in honor of the earth spirits.

S. Y. Zenith

Notes:

September 4

Monday

Labor Day (observed)

2nd ♑

☽ → ♒ 2:15 pm

Color of the day: Gray
Incense of the day: Rose

Day of Rest Spell

Labor Day is an American holiday that honors working people. What better reward for hard-working people is there than a day of rest? Regardless of whether you love your job or hate it, this is a day of rest from it. Take a small box and a piece of paper. On the paper, write the name of your workplace, your job title, and any worries or ongoing thoughts about the job. Place the paper in the box and chant: "Close the box and shut the lid. Thoughts of work are from me hid." With a deep breath, put the box on your altar and go have fun. Tomorrow, open the box and take the paper to work with you and deal with your issues, as appropriate.

Gail Wood

Notes:

September 5

Tuesday

2nd ♒

Color of the day: Red
Incense of the day: Musk

Green Grass Safety Ritual

For protective blessings, go around your home and tie small knots in the grass at the four directions or by your doors. As you tie the knots, chant or whisper:

Sweet green grass
Bless and protect me.
Troubles pass
Leaving me in safety.

Now, gather some untied grass and bring it into your home. Tie it in knots, repeating the chant and asking for the blessings of your spirit guardians. Then spread the knotted grass around your home. It is a good idea to place pieces of grass by doors and windows, vents, and under beds. Keep a piece of grass for you and anyone that lives with you to keep. Each of you may carry a knotted

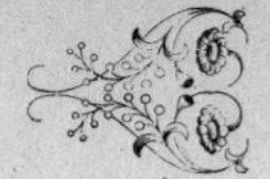

piece of grass for added protection away from home.

Kristin Madden

Notes:

September 6
Wednesday

2nd ♒

☽ → ♓ 2:56 pm

Color of the day: Topaz
Incense of the day: Pine

Light the World Spell

Assemble five small candles of various colors. As you light the first one, say: "Let drivers on the road be alert to children on sidewalks and streets." Light the second candle and say: "May all teachers renew their commitment to instructing the minds of our children. Let them teach in love and compassion." Light the third candle and say: "Bless all health workers who heal our children. Give them energy to continue their mission to heal ill and suffering children." Light the fourth candle, saying: "May parents everywhere have strength and wisdom. Give them balance, sanity, and serenity. May they recognize their mistakes and and have courage to seek help when needed. Light the fifth candle, saying: "Bless the children. Bless the children. Bless the children." Keeping watch, let your candles burn themselves out.

Luci Sophia Zain

Notes:

September 7
Thursday

2nd ♓

Full Moon 2:42 pm

Color of the day: Turquoise
Incense of the day: Chrysanthemum

Chinese Moon Festival Spell

The Chinese Moon Festival is celebrated all over China and by Chinese people worldwide this month of September. As it is a festival of lights, people gather firecrackers and glowing lanterns, and they serve special foods now. Moon cakes and special rice cakes shaped like moons are offered only at this time of the year. The origins of the Chinese Moon Festival can be traced to the fourteenth century, when Mongol rulers

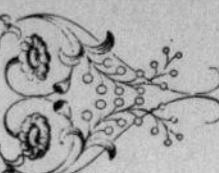

threatened to overtake China. The native Chinese fought back with a full rebellion. The time and date of attacks and troop movements were hidden in the rice cakes that were distributed among the loyal Chinese. In this way, they averted their would-be conquerers. Fortune cookies may have gotten their beginnings here as well!

Nancy Bennett

Notes:

September 8
Friday

3rd ♓
☽ → ♈ 2:23 pm

Color of the day: Rose
Incense of the day: Nutmeg

Wish for Mate Spell

Make an image of the type of mate you wish to draw to yourself. Place this in a corn peel, and wrap the silk from the corn round it three times, saying:

> Harvest magic,
> Corn of gold,
> Draw me a love to hold.
> Peel of green and silk of
> ear,
> Bring me love to cherish
> dear.

Alternatively, if you have a mate who is not communicating well with you, perform the same spell but instead saying:

> Harvest magic,
> Corn of gold,
> Let lovers speak in
> words so bold.
> Peel of green and silk of
> ear,
> Tell me of love I long to
> hear.

Nancy Bennett

Notes:

September 9
Saturday

3rd ♈

Color of the day: Brown
Incense of the day: Jasmine

Chrysanthemum Day Spell

The beautiful chrysanthemum, one of autumn's flowers, now begins to brighten flower beds and doorsteps. The Japanese revere the

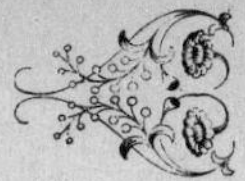

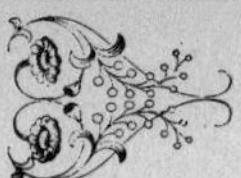

mum so much that they've set aside this day to honor the plant. The mum is a symbol of autumn, and also mystical. They are ruled by the Sun, the giver of life and protection, and protect the garden from evil. One of the mum's little-known magical qualities is its ability to bring about visions when scrying with fire. To do this, combine dried mum leaves with dried rose leaves and petals of the autumn crocus. Crush this mixture into a powder. Sprinkle it on the flames of the autumn or winter fire. Watch for any symbols, faces, names, or numbers that may appear. Hold your gaze steady as you think of your question. Set the mood by saying: "Flames dance and spark. Bring me visions from the dark."

James Kambos

Notes:

September 10

Sunday

3rd ♈

☽ → ♉ 2:30 pm

Color of the day: Amber

Incense of the day: Parsley

Golden Autumn Spell

Slowly the year wanes. The Sun still shines brightly, but less and less so each day. During autumn and winter, some people feel lethargic and depressed due to insufficient light. You can counter the effects of this seasonal light-loss by capturing the thick golden light of an autumn afternoon, when the Sun is still powerful yet attuned to the dark part of the year. For this, you'll need an Austrian crystal prism. String it on beading wire along with golden or, if you can find them, sun-shaped beads. Go outside and hold the prism up to the Sun. Now say:

Sun of honey and gold,
Sun of barley and grass,
Shine in crystalline glass.
Enter this charm I hold!

Keep the charm aloft until your arm gets tired. Then hang it in your window. When you need a reminder of the Sun, touch the prism to make it spin and sparkle.

Elizabeth Barrette

Notes:

   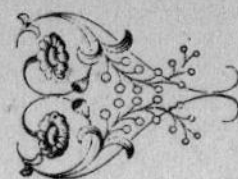 

September 11
Monday

3rd ♉

Color of the day: Lavender
Incense of the day: Daffodil

Banishing Nightmares Spell

Little children may have occasional bouts with nightmares—brought on by a scary movie, by a time of stress in the family, or sometimes for reasons that might not be obvious. Constant night terrors should be discussed with a doctor, but for the occasional bad dream a simple meditation can work. Sit with the child in bed and have the child visualize their favorite place. In a "sing-song" way (letting the child choose the tune), say together:

> **Bad dreams, bad dreams,**
> **You don't scare me!**

Talk softly with the child, adding a favorite person, a spirit guide, or pet to the meditation if the child feels more secure with the additions. After a bit, the child should be much calmer and you will find him or her drifting off to a peaceful sleep.

Boudica

Notes:

September 12
Tuesday

2nd ♐
☽ → ♑ 5:16 pm

Color of the day: Gray
Incense of the day: Neruli

Time to Part Ritual

Sometimes in a relationship we intuitively know it's time to part. There might be signs such as less affection or a lack of spark, but mostly you just know. At the same time, neither of you want to get around to talking about ending the relationship. Along with just getting up the guts to tell your lover it's time to part ways, you will likely need a spell for closure to help you move on. On this waning Moon, you can begin the process. On blue-colored paper, write your partner's name and your name, leaving some space in between, and say out loud:

> **Good times don't always**
> **last.**
> **For us, the best ones have**
> **passed.**
>
> **As I cut this paper with**
> **names of two,**
> **I do it with fond memories**
> **parting from you.**

Tear the paper, separating your names. Dispose of the two pieces in different places to seal the parting.

Emely Flak

 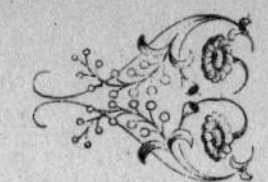   

Notes:

September 13

Wednesday

3rd ♊

Color of the day: Yellow

Incense of the day: Neroli

Hazelnut Magic

For magical purposes, nut harvesting begins September 3 and ends on the Autumn Equinox. The day after the equinox is known as the "Devil's Nutting Day." It is thought to be bad luck to use nuts harvested after the equinox for spell work. The hazel tree is one of the nine sacred trees. A symbol of wisdom, this tree is sacred to Hermes. Working with hazel nuts or the wood from the trees can bring you knowledge, luck, fertility, clairvoyance, or protection. Make a string of nine hazel nuts and hang them over a door for good luck. Or, tie a bunch of hazel twigs together for protection. Wearing a crown made of hazel twigs will deepen your divination practice. Before you begin, say:

Hermes' pride,
Hazel's grace,
Lend your wisdom
To this place.
Pool or stick,
Rune or card,
What is likely,
Plain or hard.

Lily Gardner-Butts

Notes:

September 14

Thursday

3rd ♊

4th Quarter 7:15 am

☽ → ♋ 10:53 pm

Color of the day: Crimson

Incense of the day: Evergreen

Harvest Moon Altar Ritual

This is one of many thanksgiving ceremonies employed by the Iroquois people to honor the fertility of the earth and give thanks for the harvest. Use this harvest festival as

inspiration to begin your Autumn Equinox altar. Gather about a cup of fertile soil. Put it in a pretty bowl on your altar. Pick out a few ripe gourds and squash of various colors, shapes, textures, and sizes, and place them on your altar along with some rainwater. If you are not the type to keep an altar, place these items on a nice cloth on your mantel or a windowsill. With this simple altar ritual you share thanksgiving with the Harvest Moon while preparing for the changing of the wheel at the Autumn Equinox.

Stephanie Rose Bird

Notes:

September 15
Friday

4th ♋

Color of the day: Purple

Incense of the day: Ginger

Celtic Grain Reaping Blessing

Harvest take place throughout August and September, depending on the latitude and the type of grain being grown. In Celtic countries people of old grew oats, barley, spelt, and rye. This was a time of great celebration. Everyone dressed in their finest and gathered in the fields to thank the God of the Harvest. The head of the family or group took up a sickle and, facing the Sun, cut a handful of grain. The grain was circled around his or her head three times, and everyone recited a reaping salutation. Here is a traditional Scottish reaping blessing for you to use in your autumn harvest rituals:

On the day of the feast,
At the rise of the Sun,
I go forth with my sickle
To reap the first cut.

May the gods bless my reaping,
Each ridge and plain and field,
Each ear and handful in the sheaf.

Sharynne NicMhacha

Notes:

Holiday Lore: Keirou no Hi, or "Respect for the Aged Day," has been a national holiday in Japan since 1966. On this day, the Japanese show respect to elderly citizens, celebrate their longevity, and pray for their health. Although there are no traditional customs specifically associated with this day, cultural programs are usually held in various communities. School children draw pictures or make handicraft gifts for their grandparents and elderly family friends or neighbors. Some groups visit retirement or nursing homes to present gifts to residents.

September 16
Saturday

4th ♋

Color of the day: Gray
Incense of the day: Violet

Safety at a Distance Spell

Use this to protect someone at a distance from you, helping keep him or her safe in foul weather. You will need a blue candle, a plate, and some beach sand. Also, if you have one, use a picture of the person you are trying to protect. Place the plate on a flat surface where it can be undisturbed for a few days. Arrange the photo beneath the plate. Place the candle in the middle of the plate and ring it with the sand. The candle represents the person being protected. The sand forms a ring of protection around him or her. You can think of it as a wall of sandbags, or a uncrossable line in the sand, or some such thing. Let the candle burn while you are there to supervise, until you are sure the person is safe.

Laurel Reufner

Notes:

September 17
Sunday

4th ♋
☽ → ♌ 8:15 am

Color of the day: Gold
Incense of the day: Poplar

Hathor Feast Day Ritual

Patroness of the sky, Sun, music, dance, and the arts, the ancient Egyptian cow goddess Hathor was worshipped with great music and dancing today. In honor of her feast day, surround yourself with music and beautiful creativity. From a piece of cardboard, cut out the shape of two cow horns with a circle in the

   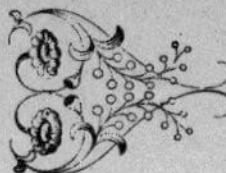 

middle. Cover this with aluminum foil. If you can find gold foil, even better! Place this in a special place in your home, asking Hathor to bless you with creativity and inspiration. Then play your favorite music and dance, even if you are simply moving to the music while seated in a chair. Dance for Hathor, for healing, and for divine inspiration. Allow this free and fun energy to flow through you, revitalizing your body and spirit.

Kristin Madden

Notes:

September 18

Monday

4th ♌

Color of the day: Silver

Incense of the day: Peony

Hestia Hearth Spell

To clean your house call upon the goddess Hestia. She is goddess of hearth and home and will aid you in your quest for a clean space. Starting in the kitchen, take a broom and sweep a circle going clockwise. Three times round go, chanting:

Hestia of the hearth,
Help me banish dust and
dirt.
Let chores go fast,
Let grime beware!
Make my space shine
With renewed care.

Follow this up with a good cleaning. You will be amazed at how well and how fast it goes. Repeat in any room where it is needed. After you are done, light a candle and leave out an offering of home-baked bread for Hestia.

Nancy Bennett

Notes:

September 19

Tuesday

4th ♌

☽ → ♍ 8:07 pm

Color of the day: Black

Incense of the day: Pine

Trivia Night Spell

Although it might sound frivolous, a Pagan trivia night is a fun way to share knowledge with your Witchy friends. You can work in pairs, or

 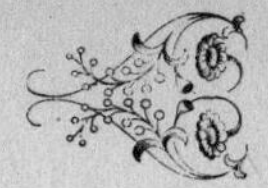  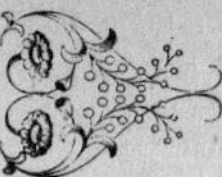 

split a larger group into teams of three or four people. To prepare, assign each team the task of organizing thirteen questions with answers and find a small prize for the winners. Each team hosts a round with their questions, going through the answers so participants can keep a cumulative score. Here are some helpful tips:

> Ask each team to include a variety of questions on topics such as mythology, magical symbols, correspondences, sabbats, etc.
>
> Ask teams to submit their questions beforehand so you can check for duplicates.
>
> Keep the questions at a level to suit your audience—whether they are novice or adept practitioners.
>
> At the event, set some simple ground rules, such as time to answer, and so on.

Have fun!

Emely Flak

Notes:

September 20
Wednesday

4th ♍

Color of the day: Brown

Incense of the day: Coriander

Wild Geese of Autumn Spell

I hear their haunting cry before I see them. Looking up, I see the dark V-formation of wild geese in the sky over the hills of the valley. They glide effortlessly across the blue September sky, heading toward the southern horizon. No other creature embodies the restless spirit of autumn. These majestic creatures own the sky. They are the nomads of autumn. Wild geese teach us that our corner of the universe is a very small place. They remind us that we, too, should expand our horizons, mentally and physically. For now I stand, my eyes turned toward the clear September heavens, humbled by the sight of these noble travelers.

James Kambos

Notes:

September 21
Thursday

4th ♍

Color of the day: Purple
Incense of the day: Dill

Fairness and Justice Spell

When evil doers seem to be succeeding while you are struggling, it's time to seek fairness and justice. Gather two measuring cups, some salt, cornmeal, and two plates. Light a white candle and a black candle. On a piece of paper, write out the unfair things in your life and place this on one plate. On another piece of paper, write all the fair things and place it on the other plate. Measure out salt to cover the negative piece of paper. Measure out cornmeal to cover the positive piece of paper. Hold your hands over the salt, and say three times: "Cleanse with salt this pile of fault." Hold your hands over the cornmeal and say three times: "Spirit of corn, justice is born." Take a small portion of salt in one hand and cornmeal in the other. Hold your hands together over the candles, and chant: "All that is wrong is transformed, and all that is right will become delight."

Gail Wood

Notes:

September 22
Friday

4th ♍

New Moon 7:45 am

☽ → ♎ 9:06 am

Color of the day: White
Incense of the day: Cedar

Giving Thanks Spell

Known as the Witch's Thanksgiving, Mabon occurs at the Autumnal Equinox. As the year shifts from light to dark, the focus shifts from the masculine to the feminine, from the God to the Goddess, and from external work to internal reflection. On this day, Lugh, honored at Lughnasadh, sacrifices himself in battle with his dark twin. In Wiccan mythology, the Goddess, full and radiant in her own abundance, waits to give birth to the new Sun god at Yule. Also known as Harvest Home, the Feast of Avalon, Wine Harvest, and the Festival of Dionysus, Mabon can also be seen as a celebration of the god of the vine. In either form, it marks the second harvest and is a time to relax, enjoy, and give thanks for the bounty of the earth. Create an altar with the colors, fruits, and flowers of fall. Decorations could include leaves, grain, acorns, apples, grapes, a cornucopia, the Empress card from your favorite tarot deck, and a picture or statute of Demeter, Persephone, Lugh, or

 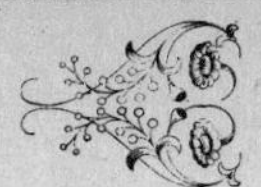  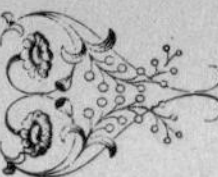 

Dionysus. Light an orange or rust candle, and reflect on all that you have harvested in the past year. Light another candle in thanks for each item or event, saying: "Thank you, Lady, for your great gift of abundance." End by raising a chalice containing a small amount of juice, wine, or mead, saying: "Thank you, Lord, for your gift of sacrifice and bounty." Take one sip, and then go outside and offer the rest in libation to the earth. Let the candles burn down and leave the altar, adding fresh items as needed, until Samhain.

Lady MoonDance

Notes:

September 23

Saturday

Mabon – Fall Equinox – Rosh Hashanah

1st ♎

☉ → ♎ 12:03 am

Color of the day: Blue
Incense of the day: Cedar

Basic Navaratri Indian Festival Ritual

While Jewish brothers and sisters observe Rosh Hashanah, Hindus around the world celebrate Navaratri beginning today until October 1. Navaratri is one of the longest popular festivals in India. It signifies the progress of a spiritual aspirant in three stages personified by the goddesses Durga, Lakshmi, and Saraswati. Navaratri translated loosely means "Nine Nights." Each three-day sequence is allocated for worshipping each of the three goddesses. The tenth day culminates as Vijaya-Dashami or "the tenth day of spiritual victory." Durga is worshipped during the first three days as the aspect of Shakti, which banishes negative inclinations. Lakshmi is next prayed to as divine mother who not only bestows peace, wealth, and abundance, but who also sees to the needs of mortals in accordance with individual karmas. Saraswati is invoked during the last three days of Navaratri. She is the goddess of knowledge, patron of the arts, studies, and music, among other qualities. Saraswati illumines supreme truth and removes inner ignorance. This basic worship ritual is an alternative for those in the West who may also wish to observe Navaratri. Find or download pictures of Durga, Lakshmi, and Saraswati. Prepare the altar and make offerings of flowers, fruit, milk,

   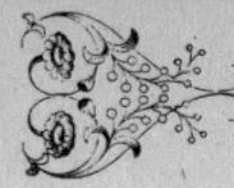 

sweets, rosewater, incense, and tea lights. Pray to or meditate on each goddess for each consequent three days. Advanced pratitioners may fast, chant mantras, and recite hymms sacred to Devi in her different forms from holy texts. On Vijaya-Dashami, the tenth day, Saraswati is invoked for blessings. Other devotees may decide to worship Durga to mark her victory over the ledgendary demon Mahishasura.

S. Y. Zenith

Notes:

September 24

Sunday

Ramadan begins

1st ♎

☽ → ♏ 9:54 pm

Color of the day: Yellow
Incense of the day: Cinnamon

Ramadan Candle Meditation

In the Muslim calendar, Ramadan begins today. This religious observance lasts one month and is a time of contemplation and worship. In our time-poor lifestyles, many of us feel that we need to be constantly occupied. Take time out for reflection with a candle meditation. Gazing into flickering flames has relaxed mankind since the discovery of fire. Candle meditations are an easy and effective way to relax your mind. Put on some relaxing music and wear something comfortable. Light a candle of your favorite color, and sit where you can comfortably gaze into the flame. Maintain your focus on the flame, even when random thoughts come and go. When you have meditated with the flame for a few minutes, close your eyes and hold the image of the candle in your mind's eye. Open your eyes slowly, and relish how relaxed you feel.

Emely Flak

Notes:

September 25

Monday

1st ♏

Color of the day: White
Incense of the day: Lavender

Celtic House Blessing

Nantosuelta is the Celtic goddess of the home. Here is a daily blessing for your home and family that calls on her:

Nantosuelta,
May your blessing be
On our home and family.

Bless us by day
And bless us by night,
And bless our children as
they sleep tight.

Boudica

Notes:

September 26
Tuesday

1st ♏

Color of the day: Maroon
Incense of the day: Juniper

Martian Spell for Struggles

Tuesday is ruled by Mars, the planetary ruler of conflict and protection. Its associated color is red. Its energy is commanding and masculine. Historically, Mars was the Roman god of war. Few of us find ourselves in the middle of a war, but everyone experiences conflict. Here is a spell to draw on the energy of Mars for victory in personal struggles. You will need a small piece of iron or steel, some pungent incense such as cinnamon or dragon's blood, and a lighter. First light the incense. Iron is the metal of Mars. Hold a piece of it in your hand and visualize it filling with fierce power. Concentrate on this until the incense burns out. Then rub incense ash on the metal. Carry the piece of metal with you. When you need extra power, touch the metal and say: "Mighty Mars, grant me victory!"

Elizabeth Barrette

Notes:

September 27
Wednesday

1st ♏
☽ → ♐ 9:16 am

Color of the day: Topaz
Incense of the day: Sandalwood

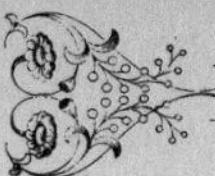

Sensual Side of Upi Spell

Venus rules the sign of Libra. During this sign, indulge your sensual side. Get a massage or pedicure, have your hair styled or colored, buy some new clothes, and beautify your home. This is a good time to redecorate your sacred space as well. Have you been using the same altar cloths for a while? Buy or make some new ones. Is your altar dusty or dirty? Clean it. Polish your candle holders. Trim the wicks on your lamps. Clean your vases and put fresh flowers in them. Look over your statues and talismans. Rearrange them or select new ones to display in your sacred space. After you've cleaned your sacred space, smudge it with sweet grasses, saying:

> With this sweet smoke,
> I reconsecrate my sacred
> space to my spiritual work
> and practice. So mote it be.

Luci Sophia Zain

Notes:

September 28

Thursday

1st ♐

Color of the day: Green

Incense of the day: Carnation

Good Fortune Spell

Michaelmas Eve celebrates Michael the Archangel's defeat of the dragon. Michael symbolizes the Sun, and the dragon, in this context, symbolizes darkness and winter. This tradition is similar to the mummer plays performed at the winter solstice, wherein Saint George defeats the dragon of winter. One custom now is to make a special dragon bread for the family. Eating this bread symbolizes overcoming the dragon.

Dragon Bread

- 1 cup white flour
- 1/3 cup whole wheat flour
- 1/3 cup fine ground oatmeal
- 1/3 cup corn meal
- 1 cup milk
- 1 beaten egg
- 1/2 cup oil
- 1 teaspoon baking powder
- 1/2 teaspoon salt
- 1/2 cup finely chopped hazel nuts
- 1/2 cup dried cranberries

Mix the ingredients together and bake in a 375-degree oven for twenty-five minutes, or until a toothpick comes out clean. Allow to cool for

 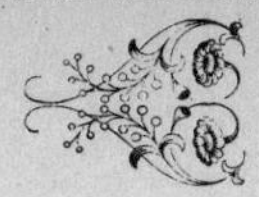   

five minutes before serving warm.

Lily Gardner-Butts

Notes:

September 29
Friday

1st ♐

☽ → ♑ 6:01 pm

Color of the day: Coral
Incense of the day: Ylang-ylang

Quarter Days Cleaning Spell

Today is one of the British Quarter Days, which honor the change of seasons. The wheel always turns, but Quarter Days remind us to stop and do some cleaning. For this simple cleansing, you will need a white taper candle and holder, salt water, a smudgestick, and a feather. Set up a small altar and place the items on it. Take the smudgestick and feather and walk around the house counterclockwise. Using the feather, blow smoke into every corner of the house. Say: "I ask air and fire to clear this house of any negativity." After you've smudged, take the saltwater and repeat your path. As you walk, say: "I ask water and earth to clear this house of any negativity." Return to the altar and say: "Lord and Lady, this place is clear. Bless all the occupants and hold them dear. So mote it be!"

Olivia O'Meir

Notes:

Holiday lore: The Feast Day of St. Michael the Archangel is celebrated in Western churches on September 29. In the Eastern (Orthodox) Church, it is observed on November 8. The cult of Saint Michael first began in the Eastern Church during the fourth century. It spread to Western Christianity in the fifth century. Saint Michael was the leader of all the heavenly armies. The veneration of all angels was later incorporated into his cult. He was highly revered as a protector against dark forces. By Michaelmas, harvests were completed and fresh cycles of farming would begin. It was a time for beginning new projects, balancing accounts, and paying annual dues.

   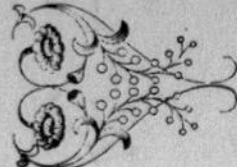 

September 30

Saturday

1st ♑

2nd Quarter 7:04 am

Color of the day: Indigo
Incense of the day: Patchouli

School Bus Security Charm

Riding the bus can be scary, both for little kids uncertain of what to do and for parents worried about bullies and other safety threats. This beaded charm adds to both safety and security to a child's daily transit. Your child can even assist in making it. Decide on how it will be carried—as a necklace, bracelet, keychain charm, or maybe just a totem carried in a safe spot in a backpack. Since this is an individualized charm, have the child pick out bead colors. Just make sure they aren't plastic, as plastic feels inert when it comes to bead magic. Add an animal fetish—that is, a bead shaped like an animal known for strength, such as a tiger, dragon, bear, and so on. After making your piece of jewelry, let it sit for twenty-four hours where it can catch both sunlight and moonlight.

Laurel Reufner

Notes:

October is the tenth month of the year, its name derived from the Latin word meaning "eight," as it was the eighth month of the Roman calendar. Its astrological sign is Libra, the scales (September 23–October 23), a cardinal air sign ruled by Venus. In October we enter the glorious late afternoon of the year. Bittersweet berries turn brilliant orange, and the woodland blazes with vibrant colors reminscent of a Persian carpet. As October passes, the door to the otherworld opens wider. We become more receptive to spiritual energies and feel drawn to bond with our ancestors. The main holiday of October, and one of the most magical nights of the year, is Samhain, or Halloween. This is a traditional time to honor our ancestors. Many seasonal decorations can help do this. The jack-o'-lantern illuminates a path so the spirits of our ancestors can find their way. Apples are used to feed the dead, so leave an apple near your door or on a plate at your table. The name of October's Full Moon, the Blood Moon, comes from this urge to connect with ancestors. When the Blood Moon rises, it smolders like an ember in the autumn sky. She is a beacon for spiritual energy. Thank her by leaving an apple beneath a tree, or by burning some dried wormwood in a dish and meditating on your deceased loved ones.

   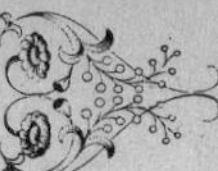 

October 1
Sunday

2nd ♑

☽ → ♒ 11:24 pm

Color of the day: Orange
Incense of the day: Sage

Acorn Lore

The goddess Artemis, patron of the forests, wild animals, and the Moon, was often depicted wearing a necklace of acorns. Fruit of the oak tree, acorns were sacred to the Druids and formed the tip of a priapic wand. The acorn symbolizes prosperity, fertility, and the fruition of long-term projects. If you find an acorn rattling in its cup, pocket it and it will halt the aging process for as long as the acorn stays shiny and smooth. An acorn on the windowsill is said to guard the house from lightning strikes. An old form of love divination is to place two acorns in a glass bowl filled with water. The acorns represent you and your love. If the acorns drift together, you will have a long and happy relationship.

Lily Gardner-Butts

Notes:

Holiday lore: According to Shinto belief, during the month of October the gods gather to hold their annual convention. All of the *kami* converge on the great temple of Isumo in western Honshu, and there they relax, compare notes on crucial god business, and make decisions about humankind. At the end of this month, all over Japan, people make visits to their local Shinto shrines to welcome the regular resident gods back home. But until then, all through the month, the gods are missing—as a Japanese poet once wrote:

> The god is absent;
> the dead leaves are piling
> up,
> and all is deserted.

October 2
Monday

Yom Kippur

2nd ♒

Color of the day: Gray
Incense of the day: Maple

Soul Cleansing Spell

On this Jewish Day of Atonement, people all over the world wear white and undergo serious physical and spiritual cleansing. No work is permitted on this day, and believers atone for sins between them and their God. While this may not be

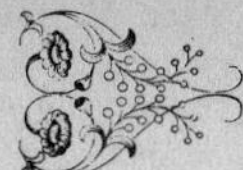

your tradition, now may be a good time to consider your actions and your path. Are you living your spiritual beliefs? List all the things you do and say. Include your reactions to stressful situations. If anything is not compatible with your truth, try a cleansing ritual. Smudge yourself and your home, bathe in salt water, eliminate junk food, and meditate to clear your mind. Then decide what aspects of your life you will adjust first. Pick one or two simple ones, then make a practical plan that realigns you with your spiritual path.

Kristin Madden

Notes:

October 3
Tuesday

2nd ♒

Color of the day: White

Incense of the day: Honeysuckle

Blood Moon Ritual

On the eve of the third day before Blood Moon prepare by ceremoniously pourly a libation to celebrate the earth and sky. All participants should wear white or silver robes or gowns, as well as jewelry containing carnelian or moonstone with silver accents. The coven leader will clean a chalice with rose water and dry it. Pour a cup of red wine into the chalice. Slice a ripe pomegranate in half and squeeze the juice into the chalice. Add a teaspoon honey, and have each member of the circle stir the potion with a magic wand. Go outside. Form a circle holding hands. The leader lifts the chalice, gives humble praise to the approaching Blood Moon, then takes a sip and passes the chalice clockwise around the circle. Each member also toasts the Blood Moon and drinks.

Stephanie Rose Bird

Notes:

   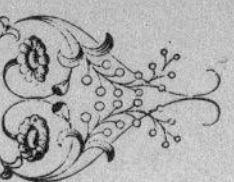 

October 4
Wednesday

2nd ♒

☽ → ♓ 1:33 am

Color of the day: Yellow
Incense of the day: Eucalyptus

Rowan Lore

The rowan tree was very magical in the Celtic tradition. Its reddish-orange berries appear in late summer and into the fall and can be made into a delicious jelly. Trees with red colored fruits and white flowers—such as apple, hawthorn, and rowan—were especially sacred, as red and white were two of the most important otherworld colors. Rowan was used in magic throughout the year, especially for protection. Gather fallen rowan branches and place these above the doorway. You might also want to create magical hoops or wreaths out of rowan and other sacred plants to decorate your home or altar at this time of year.

> Rowan tree,
> O rowan tree,
> Red berries of life and birth,
> Bring to us the power of three.
> Gods, ancestors, and earth
> Guard us in wholeness,
> Ground us with lore,
> Bring us together
> In wisdom once more.

Sharynne NicMhacha

Notes:

October 5
Thursday

2nd ♓

Color of the day: Turquoise
Incense of the day: Geranium

Prosperity Signature Ritual

Ancient principles of Chinese calligraphic art, ritual, and practice—particularly concerning the upwards and downwards strokes of the brush—can be adapted for modern-day use. Calligraphy is an artistic form of expression and a science that deals with each person's individual pen-strokes. This ritual will be especially beneficial for those who write and sign many personal checks but find their bank accounts constantly overdrawn. Set up a small table with a new pen, paper, a vase of flowers, incense, a votive candle, and a glass

   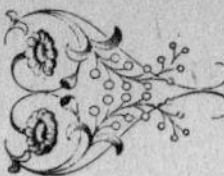 

of water. Sit in a comfortable position, then inhale and exhale nine times. Take a sip of the water and meditate upon fresh beginnings. Visualize money regularly flowing into your bank account, covering every check you write and also filling your account with surplus cash for incidental expenses. There will even be enough left over to save. When ready, smell the flowers and pass the pen and paper over the votive candle. Create a new signature that begins and ends with a firm upwards stroke to draw money luck. Continue practicing until you are able to use this signature with ease, and then use it for all your money transactions.

S. Y. Zenith

Notes:

October 6

Friday

2nd ♓

☽ → ♈ 1:32 am

Full Moon 11:13 pm

Color of the day: Pink

Incense of the day: Almond

Old Button Spell

Everyone has a box of old mismatched buttons from old clothes long forgotten or passed down from aunts and grandmothers. During the Blood Moon, when we reflect on our ancestors, you can use the buttons for magic. On a rainy day, give your kids some paper, glue, and kid-safe scissors. Begin by letting the children explore the buttons by running their fingers through them. Soon they'll ask questions such as: Where did this button come from? You can begin telling them about family history. For example, maybe a button came from grandpa's musty old favorite sweater, or from the dress of crazy Aunt Ellen who loved to dance all the time. Let them visualize who these people were. Next, let them create art with these buttons by gluing them to the paper to make pictures. Or, you can supply string to turn them into jewelry, or you can let them decorate an old cigar box. This magical exercise will give you time to bond and teach children simple visualization techniques.

James Kambos

Notes:

 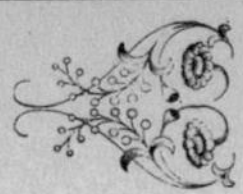   

October 7

Saturday

Sukkot begins

3rd ♈

Color of the day: Brown

Incense of the day: Lilac

Jade Magical Lore

Jade is revered as a sacred and auspicious stone in China. In the ancient dynasties, jade ornaments were coveted by emperors, empresses, princes, princesses, high-ranking officials, the nobility, and other wealthy families. Art objects, hair accessories and adornments, musical instruments, and various other items were fashioned from jade and were often used during important or auspicious rituals and events. Signatures were engraved on jade, and red ink was applied to use as a seal for decrees of command. Altars of the time were also intricately carved from jade, as were images of Buddha in various forms, and other Chinese deities such as Quan Yin, the goddess of mercy. In engagement ceremonies, ladies presented a gift of jade to fiances. Before the wedding, grooms gave future brides a piece of valuable jade as a gesture of promised upcoming nuptials. As a stone that possesses numerous qualities, jade continues to be utilized in modern times as a status symbol or in assorted magical rituals. Singles wishing to attract love can wear a jade butterfly pendant against the skin. Such an item can be gifted to one who takes your fancy in hope of reciprocation. If you are already in a relationship, the exchange of jade pendants between partners symbolizes long-term togetherness, harmony, and loyalty. In healing rituals, consecrate and wear a jade pendant or bangle to facilitate speedy recovery and physical regeneration. The Chinese also wear jade for prosperity, longevity, and good health. It is also worn for protective purposes and general good luck in all endeavors. You can enhance positive feng shui, tranquility, and harmony in the home by installing a jade Buddha. This generally assists with meditation and reducing stress levels. Light sandalwood incense and candles in front of the Buddha. Make regular offerings of fruit and flowers. Eventually the blessings received will go from good to excellent!

S. Y. Zenith

Notes:

 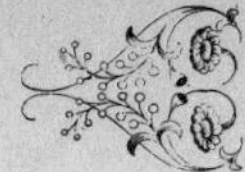  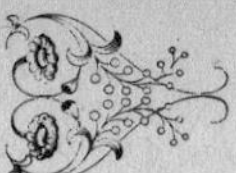 

October 8

Sunday

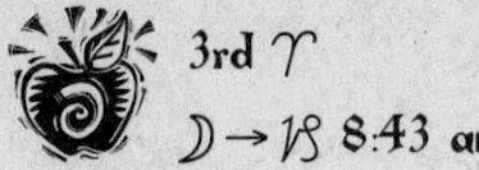

Color of the day: Gold
Incense of the day: Clove

Iron Invigoration Spell

Gather several small items made of iron and place them around you in a circle. Sit in the middle of the circle on a red cloth. Light a red candle and use this as a focal point. Clear your mind, watch the flame, and say:

> Iron strong encircles me,
> Flame of red strong it be.
> Exhaustion fade by light
> of Sun,
> I awake renewed!
> My will be done!

Gather the items in the cloth and blow out the candle. Wrap the items and seal the bundle with red wax. Place the bundle beneath your bed and the candle on your altar. Drink a glass of red wine or eat some iron-rich food before going to bed. You will awake invigorated and ready for your day.

Nancy Bennett

Notes:

October 9

Monday

Columbus Day (observed)

3rd ♉

Color of the day: Lavender
Incense of the day: Chrysanthemum

New Home Cleansing Ritual

Whether your home is a new apartment or a new house, you should clean it not just with soap and water, but also in a spiritual way. To start, smudge the home. For this, I prefer a sage and lavender smudge. Visualize warm thoughts of how you will spend time here with your family and friends. To ground and clear the home, use a mix of pine needles, mint leaves, salt, crushed cedar shavings, and lavender buds to sprinkle on the floors and carpets. Leave this mixture in place for twenty-four hours before sweeping and vacuuming, and you will draw out negativity. As soon as you are finished vacuuming, dump the bag to rid the house of any energies from the previous residents. Next, steep a handful of dried burdock (*Arctium lappa*) in water and wash your floors with this to purify, protect, and ward off negativity. Sinks, drains, and toilets benefit by mixing lavender oil and salt with water and allowed to stand over night before rinsing.

Boudica

   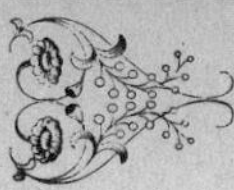 

Notes:

October 10

Tuesday

3rd ♉
☽ → ♊ 2:06 am

Color of the day: Red
Incense of the day: Evergreen

Get Good Grades Spell

School is in full swing now, and we're starting to take tests and do homework. Even if students are not enrolled in classes now, life has a way of testing us and finding new ways to assess our competence. To study well in order to do well on tests, either academic or in life, you will need an apple, any nonfiction book, and a yellow candle. Place the apple and the candle on top of the book. Light the candle and repeat the chant below several times. Keep chanting until the intention is firm.

> Study hard,
> Think well.
> Do the best,
> Pass the test.

Eat the apple while hearing the chant inside your mind. When you're done, thank all the spirits that have assisted you. Extinguish the candle and hit the books!

Gail Wood

Notes:

October 11

Wednesday

3rd ♊

Color of the day: Brown
Incense of the day: Cedar

Career Hunt Spell

Whether you're looking to get started in your chosen career or to change the path you're on, looking for a job these days is getting harder and harder. Take advantage of Gemini in Libra to add extra charm to your job search. Nothing inspires confidence like a bright smile, so for this spell you'll need a new toothbrush and a tube of toothpaste that only you use. Charge the toothbrush and toothpaste with energies that bring forth your natural exuberance and that show off

 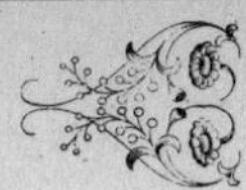   

your best talents and skills. Focus on providing yourself an extra boost of confidence when you talk with someone in person or on the phone. Use this toothpaste and toothbrush every morning. Now go out and apply for those open positions.

Laurel Reufner

Notes:

October 12
Thursday

3rd ♊

☽ → ♋ 6:21 am

Color of the day: Green
Incense of the day: Cedar

Tarot Card Prosperity Spell

For this spell you'll need the King of Pentacles card from your favorite tarot deck. On your altar light an orange or gold candle with a spicy scent. Place the card in front of the candle. Decorate your altar with symbols of the season—pumpkins, apples, mums, and so on. Also gather a sheet of white paper, an envelope, and a metallic gold ink pen. Meditate on the card. Imagine you are also surrounded by abundance. Write out your wish or goal with the gold ink pen in the form of an affirmation. When you are done, fold the paper and place it in the envelope. To enhance the spell, place the following seasonal prosperity-attracting materials in the envelope: one colored maple leaf, one oak leaf, and a bit of goldenrod flower. Seal all in the envelope and put it in a place where you keep spare change.

James Kambos

Notes:

October 13
Friday

Sukkot ends

3rd ♋

4th Quarter 8:25 pm

Color of the day: White
Incense of the day: Nutmeg

Wishing Well Spell

In ancient Rome, today was the celebration of Fontinalia. This festival was dedicated to the god Fons,

 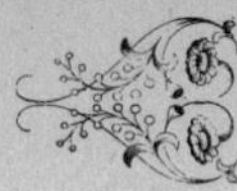  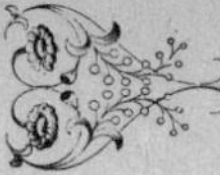 

lord of wells and springs. Garlands of ivy and flowers were thrown into the well today. Honor Fons and ask for his blessing. You will need: a coin, a sharp nail, and your desire. Go to any well, even if it's only a mall fountain. Take the nail and scratch a symbol of your desire on the ground near the fountain. Use any symbol you think is appropriate. Be sure you won't leave a permanent mark. Sit by the fountain and hold the coin in your closed palms. Focus on your wish. See yourself achieving it. When you are ready, toss the coin into the well and ask Fons to bless your wish.

Olivia O'Meir

Notes:

October 14

Saturday

4th ♋

☽ → ♌ 2:38 pm

Color of the day: Gray

Incense of the day: Juniper

Make You Invisible Spell

Is there someone in your life who is harassing or stalking you? If you face this difficulty, try this spell on the waning Moon to disconnect from your persistent admirer. Light a gray candle, or black and white candles. Gray represents invisibility and neutrality as it contains equal amounts of black and white. Light some frankincense incense for protection, then visualize a protective circle made of a mirror that you can see out but others cannot see through to you. This makes you invisible to your disillusioned admirer. The mirror will reflect energy back to anyone who looks in. While visualizing, recite:

> The energy you send
> Cannot see or reach me.
> It cannot find the target,
> Behind the wall you can-
> not see.

If you own anything that reminds you of this person, wrap it in gray material and bury it where it will not be disturbed or dug up.

Emely Flak

Notes:

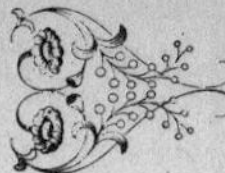

October 15
Sunday

4th ♌

Color of the day: Amber

Incense of the day: Basil

Hawaiian New Year Spell

Today marks the Hawaiian New Year, called Makahiki. According to myth, Po (Chaos) created Wakea (Father Sky) and Papa (Mother Earth). Wakea and Papa then created the Akua, or the gods and goddesses. Makahiki celebrates this act of creation. Traditional activities now include family feasts, storytelling, and outdoor games such as dart sliding. A new year festival in any culture is a time of renewal, and the Hawaiian tradition places an especially strong emphasis on people's connection to the land. Make some time today to bond with the land where you live. Go outside to your yard or to a nearby park. Sit on the ground. Touch your bare feet or hands to the soil, then say:

> Birth to death,
> Death to birth,
> I belong to the earth.
>
> Death to birth,
> Birth to death,
> I bless her with my
> breath.

Let the land's power fill you and strengthen your connection to the earth, until you feel wholly and completely renewed.

Elizabeth Barrette

Notes:

October 16
Monday

4th ♌

Color of the day: White

Incense of the day: Frankincense

Middle Way Spell

Qabalists tell us to find the middle way between mercy and severity. Mercy, out of balance, is weak and allows evil to flourish. Severity, out of balance, is harsh, often doing great injury. They advise finding the middle way. This middle way in tarot is symbolized by the tarot card Justice, which is assigned to Libra. Place three candles on your altar. If possible, have one white, one black, and one gray. Place the gray candle in the middle. Light the white candle and pass your right hand through the flame, saying: "I embrace mercy. I show compassion and charity to

 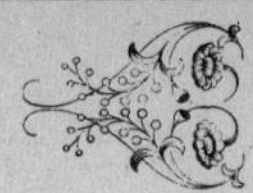  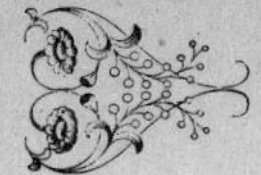 

the world." Light the black candle and pass your hand through the flame, saying: "I embrace severity. I show firmness and stability to others." Light the gray candle and pass your hand through the flame, saying: "I temper mercy with severity. I temper severity with mercy. I walk the middle path."

Luci Sophia Zain

Notes:

October 17
Tuesday

4th ♌
☽ → ♍ 2:15 am

Color of the day: Black
Incense of the day: Sage

Sacred Bore Lore

In Celtic spiritual tradition, the boar was one of the most sacred animals of the Samhain season. It was especially associated with the Sacred Hunt that took place in the weeks leading up to the Celtic New Year on November 1. The boar represented strength, courage, and determination. Magical boars appeared in the forest to lead people into magical adventures. In Welsh legend, King Arthur and his warriors pursue the supernatural boar Twrch Trwyth. The Gaulish goddess Arduinna, who presided over the Ardennes forest, was portrayed riding a wild boar. Recite this prayer to invoke personal power and the wisdom of nature, especially that spiritual power which comes from otherworld encounters:

I will wash my face in
the nine rays of the Sun.

I will travel in the name
of the gods.

In likeness of deer,
In likeness of horse,
In likeness of serpent,
In likeness of boar.

Sharynne NicMhacha

Notes:

October 18
Wednesday

4th ♍

Color of the day: Topaz
Incense of the day: Maple

Clean Water Libation Ritual

Today is the anniversary of the enactment of the Clean Water Act. Water is precious to Pagans of various paths and to all because it is the elixir of life. Pour a libation outside from a crystal chalice filled with pure spring water. Pull together your coven or a circle of earth-wise friends. Have the group recite while pouring the libation:

> We honor the God. We
> honor the Goddess We
> salute the spirits that
> animate nature. We
> remember and appreci-
> ate the ancestors.

Lift the cup, then begin pouring again.

> In honor of the elementals,
> precious water to each of
> you we extend.

Stephanie Rose Bird

Notes:

October 19
Thursday

4th ♍
☽ → ♎ 3:19 pm

Color of the day: Purple
Incense of the day: Jasmine

Chinese Gods of Wealth Ritual

Chinese homes, restaurants, and other enterprises usually have an altar on the premises made of various materials such as ceramics, brass, bronze, crystal, jade—even gold if the owner is affluent. The most common gods of wealth in Chinese culture are Tsoi Sun Yeh, whose vehicle is the tiger, Kuan Kung, and the three stellar gods named Fook, Lok, and Sow. The first two deities are usually displayed separately, but Fook, Lok, and Sow are most often displayed standing next to each other as a set. These deities are useful for attracting a continuous flow of good luck, for smoothing any monetary transactions, and for promoting evergreen prosperity. Images and figures of them can be purchased around the world in Chinatowns. Make regular supplications and offerings to them after installing. Most Chinese use flowers, oranges, mandarin oranges, pears, apples, red candles, sandalwood incense, rice wine, and tiny cups of Chinese tea. Always give thanks and make regular donations to charity.

S. Y. Zenith

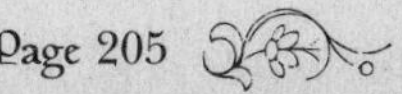

   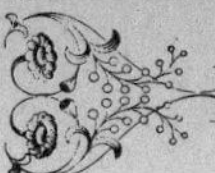 

Notes:

October 20
Friday

4th ♎

Color of the day: Rose
Incense of the day: Ginger

Affirming Love Spell

This spell honors Hulda, an old Germanic goddess of marriage and fertility. When it is snowing, it is said Hulda is shaking the sheets. To further encourage this spell, drink elderberry wine with someone you love. Elderberry is sacred to Hulda. To start, pick a time when you have the house to yourself. Light some white candles in the bedroom and strip down the bed. Get out some clean white sheets and put on the bottom sheet, spreading it out in a clockwise motion. Take the ends of the top sheet and lay it straight on the bed. Holding the ends of the sheet, lift it it up and down three times, saying:

> My love who lies between
> these sheets,
> A love that nothing can
> defeat.
>
> May our passion be pure,
> And our nights be long
> From this day forward,
> Our love grows strong!

Nancy Bennett

Notes:

October 21
Saturday

4th ♎

Color of the day: Blue
Incense of the day: Pine

Remnants Ritual

The year is ending and the harvest is nearly done. We are surrounded by remnants of projects that prey on our minds as half-finished spectres. Our anxiety over this creates crises

   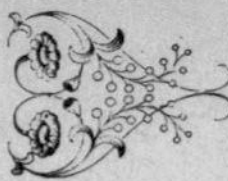 

and endangers the completion of the harvest. To tie up loose ends and finish the harvest, find a piece of loosely woven cloth, such as burlap or linen, in a color reminiscent of fall. Decorate the center of the cloth with symbols of the craft and of harvest. Then pull threads from the two raw edges to make a fringe. When the fringe is long enough on both sides, make knots in the fringe, envisioning your anxieties being blocked. With each knot, chant: "This knot is tied and harvest survives." Use the cloth at Samhain to celebrate the ending of the old and the beginning of the new.

Gail Wood

Notes:

October 22

Sunday

4th ♎

New Moon 1:14 am

☽ → ♏ 3:54 am

Color of the day: Yellow

Incense of the day: Coriander

Rosewater Beauty Spell

The New Moon is a good time for a new beauty start. For this spell, find the most scent-filled, pesticide-free, old-fashioned rose that you can get your hands on. Fill your prettiest bowl you have with some fresh spring water and float the lovely scented rose petals on the water. Let the water sit out somewhere warm for the next week, letting it catch the moonlight from the waxing Moon if possible. Finally, strain out the rose petals and store the water in a pretty spray bottle. Give yourself a refreshing spritz whenever you need an extra boost of beauty confidence.

Laurel Reufner

Notes:

October 23

Monday

1st ♎

☉ → ♏ 12:38 pm

Color of the day: Silver

Incense of the day: Myrrh

 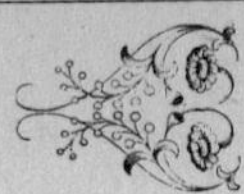   

Dark Side of the Moon Spell

With so many planets in Scorpio tonight, this is an ideal time to explore how your hidden self affects your family and friends. To do this, imagine you are standing under a Full Moon. The light shines brightly, then slowly wanes to dark. Ask to be shown what the dark side holds now—especially ask for any information that can help you to improve your relationships. Feel yourself being pulled to the Moon, and see that the orb reflects the shadows within you. Most of these shadows are very dark and you pass by without stopping. But eventually you will find one small image that speaks to you. Ask what message it holds for you. Take note of any images, messages, memories, or feelings that come up. When you understand something of the message or have received all that is offered, see light return to this place. Gently return to your body. Light and understanding fill you as the Moon waxes brighter.

Kristin Madden

Notes:

Lore for an October day: Maples are among the most stunning trees in nature, often very brightly orange and red. In October, trees are in their full glory and natural beauty (as the green of chlorophyll fades from tree leaves, only the natural color of the leaves remains). Cadmium-colored sumac gathers on roadsides and riverbanks, and provides contrast to the still-green grass and clear blue skies. The first fires have now been kindled inside to fight the coming chill at night, and days suddenly seem very short. Quilts have been pulled from cupboards to warm cold beds; our bodies begin to change in metabolism at this time of year, and our consciousness shifts from an actively mental state to a psychically receptive state appropriate to the dark half of the year. This is the time of the apple harvest; and apples fill fruit bowls or are stored in the root cellar. The house is scented with applesauce laced with cinnamon. Apples have always been magically important—playing a key role in the "wassailing" ceremonies meant to ensure a bountiful harvest in the coming year. Wassail was traditionally made with hard cider heated with spices and fruit—and a ritual imbibing of this drink was likely performed at Halloween and Samhain, and at Yule. Candy apples are a modern treat celebrating the magic of the apple harvest—these treats are eaten often

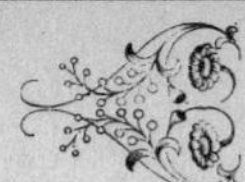

at Halloween even today. Bobbing for apples, too, has a long tradition as a celebratory ritual. Apples have ancient associations with healing (thus the phrase "An apple a day . . .") and were said to be useful for curing warts. The interior of an apple, sliced horizontally, reveals a five-pointed star. The final harvest of the year is the hazelnut harvest. Gather the nuts in wickerwork baskets to cure until they can be stored properly. The hazel tree was long held sacret and is symbolic of secret knowledge and divination. Forked hazel rods are useful for dowsing for sources of water or for underground minerals, and hazel is a traditional wood for magical wands.

October 24

Tuesday

Ramadan ends

1st ♏

☽ → ♐ 2:53 pm

Color of the day: Gray
Incense of the day: Musk

United Nations Spell

On this day in 1945, the United Nations was formed. This international organization was created to help prevent future conflicts and to offer humanitarian aid around the globe. For this spell you'll need no ritual tools, candles, nor herbs. Since international peace begins at home, the only things you'll need are an open heart and an open mind. To observe this day, try visiting an ethnic neighborhood in your community, especially one you know little about. Talk to the residents, visit their food markets, and eat at a restaurant. By now you've probably also noticed the familiar black and orange Trick-or-Treat for Unicef collection boxes. Give to them whatever you can afford now. End the day by remembering this: Open hearts and open minds will always open doors.

James Kambos

Notes:

October 25

Wednesday

1st ♐

Color of the day: White
Incense of the day: Neroli

Shoe Prosperity Spell

How you wear shoes and where and when you take them off can spell anything from prosperity to pregnancy

 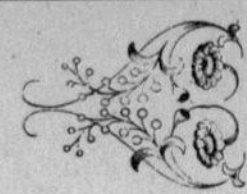   

to a death in the family—or so says an old Suffolk rhyme says:

Tip at the toe,
Live to see woe.

Wear at the side,
Live to be a bride.

Wear at the ball,
Live to spend all.

Wear at the heel,
Live to save a deal.

Today is the feast of Crispin, patron saint of cobblers. Since the fourteenth century, people have bought a new pair of shoes today for good luck and prosperity for the year. Why not give it a try? Before you wear your new pair, sprinkle a tiny bit of ginger powder inside the shoes. Be sure they are on the floor and not on the table when you sprinkle, as that will bring bad luck to the household. Slip your feet into the shoes, stand on your tiptoes, and say:

Saint Crispin, grant me
a boon: Good luck and
plenty, from October this
to October next.

Lily Gardner-Butts

Notes:

October 26

Thursday

1st ♐
☽ → ♑ 11:47 pm

Color of the day: Crimson
Incense of the day: Carnation

Acknowledging Errors Spell

Ralph Waldo Emerson said: "A man should never be ashamed to own he has been wrong, which is but saying in other words that he is wiser today than he was yesterday." Sometimes, when we are on a spiritual path, we discover that we have made mistakes, poor choices, and simple misjudgments. It is wise in such cases to acknowledge our errors and to change our ways, rather than clinging to our old choices through pride or fear of being teased or scolded. Changing our minds is just a way of showing that we are wiser today than we were yesterday. Today's simple ritual acknowledges a new insight about the nature of wisdom and a change in direction in how we consider our choices. To start, face the north, saying:

I have followed a path
for some time I believed
was best. I have found a
better, truer path. I now
begin my journey on this
new path.

Turn to face east and take a step forward, secure in knowing you now have a new wisdom and outlook.

Luci Sophia Zain

Notes:

October 27
Friday

1st ♑

Color of the day: Coral
Incense of the day: Parsley

Lots of Flowers Love Spell

Nothing says love more clearly than a bouquet of flowers given when it's not a birthday, anniversary, or other special day. For a loved one, be it a wife, husband, child, parent, or a special friend, find a bouquet of flowers or a flowering plant to offer as a simple gift—with no strings or expectations attached. Something with color is always cheery. It makes no difference what the flowers are, you need not be specific. Whatever is available at the time is usually perfect. You will be surprised at the quick response to this simple offering spell.

Boudica

Notes:

October 28
Saturday

1st ♑

Color of the day: Indigo
Incense of the day: Parsley

Spiritual Path Reaffirmation

During the Witches' New Year, or Samhain, take time to stop and evaluate your faith and beliefs. Make a sacred ritual or retreat out of this evaluation. Light white candles and burn sandalwood, myrrh, or frankincense. Brew a cup of herbal tea. Sit down and ask the God and Goddess to guide you on your path. Write down your beliefs in a journal or your Book of Shadows. Some questions you can meditate on are: What is life? How do I view the universe? Why am I here? What affirms my spirituality and what lessens it? How can I bring spirituality into my everyday life? After writing, you can create a statement of faith based on your answers to the questions. Recite what you write

   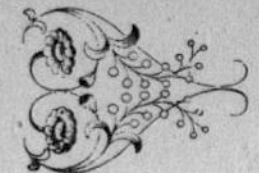 

by candlelight for the universe to hear. Rediscover and rededicate yourself to your spirituality.

Olivia O'Meir

Notes:

October 29

Sunday

Daylight Saving Time ends 2 am

1st ♑

☽ → ♒ 5:17 am

2nd Quarter 4:25 pm

Color of the day: Orange
Incense of the day: Poplar

Moon of Hecate Spell

The twenty-ninth day of each month is known as the Moon of Hecate, regardless of the Moon cycle at the time. Hecate, Greek goddess of the underworld, is sometimes misunderstood and aligned with dark forces. Hecate is actually a symbol of empowerment for many women. Her image is represented as a woman who faces three directions, expressing the Triple Goddess of maiden, mother, and crone, whose wisdom can also see in all directions. Today, two days before Samhain, invoke the energies of Hecate to uncover secrets that are hidden from you, or to help find an answer to a question you need to have answered. Speak these words:

> Hecate,
> Come help me unfold,
> What has remained
> untold.
> With your vision help me
> see what remains unseen
> by me.

Meditate and allow thought to flow freely, taking note of whatever enters your mind.

Emely Flak

Notes:

Holiday lore: Many villages in the English countryside share the tradition of "lost-in-the-dark bells." Legend tells of a person lost in the dark or fog, and heading for disaster,

who at the last moment was guided to safety by the sound of church bells. The lucky and grateful survivor always leaves money in his or her will for the preservation of the bells. This day commemorates one particular such case, a man named Pecket in the village of Kidderminster, in Worcestershire, who was saved from plummeting over a ravine by the bells of the local church of St. Mary's. In honor of this event, the bells still ring every October 29.

October 30
Monday

2nd ♒

Color of the day: Ivory
Incense of the day: Rose

Celtic Elemental Scrying

As we move from a time of light and action into a time of darkness and contemplation, now is a great time to perform the centuries old art of scrying. Since tomorrow marks the Celtic New Year, this technique pays homage by drawing up the elements sacred to the Druids: fire and water. This is best performed in a darkened room where you are comfortable. Fill a black or dark blue ceramic bowl with spring or rain water. Nearby, so that its flame is reflected within the bowl, place a lighted candle. Relax your body and allow your mind to "zone out" while gazing into the water. Have a pad of paper and a pen nearby for you to write notes after you've received your impressions from the flame's reflection in the water. Give yourself a moment or two to ground and reconnect before going on to other things.

Laurel Reufner

Notes:

October 31
Tuesday
Halloween – Samhain

2nd ♒
☽ → ♓ 9:10 am

Color of the day: Green
Incense of the day: Gardenia

Mask Exploration Ritual

Tonight is Samhain, the night of spirits. People dress up in masks to prevent malign entities from recognizing anyone and to scare them away. Masks can reveal who we are deep inside, or allow us to impersonate something we're not. Masks employ

some of the oldest magic known to humanity. They even appear in cave paintings! Find two plain white masks. Collect some art supplies, such as colored pencils or markers, glitter-glue, sequins, feathers, and so on. One mask is meant to represent your true nature and your inner self. The other represents your outer self, the face you present to the world. Decorate your masks, one at a time, taking care to express in each mask these different aspects of yourself. Now explore. Try on the masks and look in a mirror. How does each make you feel? Hold the masks so that they are facing each other. What might your inner and outer selves say to each other? The first rule of magic is "To know," so start by knowing yourself!

Elizabeth Barrette

Notes:

November is the eleventh month of the year. Its name is derived from the Latin word for "nine," as it was the ninth month of the Roman calendar. Its astrological sign is Scorpio, the scorpion (October 23–November 23), a fixed water sign ruled by Pluto. November reveals signs of winter. The raw winds sweep up the valleys and over the hilltops. The wild grasses along the lanes are bleached to a tawny color. Nature is stripped to its bare essence. Now is a time of simple beauty. The trees reveal the shapes of their naked branches, and dried leaves flutter up the roads in the late autumn breeze. The spirit realm is closer to us now and more active. Dusk settles quickly. The season's first fires glow on the hearth, and blue-gray smoke curls from the chimney. Traditional magical activities include scrying with fire, smoke, or a magic mirror. The harvest is complete, and we gather for Thanksgiving to share the bounty—especially turkey, sweet potatoes, cranberries, and pumpkin pie. November nights are magical. We can hear the stark voice of an owl hooting from out of the woods. In the darkness, the hard frost sequins the grass and bare tree branches with a silver jacket—giving November's Full Moon its name, the Frost Moon. To honor her, scry into a black cauldron filled with water and one silver coin.

November 1

Wednesday

Day of the Dead – All Saints' Day

2nd ♓

Color of the day: Yellow

Incense of the day: Coriander

Winter Is Coming Magic

The Callieach, Celtic hag of winter, begins her reign today. Legend says that on this day, she strikes the earth with a giant hammer, and cracks of frost spread out from wherever she strikes. Northern cultures offer numerous spells and charms to aid people's in their efforts to survive and stay wall through this dark time of the year. Still, you should know the winter season offers gifts as well—the benefits of reflection and rest. Winter is an excellent time to plan, to study, and to dream. Offer the Callieach an apple on your altar and burn a white candle. Ask this goddess to send you visions of the coming year. Allow yourself an hour of meditation. Feel yourself sinking into the earth, your roots reaching ever deeper. Slow your breathing and quiet your mind. Look forward to the next year. What thoughts surface? At the end of the hour, write in your journal what thoughts came to you. Fold the paper and plant it in your garden or in a flower pot.

Lily Gardner-Butts

Notes:

Holiday lore: The time between sundown on Samhain to sundown today, the Day of the Dead, was considered a transition time, or "thin place," in Celtic lore. It was a time between the worlds where deep insights could pass more easily to those open to them. Through the portals could also pass beings of wisdom, of play, and of fun. And while in time these beings took on a feeling of otherness and evil, as our modern relationship between the realms has been muddled, today can be a day to tap into the magic and wonder of other worlds.

November 2

Thursday

All Souls' Day

2nd ♓

☽ → ♈ 10:46 am

Color of the day: Green

Incense of the day: Sandalwood

Death Card Transformation Spell

Today is the Christian All Souls' Day, a holiday very similar to the Celtic Samhain. It is a day for remembering friends and family who have died. The Sun is in Scorpio today, and appropriately, the tarot card appropriate to this day is the Death card. The Death card can indicate physical death, but it more often means transformation. It focuses on the death of an old way of living or thinking and on the birth of a new way of life or thinking. Today, put aside any outdated or unhealthy ways of thinking or behaving. Begin fresh and think healthy thoughts and promote beneficial behaviors. For inspiration, look to friends, family members, heroes, mentors, and teachers who have passed on. How can you be inspired in your transformation by their lives? Be grateful for their example in your life.

Luci Sophia Zain

Notes:

November 3

Friday

2nd ♈

Color of the day: White

Incense of the day: Dill

Attract a Partner Ritual

If any of your recent romantic partnerships were fraught with negativity and bitterness and ended with regret, use this ritual to attract a mate who is right for you and likely to be your soulmate. Apply intuition and common sense when dating new people. Use logic rather than letting the heart run amuck. Resist the temptation to fall head over heels until you've had a chance to get to know the person. A compatible partner is not one who causes heartache, harm, or provocation. Write down on a piece of paper a personal affirmation about not falling for troublesome types with unusually fiery temperaments, self-serving tendencies, and a history of abusiveness. Be concise with your wording, and when you are satisfied cut nine squares from a large piece of paper. Write the same affirmation on each piece. Every evening, dab basil oil on the four corners of the paper and burn it at your altar on a heat-proof dish. Bury the remains a few miles away from your home.

S. Y. Zenith

  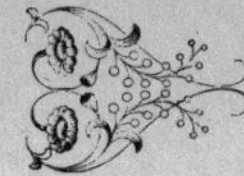 

Notes:

November 4
Saturday

2nd ♈

☽ → ♉ 11:05 am

Color of the day: Brown
Incense of the day: Jasmine

Ancestor Invocation

This day is very close to both Hopi and Zuni Ancestor Days. It is a good time to make an offering. Bring fresh fruit and vegetables of the season, a white candle, and matches to the closest body of fresh water. Those without a body of water can still pay tribute using a freshwater fountain. Set out fruit that is special to your family or heritage. Clear a space down to the dirt to place the candle, and light it. Begin your prayer of thanks:

> I know that you were here
> in my beginning and that
> you will be here in the end.
> Blessed be. Thank you for
> always being with me,
> for influencing, shaping,
> and making me whole.
> Blessed be. I lay these
> fruits out for you to par-
> take in our elixirs of life.
> Blessed be. I am yours
> you are mine—in body, mind,
> and spirit. Blessed be.

Bow your head. Listen to the ancestor's response. When you are ready, extinguish the candle and take it with you. Leave the fruit out as an offering to the ancestors.

Stephanie Rose Bird

Notes:

November 5
Sunday

2nd ♉

Full Moon 7:58 am

Color of the day: Gold
Incense of the day: Clove

Antiterrorism Fire Spell

November 5 is Guy Fawkes' Day in Britain. Some may ask: Why do people across the world still gather around bonfires to burn effigies and watch fireworks in order to celebrate the discovery of Fawkes' Gunpowder

Plot to blow up the Houses of Parliament on this date in 1605? The answer: Freedom. In the early days of the United States, the celebration was called by the alternative name "Pope's Day," referring to the fact that it blew a hole in British Catholics' plot to gain greater religious freedom. Some writers believe that these celebrations of freedom brought together American protestors and paved the way for the War of Independence. In fact, some of our founding fathers, including General George Washington, were considered "Enemies of the Bonfire." Now that Britain is our ally, standing beside us in the battle against terrorism, it makes sense to reclaim this as day to celebrate freedom from the fear created by terrorists. This is true no matter what religious beliefs might be driving their cause, but we can also pause today to ask for religious freedom that is more rational. On this night, coming just before election day, light a fire—whether it be bonfire, hearth-flame, or candle—and ask:

> May all of our leaders be guided toward a world that honors the spirit in everyone, and accepts any differences in people's beliefs, lifestyles, and cultures. May no one religion seek to oppress others, whether it be by terrorism or by dictatorship. So mote it be.

Lady MoonDance

Notes:

November 6
Monday

3rd ♉
☽ → ♊ 11:26 am

Color of the day: Lavender
Incense of the day: Peony

Easing Your Labor Spell

There are many folk remedies for easing or speeding along labor, especially when delivery is proving long or difficult. One of the most popular methods is to remove all fastenings and ties by using a form of sympathetic magic. If you can stand it, let your hair flow loosely about your shoulders. Remove any jewelry you might still be wearing. Other women in the room, if in a position to do so, can follow suit, offering further encouragement to the baby. Folks in the medieval period believed that an emerald tied about a woman's thigh helped speed labor. For those

of you who don't have an emerald handy, an onyx will also work. Try using one as a focal point during your breathing to help you relax and move your labor forward.

Laurel Reufner

Notes:

November 7

Tuesday

Election Day

3rd ♊

Color of the day: White

Incense of the day: Ginger

Election Day Spell

Today is Election Day in the United States. The opportunity to vote is an honored trust and an act of magic. The spirits of the founding fathers of the United States and the suffragettes of the last two centuries gather on this day to bless your actions, however you choose to vote. Our civic lives are as important as our magical ones. To find wisdom in your life as a citizen, place a newspaper on your altar. Draw or write your concept of a free and open society on the newspaper. For wisdom burn some sage and smudge the newspaper, asking for the wisdom to understand the issues of society, then chant:

> Ancient ones of power
> and wisdom, give me
> understanding of my
> world and how to use
> my rights wisely. For
> the good of all and the
> harm of none. Blessed be.

Gail Wood

Notes:

November 8

Wednesday

3rd ♊

☽ → ♓ 7:22 pm

Color of the day: Brown

Incense of the day: Eucalyptus

Tree Wisdom Spell

To the ancient Celts, the hazel tree and hazelnuts were symbolic of divine wisdom. Hazel trees often grow near water, which was also associated with knowledge, wisdom, healing, purification, and transformation. In Ireland, the Well of Wisdom was described as existing in the otherworld. It was surrounded by nine

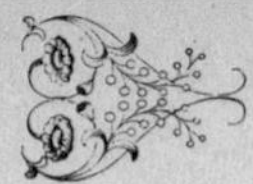

purple hazel trees. The trees dropped their nuts into the water, and the Salmon of Wisdom ate the nuts. Five streams flowed from the well, and these symbolized the five senses through which wisdom could be obtained. Chant this invocation to connect with the power of the sacred hazel trees and Well of Wisdom:

I seek to join you,
Fountain of knowledge,
Wellspring of lore.
As a seawave flowing,
And the nine wells of
Mannan'n mac Lir,
The gods guide the
pathway I follow.

Sharynne NicMhacha

Notes:

November 9
Thursday

3rd ♋

Color of the day: White
Incense of the day: Chrysanthemum

Let Prosperity Flow Spell

Prosperity spells are among the most popular of all spells. Still, many people complain when the spells don't work quickly enough. Here are some magical tips to get your prosperity spells to work more quickly.

Start small. Ask for tiny amounts of abundance first.

Be realistic. Don't ask for a house and expect it to happen today.

Don't repeat a spell too often. Doing this creates negativity that can slow things.

Ask for your spell to manifest with perfect timing.

Trust the divine power to manifest the spell wisely.

Ask for "just enough" prosperity to come to you.

Be sure your prosperity magic will harm no one.

After you cast the spell, visualize your request flowing down a stream or waterfall to completion.

James Kambos

Notes:

November 10
Friday

3rd ♋

☽ → ♌ 9:34 pm

Color of the day: Pink
Incense of the day: Thyme

Falling Leaves Spell

Druids honor all kinds of trees, but the oak is most important in this religion. A triad of oak, ash, and thorn marks where the fair folk gather. Other sacred trees include birch, rowan, alder, willow, hazel, apple, and elder. Every autumn leaves fall from trees, thus releasing energy held in potential. Stand under a tree now, and wait for a breeze. When the leaves flutter down, catch one before it touches the ground. Hold it and make a wish, visualizing your desire completely. Then toss the leaf into the air. If you can catch the very last leaf to fall from a particular tree, it will hold extra power, like the last sheaf of grain gathered from a field.

Elizabeth Barrette

Notes:

November 11
Saturday
Veterans Day

3rd ♌

Color of the day: Gray
Incense of the day: Violet

Drain of Jealousy Spell

Jealousy eats away at us emotionally. When someone is jealous of us, he or she drains us with toxic thoughts. Jealousy also breeds unnecessary malicious gossip. While the Moon is in its waning phase, take steps today to remove the negative effects of jealousy from your life. A spell to banish jealousy involves no harmful intentions. Light a green candle to represent the person who is envious of you. Walk around the room thrice in a counterclockwise direction imagining a protective shield of blue light around you. When the candle is nearly out, tie a blue ribbon around it to bind your spell and say:

No harm to this person.
No harm to me.
I bind this spell.
So mote it be!

Emely Flak

Notes:

Historical lore: Veterans Day commemorates the armistice that ended the Great War in 1918. Oddly, this war ended on this day, November 11, at 11 am (the 11th hour of the 11th day of the 11th month). Though Congress changed Veterans Day to another date in October at one point during this century, in 1968 they returned the holiday to November 11, where it stands today. The number 11 is significant. In numerology, it is one of the master numbers that cannot be reduced. The number 11 life path has the connotation of illumination and is associated with spiritual awareness and idealism—particularly regarding humanity. It makes sense then that this collection of 11s commemorates the end of an event that was hoped to be the War to End All Wars. Unfortunately, it wasn't the last such great war, but we can at least set aside this day to ruminate on notions of peace to humankind.

November 12

Sunday

3rd ♌

4th Quarter 12:45 pm

Color of the day: Yellow
Incense of the day: Sage

Simple Bird Spell

Remember the old days when animals worked closely with us? Well they still can if you are attentive to them and thank them for their contributions. I like to work magic with birds, my namesake. You may find that you do as well. Here is one of my favorites, a simple bird spell. All you need is a large bag of birdseed, a bowl, some water, and a photograph representing what you need. Go to a place that is not used often by humans, and put out the picture at high noon. Put your power stone or crystal atop the picture. Cast a large circle using wild bird food, and write out a simple wish in bird food inside the circle. Put out a little dish of fresh water and leave the location. Return the next day, retrieving your picture and power stone. Expect your wish to come true within a fortnight. If it doesn't, try it again in a different place. If you want to do bird magic often, try keeping a birdbath or grow a garden containing flowers, berries, and wild grasses.

Stephanie Rose Bird

Notes:

November 13

Monday

4th ♌

☽ → ♍ 8:18 am

Color of the day: Silver
Incense of the day: Lavender

Comfort Food Spell

We all have foods that we think of as special, and that make us feel better when we are sick or the weather is bad. Nothing warms me faster than a bowl of hot soup on a cold winter day. We can weave a magic around such comfort foods. If you or someone you love has a cold, some hot broth or hot tea will make them feel warm or keep them from dehydrating, even if they don't feel like eating or drinking much. Chicken soup is always a favorite. Cold evenings also cry out for a cup of hot cocoa. Top it with cinnamon or whipped cream for a touch of special magic. Share comfort foods with your family that will weave a spell of warmth against the growing cold.

Boudica

Notes:

November 14

Tuesday

4th ♍

Color of the day: Black
Incense of the day: Poplar

Raising Energy Spell

This is the time in Inuit tradition of the Asking festival. In the spirit of this tradition, find a drum or a rattle now. Make a sacred circle with white candles or white objects of power such as carved stones, statues, and the like, and stand in the middle. Slowly beat the drum or shake the rattle, breathing in and out and visualizing the energy flowing from the beat. Feel the strength raise as you drum or shake faster and faster. When it has reached the zenith do one final crash and raise your arms, shouting "Yes!" as loudly as you can. Feel the surge of power come through you now. Slowly bring the energy down and ground by touching your head to the floor. The energy is now there and the power is part of you. When you need it, simply ask.

Nancy Bennett

Notes:

November 15
Wednesday

4th ♍
☽ → ♎ 9:14 pm

Color of the day: White
Incense of the day: Cedar

Seven-Three-Five Spell

In Japan, today is Shichi-go-san, or "seven-three-five," a festival honoring children aged three, five, and seven. Prayers are offered now for the long life of the children. They are given bags of candy decorated with cranes and turtles, which symbolize longevity. You are likely older than seven now, but you can still create a long and happy life for yourself. Buy your favorite type of candy for dessert tonight. Decorate with images and words for turtle and crane. At dinner, toast seven times to turtle and crane. Before dessert, chant these six lines three times:

Sacred turtle
And honored crane,
I ask for a long, rich life.
Happiness shall not wane.
My life will be strife free,
Thanks to you.

Kristin Madden

Notes:

November 16
Thursday

4th ♎

Color of the day: Turquoise
Incense of the day: Evergreen

Relighting the Inner Flame Spell

Today marks the Dewali, the festival of lights celebrating the Hindu New Year. This event, coupled with the Witches' New Year at Samhain, makes now a good time to refocus and relight your inner flame. Create an altar to the element of fire. It should have lots of candles, preferably colored red or orange. Burn incenses like dragon's blood, cinnamon, ginger, damiana, rosemary, or dill. Place pictures of fire creatures like salamanders, iguanas, or chameleons next to the candles. Use any symbol, like a Sun or a hearth, that connects with fire. Add images of fire deities, like Pele. Light the candles and say: "Inner flame burn bright, never lose your light." Feel yourself become hot and your inner fire burn. Know that it is always lit.

Olivia O'Meir

Notes:

November 17
Friday

4th ♎

Color of the day: Rose
Incense of the day: Sandalwood

Braid Spell for Change

What would you like to change in your life? Your love interest, your affluence level, your career, or a bad habit? Buy three lengths of cord in a color that symbolizes for you the element you'd like to change. As you braid the cord, speak to it of your frustrations. Cry over it, tie knots in it, infuse it with your unhappiness. Holding this cord, say:

> Unravel cursed threads,
> So I can wind a better way.
> Old ways are now in
> shreds,
> A better life begins today.

Turn in a widdershins direction. After chanting, dig a hole in the earth and bury the cord.

Lily Gardner-Butts

Notes:

November 18
Saturday

4th ♎
☽ → ♏ 9:46 am

Color of the day: Blue
Incense of the day: Patchouli

Jamaican Sleeping Potion

As the first day of week's end, today is a day we do all those little things we are too busy to do during the week. Increasingly, many of use are overwhelmed with work and other duties. We get little sleep, especially high quality sleep. A tasty brew that hails from the highlands of Jamaica harnesses the calming quality of warmed milk and the exotic cardamom pod. Make the potion for as many people as need it. Take one white cardamom pod for each person and grind them using a mortar and pestle. Remove large parts of the husk of the pods, and discard. Add the powder to a clean cauldron or pot. Add one cup of milk (cow's milk or goat's milk, preferably) for each person. Warm this brew over medium heat, but do not bring to a boil. Strain it and pour into cups. Sprinkle the top with nutmeg, another spice with a marked tranquilizing effect. Before you know it, you'll all be nodding off for a sound night of uninterrupted sleep.

Stephanie Rose Bird

  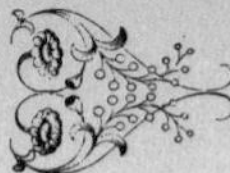 

Notes:

November 19
Sunday

4th ♏

Color of the day: Orange

Incense of the day: Clove

Magic of Darkness Meditation

There is magic in the darkness if only we can allay our fears of it. It is only the unknown we fear and once we understand that mystery is revealed in the dark, we can relax and find the enchantment of the place. To do this, after sunset today find a place that will be in darkness when the lights are off. Light some patchouli incense to promote deep awareness. Tone a single note to yourself, and settle down into a meditative state. Turn out the lights and close your eyes. Continue to intone softly and breathe deeply. Open your eyes in the darkness. Do not strain to see. Extend the awareness of your psychic senses outward and feel the texture of the night. Breathe deeply and rest in the darkness. Let the messages come to you as you rest in the deepest dark. When you are finished, go back to a ordinary state of consciousness and to your normal activities.

Gail Wood

Notes:

November 20
Monday

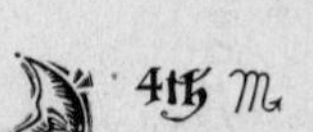

4th ♏

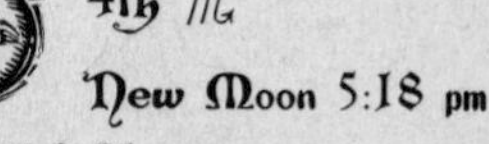

New Moon 5:18 pm

☽ → ♐ 8:15 pm

Color of the day: Ivory

Incense of the day: Maple

Know Your Own Darkness Spell

The New Moon in Scorpio occurs just as we are about to leave this particular Sun sign. What have you learned about your own darkness in these last weeks? This Plutonian sign holds knowledge, magic, and power, but here is also found intensity, passion and sometimes even a recognition of our own cruelty. Sit in the darkness, by the light of a single candle,

and ask yourself: What part of yourself are you afraid for the world to see? How do you respond to this fear? Do you put up walls or attempt to impose your will on others? To change the world around you, you have to change yourself first. But that change won't happen when you are ruled self-ignorance, fear, or anger. It will come only when you know and understand even those parts of yourself you would rather hide. We all have dark urges, the real test of character is how we choose to act on them. We must first acknowledge these impulses or we will unconsciously act out on them. Wrap yourself in a warm, cozy blanket surrounded by pillows, and talk to the dark place in your soul. Envision it curled up in your arms, and express your love. Not that you love the negative urges, but that you love the dark spot regardless of the negative side. Say you understand the fear and hurt that often underlies this. Promise yourself that you will be a good parent to your dark side—giving it protection and acceptance, while not allowing it to be harmful to others.

Lady MoonDance

Notes:

November 21
Tuesday

1st ♐

Color of the day: Maroon
Incense of the day: Pine

Bloodstone Spell

Bloodstone has various uses in spellwork—including healing, gaining inner physical strength, wealth, courage, longevity, and removing fear and inhibitions. It is also used in folk remedies for stopping bleeding, soothing difficult menstrual cycles, preventing miscarriages, easing childbirth, easing nosebleeds, purifying bloodstreams, and providing relief for those generally afflicted by blood disorders. In ancient times in Babylonia, bloodstone was carried for overcoming enemies. Egyptians used it for breaking bonds and banishing undesirable ties. In modern times, bloodstone is applied for eliminating anger, cooling fiery tempers, dissipating fear, and for gaining victory in court or legal affairs. Basic magical rituals using bloodstone require only a few simple tools such as a pair of red candles consecrated with bayberry or basil oil, several pieces of bloodstone, some incense, and a bowl of spring water. Use your imagination and creativity when you design personalized bloodstone spells. Remember that the most important factor is focus and single-mindedness.

S. Y. Zenith

   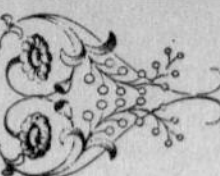 

Notes:

November 22
Wednesday

1st ♐
☉ → ♐ 6:02 am

Color of the day: Topaz
Incense of the day: Neroli

Holiday Stress Spell

In the United States, today is the day before Thanksgiving. Often, as we prepare for holidays, there is a great deal of stress. We wonder: "How will I ever get it all done—the cooking, the cleaning, the preparations?" In the midst of your busy preholiday busyness, take just a few moments for a quick calming spell. Have handy some lavender essential oil, diluted with a carrier oil. Pour a few drops into your palms. Sniff, then sniff again. Take the oil and massage some into your hands. Pay attention to the webs between fingers, particularly between your index finger and thumb. Massage your feet in a like manner. Then, massage some oil into the back of your neck. As you massage yourself, say: "I banish tension, stress, and worry. I attract calm, peace, and serenity."

Luci Sophia Zain

Notes:

November 23
Thursday
Thanksgiving

1st ♐
☽ → ♑ 4:25 am

Color of the day: Purple
Incense of the day: Dill

Thankful Thinking Spell

Thanksgiving is the traditional time for gratitude and reflection. Too often, we worry about small problems and petty disagreements. Rarely do we reflect on the positive aspects of what we have. Instead, we spend a great deal of time pining for something or someone we don't have. Today is a day to focus on the wonderful things we do have. Thanksgiving is a good time to realign our perspective and appreciate the many gifts in our life: our family, friends, job, children, country, and

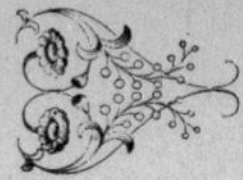

spiritual freedom. Appreciate simple gifts of nature we take for granted, such as the warmth of the Sun on your face, walking through grass or sand with bare feet, or sipping your favorite cold beverage under a shady umbrella. Write this affirmation on a small card and keep it somewhere visible: "I enjoy and value the precious gifts and moments in my life."

Emely Flak

Notes:

November 24
Friday

1st ♑

Color of the day: Coral
Incense of the day: Ylang-ylang

Holiday Stress-Busting Spell

Yesterday was Thanksgiving. The holiday rush is on now. To avoid getting stressed out this holiday season, perform this spell as needed. Light a pale blue candle and run a bath scented with lavender. Take the phone off the hook or shut off the cell phone. Draw the blinds. Say to yourself: "This is your time." As you soak, visualize your holiday tasks diminishing. Instead of worrying about cooking for everyone, decide here and now to have each guest bring a dish. Instead of visiting everyone on your list on or before Christmas, plan visits between Christmas and New Year's Day. Spreading out holiday events is a pleasant way to extend the spirit of the holidays and reduce stress at the same time. Finish your bath knowing that this year you won't spread yourself too thin.

James Kambos

Notes:

November 25
Saturday

1st ♑
☽ → ♒ 10:41 am

Color of the day: Indigo
Incense of the day: Lilac

Keeping Warm Ritual

As cold weather approached in olden times, stores of wood and fuel were gathered to keep the tribe warm during winter months. Fallen branches and logs were taken first,

   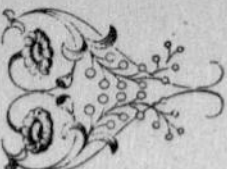 

supplemented by other branches for which thanks were offered to the spirits. It was therefore important to know what kind of wood burned well, which could be burned wet to give instant warmth, and which had to be dried before use. An intimate knowledge of trees and the properties of their wood was important in both a practical and spiritual sense. Here is an old Scottish rhyme about which types of wood should be gathered and revered:

> Choose the willow of the streams;
> Choose the hazel of the rocks;
> Choose the alder of the marshes;
> Choose the birch of the waterfalls.
>
> Choose the ash of the shade;
> Choose the yew of resilience;
> Choose the elm of the brae:
> Choose the oak of the Sun.

Sharynne NicMhacha

Notes:

November 26
Sunday

1st ♒

Color of the day: Amber
Incense of the day: Basil

Clarity for the Season Spell

At the start of the holidays, it is easy to feel overwhelmed by just a glance at your to do list. Take a few minutes to organize yourself. Sit down with your planner or calendar, your gift lists, some extra paper, and a pen. Light a yellow candle and some rosemary incense, saying: "Lord and Lady, help me to clear my mind and organize myself so that I can enjoy the season more." Now, make a list of everything you have to do and what presents to buy. Take that list and break it up into smaller, manageable steps. Now, take those tasks and examine them. How much time will it take to achieve each goal? Be honest. Find ways to save time. When you are ready, plot your tasks on a planner or calendar. Know you will have enough time to finish them and enjoy the holidays.

Olivia O'Meir

Notes:

November 27
Monday

1st ♒
☽ → ♓ 11:33 am

Color of the day: Gray
Incense of the day: Frankincense

Hermes and Aphrodite Celebration

In ancient Greece, people celebrated the feast of Hermes and Aphrodite on this day. Rather than focusing on romantic or physical love, this holiday emphasizes partnership. It honors the divine masculine and the divine feminine coexisting in harmony. On a more subtle level, it suggests the interdependence of mind and heart, intellect and emotion. Today, pay attention to your interactions with the opposite sex. Be open to opportunities for showing partnership and cooperation. Women may begin the day with this verse:

> Aphrodite,
> Goddess bright,
> Rising from the brine.
> Let my brothers turn to me.
> Let me be their guiding
> light.

Men may begin the day with this:

> Hermes,
> Lord of speed and sky,
> Skimming through the air.
> Let my sisters hear my
> prayer.
> Let me guard them as
> they fly.

Remember to look for the Goddess in each woman, the God in each man.

Elizabeth Barrette

Notes:

November 28
Tuesday

1st ♓
2nd Quarter 1:29 am

Color of the day: Black
Incense of the day: Juniper

Home Protection Spells

Black is the color most commonly associated with protection. The use of black stones, black candles, and black clothes are associated with protection spells. I like keeping a piece of irradiated smoky quartz near my front door to keep out any unwelcome intruders. Plant holy thistle (*Silybum marinanum L.*) around the house to turn away thieves. This herb is most commonly found in California, but in cooler climates, plant it in a large container out in front of your house. This will also prevent it from going

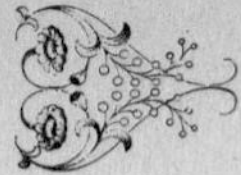

wild all over your property. Sprinkle betony at doors and windows for some extra protection. Burn fiddleheads, or uncurled fern fronds, indoors as a smudge for a strong wall of protection.

Boudica

Notes:

November 29
Wednesday

2nd ♓

☽ → ♈ 6:30 pm

Color of the day: Yellow
Incense of the day: Coriander

Hecate Crossroads Spell

As we travel we are all faced with choices. Hekate is the goddess of the crossroads. Go to her if you need to make a decision in matters having to do with travel or life opportunities. Take three apples and go to a crossroads that is not busy with traffic, ideally at night. Cut each in half so the pentacle formed of the seeds is showing. Thinking of your choices, place one-half of an apple at each intersection. Then make your wish and place the last two halves where the roads join. Ask for Hekate's help in making your decision. Go home and eat an apple or drink an apple beverage before bed. Dream of possibilities. Save the seeds to plant in the crossroads area next spring, and ask again for Hekate's blessings.

Nancy Bennett

Notes:

November 30
Thursday

2nd ♈

Color of the day: Crimson
Incense of the day: Carnation

Stones of Change Spell

Grow your finances, a pebble at a time. This spell uses a small bowl you make yourself to change your financial prospect. You'll need a small glass as the mold, about two inches in diameter. Cover the bottom with a layer of petroleum jelly so it runs about one inch up the side. Using a mixture of four parts white glue to one part water, coat small strips of

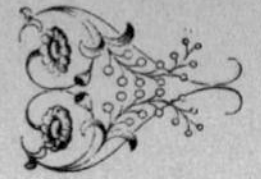

green or brown paper and place them on the glass. Picture yourself having the money you need. Build up at least three or four layers of paper so your bowl will hold up. Allow this to dry overnight, then ease the paper bowl off of your mold and trim any edges. Wipe off the petroleum jelly. Place the bowl on your altar or near where your money is kept. Start collecting small pebbles when you're out walking. Trust yourself to know when a rock is calling out to you. Place these stones in your bowl and money will begin to collect.

Laurel Reufner

Notes:

December is the twelfth month of the year, its name derived from the Latin for "ten," as it was the tenth month of the Roman calendar. Its astrological sign is Sagittarius, the archer (November 23–December 22), a mutable fire sign ruled by Jupiter. Winter owns the land now. Snow covers the land, and ice silences the streams. Still, this is a month of joy and renewal. Holiday lights glitter, and kitchens fill with spicy fragrances from holiday season sweets and pastries. Yule, Hanukkah, Kwanzaa, and Christmas are the holidays of December. At Yule we celebrate the return of the Sun God and burn the Yule log to honor the strengthening Sun. As we decorate the Yule tree, we honor the evergreen as a symbol of eternal life. The decorations we use on the Yule tree are rich with symbolism. The lights represent stars, fruit-shaped ornaments represent fertility, and the star atop the tree is a symbol of the divine spirit. December's Full Moon, the first of the winter season, is known as the Cold Moon. It is a white, distant Moon that shimmers above the frozen landscape. Acknowledge her by lighting a single white candle in a window. As the wheel of the year makes its final turn, we arrive at New Year's Eve, a time to honor our past and think of the future. The endless rhythm of the seasons continues.

December 1

Friday

2nd ♈

☽ → ♉ 8:26 pm

Color of the day: White
Incense of the day: Nutmeg

Spread Peace Spell

As we begin the month when the light of the Sun returns to the Northern Hemisphere, let us use this time to spread peace and love through the world. Decorate a white candle with evergreens. Carve symbols and words for peace and love into the side of the candle. Anoint the candle with gardenia or lavender oil, visualizing peace and love starting with you and spreading to others. As you light it, chant:

> May I find the peace and
> love that resides in me.
> May I feel the peace and
> love of nature and of the
> spirits. May I share peace
> and love with all. May I
> know peace and love
> everywhere I go.

Then let the candle burn itself out.

Kristin Madden

Notes:

December 2

Saturday

2nd ♉

Color of the day: Brown
Incense of the day: Pine

Lord Shani Rituals

The planet Saturn is considered by *Jyotishis,* or Indian astrologers, to be a naturally malefic planet. When it is ill placed in a birth or Moon chart, Saturn causes strife, illness, and prolonged hardship. Saturn is worshipped as a planetary deity called Lord Shani in India. Its sacred gem is blue sapphire. Jyotish astrology ascribes that each mortal has to go through three stages of *sadhe sati,* or "Saturn return." There are other minor Saturnine subperiods known as *shani dasa.* When entering cycles where Saturn is strongly posited in the personal astrological chart, a simple but effective ritual can help lessen the negative effects of Saturn. Find a picture of the shani yantra, a mystical diagram or talisman, and place it on a black cloth on your altar. Offer fruit, flowers, oil lamps, incense, milk, palm sugar, and some coconut. Two hours before sunset, recite the mantra for Lord Shani 108 times or continue over a period until 23,000 rounds are achieved. Beginners can fill a box with 108 toothpicks

   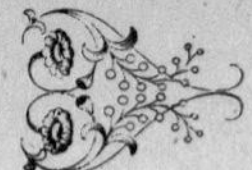 

and take one out upon completion of one round of mantra. Those who own traditional Hindu *japa malas,* or rosaries consisting 108 beads, may use it for counting. Advanced practitioners or adepts can formulate their own rituals for worshipping Lord Shani. The short version of Saturn's mantra is:

> Om sham sha–na–ish–
> cha–ra–ye namah Om

S. Y. Zenith

Notes:

December 3
Sunday

2nd ♉
☽ → ♊ 10:05 pm

Color of the day: Orange
Incense of the day: Parsley

Beauty of the Season Spell

Winter can be the harshest season. It burns your cheeks with cold and dries out your skin. But winter can also be the most beautiful season. Bundle up and take a walk down the street or to your favorite park. Notice how different winter's quiet repose seems from spring's new beginnings, summer's hot vitality, and fall's sharp decay. Enjoy the freshness of the snow. Hear how it crunches underfoot, and feel the chilling freeze on your cheek. Let the beauty fill your heart with love. Take this love with you to your holiday celebrations and share it with friends and loved ones. Thank the goddess Aphrodite for the beautiful scenery by leaving food out for the birds, giving money or food to charity, or sharing the holiday with someone less fortunate.

Olivia O'Meir

Notes:

December 4
Monday

2nd ♊
Full Moon 7:25 pm

Color of the day: Lavender
Incense of the day: Myrrh

Feast for Our Protectors

December 4 is feast day for Pallas Athena, Chango, and St. Barbara. All three of these are associated with warriors and offer protection against

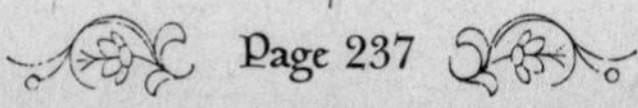

lightning. This protection can be extended to include protection from fire, explosions, and sudden deaths of all sorts, including on the battlefield. The Greek goddess Athena is the patroness of not simply war but also of strategy. Like her Roman counterpart, Minerva, she is also associated with wisdom and knowledge. St. Barbara was a girl who was locked away in a tower by her father because of her extreme beauty. Her father was struck down by lightning after having her beheaded for her spiritual beliefs, whereas Athena sprang forth from her own father's head after he tried to kill her by swallowing her mother, Metis. On the other hand, Chango is the playboy of the Orishas and a man of passion and power, war, and dance. Like Athena's father Zeus, he controls lightning and thunder. Set up a feast in honor of these protectors–including olives for Athena, cornbread, okra, bananas, and apples for Chango, and a chalice of dry, red wine or juice for St. Barbara. Invoke your preferred deities, and invite them to dine with you. Make up a separate plate and chalice for them and place it across the table from you before you eat. As you sit there, express your anger and your concerns with the world and its future. Ask the protectors for their strength, protection, and guidance on the occasion of their feast day.

Lady MoonDance

Notes:

December 5
Tuesday

3rd ♊

Color of the day: Black

Incense of the day: Neroli

Make a Witch Ball Spell

Years ago Witch balls hung in the windows of many homes. These were glass balls similar to the gazing balls you see today in many gardens. The purpose of these balls was to repel the evil eye. Here's how you can make your own. Purchase clear glass or plastic Christmas ornaments from a craft store, along with bottles of liquid gold and silver metallic craft paints. You can also purchase other colors of paint–it's up to you. Next, remove the wire loop at the top of the ornament. Squeeze small amounts of the paint on to the ornament, in pleasing combinations of colors. Swirl the ornament around, so the paints blend and coat the interior of the ornament. Leave it to dry overnight. On the next day, replace the wire loops at the top of the ornament and charge it with your magical intent. Hang it with

a pretty cord in your window or on a holiday tree. The pattern made by the paints will trap and hold any negative energy.

James Kambos

Notes:

December 6
Wednesday

3rd ♊

☽ → ♋ 1:00 am

Color of the day: White
Incense of the day: Sandalwood

Pasty Recipe Spell

Ancient people gathered as much food as possible so it would last them throughout the long winter months. Hearty food was often served in Celtic countries in the winter. This included oatmeal with butter and milk, soft cheeses, root vegetables, nuts and berries, bread, and dried or salted fish and meat. In later times, pasties or pastry pies were served. These consisted of baked dough toasted around a meat, fish, or vegetable filling. These were so popular that it was said the devil would not come to Cornwall for fear of being put into a pie! Here is a recipe for traditional pies to share at your winter rites and ceremonies. Combine one pound of flour with a half pound of butter, three eggs, and hot water. Roll out the dough on a board three times. Then cut it into six-inch circles, place the filling in the center of the circles, and fold them over to make a half moon shapes. Cook at 350 degrees until they are golden.

Sharynne NicMhacha

Notes:

December 7
Thursday

3rd ♋

Color of the day: Green
Incense of the day: Geranium

Jupiter Security Spell

Thursday is ruled by Jupiter, the planet of stability, authority, and money. This makes Thursday auspicious for spells relating to security or finances. In winter, the conifers remind us of life everlasting. Their green needles bring us hope during the bleak weather. The colors green and gold likewise stand for life and wealth.

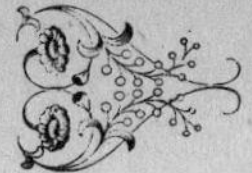

Carefully pull a few needles from a live evergreen tree. Lay a dollar bill flat and place the needles along the short edge of the bill. Roll it into a tight tube around the needles, then secure it with a rubber band. Say:

> Evergreen, evergreen,
> Growing so high,
> Grant that my money
> grows
> Up to the sky.
> All through the winter
> Let it endure,
> Growing toward the Sun
> Golden and pure.

Store the rolled dollar wherever you keep your money—in your purse or wallet, in a coin dish, and so on.

Elizabeth Barrette

Notes:

Holiday lore: Cultures around the world have shared a penchant for the ritual burning of scapegoats, enemies, and devils. There is something primal about the roar of a large bonfire and its ability to bring purging light to a community. Today is such a day in the highland towns of Guatemala. Men dress in devil costumes during the season leading up to Christmas, and children chase the men through the streets. On December 7, people light bonfires in front of their homes, and into the fires they toss garbage and other debris to purify their lives. At night, fireworks fill the air.

December 8
Friday

3rd ♋
☽ → ♌ 6:52 am

Color of the day: Pink
Incense of the day: Ginger

Winter Blessing Incense

In December, there is beauty, stress, anxiety, strife, and love all rolled into one month. We who work magic can depend on the gifts of the herbal kingdom to provide a wonderful balancing energy for December. This blessing incense can be burned to imbue all those who come into your space with warmth, strength, purity, and energy. It is truly a blessing for the winter season. Gather two pinches of each of the following ingredients: frankincense, myrrh, sandalwood, cedarwood, lavender, juniper berries, pine or fir needles, mugwort, cinnamon, and cloves. Grind the ingredients in a mortar and pestle until they are

 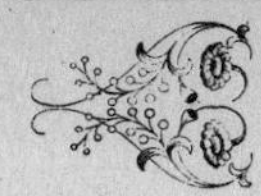  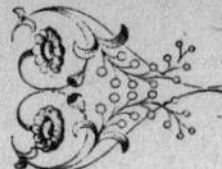 

a coarse powder. To use, prop open a window or door just a crack. Place a bamboo charcoal in a censor. When the charcoal begins to turn white, add a few pinches of the blessing incense until the desired effect is achieved. Enjoy this aromatic blessing with your coven, family, or circle of friends. Store the powder in an air-tight container away from the Sun when not in use.

Stephanie Rose Bird

Notes:

December 9
Saturday

3rd ♌

Color of the day: Black
Incense of the day: Lavender

Igniting Passion Spell

To ignite the passions of love and sensual pleasure, you will need a red candle and a pink candle, a bowl of cinnamon candy, some rose petals, and jasmine incense. Set the scene by decorating your space. Play sensuous music at a very low volume. Turn the lights down very low. Stand before your altar and spread the rose petals across it, chanting: "Enliven love with passion." Light the pink candle and chant: "Burn tonight in love's delight." Light the red candle, chanting: "With this burning fire, bring to me love's desire." Light the jasmine incense and breathe in the scent of sensuality and pleasure. As the scent fills your body, eat the some of the cinnamon candy, and envision sweet and fiery passion filling you with delight. Turn up the volume and dance with passion.

Gail Wood

Notes:

December 10
Sunday

3rd ♌

☽ → ♍ 4:31 pm

Color of the day: Yellow
Incense of the day: Poplar

Healthy Habits Spell

Choose an item that represents a habit you want to break today. Wrap it in a black cloth and wrap the cloth with a paper chain. Say in a firm voice:

   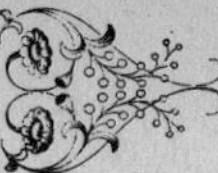 

I break this pattern,
Which causes me such
strife.
My self is worth much
more to me.
I break this chain and
set me free!

Break the chain of paper. Crush the item inside the black cloth if you can. Bury it under a large stone. Keep the chain on your altar as a reminder of your strength. Today is Nobel Prize Day when awards are give for inventions or activities that promote peace and the overall good of mankind. When we do spells we should recall we are also inventors. Put your positive powers to work today to create good that will give to the world.

Karen Follett

Notes:

December 11

Monday

3rd ♍

Color of the day: White
Incense of the day: Rose

Family Event Destressing Ritual

While many times a family gathering may be a happy event that is well planned and anticipated with much joy, it can also sometimes be a nerve-racking event, especially if you are the one hosting. Before the guests arrive, make time for yourself. This should last about an hour, and you should be the only focus. Take a hot bath with some grounding, calming bath salts. Center and relax. All the planning is done. The focus is now on you. In the bathroom, burn candles that give off calming scents. Gingerbread, vanilla, lavender, and apple spice are good aromatherapies. Place a piece of sodalite in your pocket to remind you to be personable with your guests. A quick prayer to Hestia is helpful too.

Boudica

Notes:

December 12

Tuesday

3rd ♍
4th Quarter 9:32 am

Color of the day: Red
Incense of the day: Evergreen

   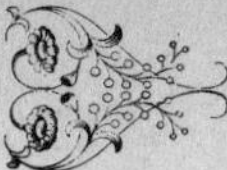 

Find an Item Spell

This time of the year can be rather hectic with socializing and family gatherings and so on. It's easy now to lose or misplace an item. Use Mercury's energies of clear thinking today for a spell to help you find your lost item. To do this you will need a mirror and a small magnet, two candles—one black, representing loss, and one orange, representing memory—and some patchouli incense. Set up the candles in front of the mirror, and place the magnet in the middle of the mirror. Walk around the room clockwise with the lit incense three times, saying:

> I invite the elements
> As I walk around
> To help my lost item
> Be soon found.

Touch the magnet as you recall when you last saw the item. While the candles are burning, try to find it.

Emely Flak

Notes:

December 13

Wednesday

4th ♍

☽ → ♎ 5:00 am

Color of the day: Topaz

Incense of the day: Eucalyptus

Saint Lucy's Divination Spell

Saint Lucy's name means "light" and has the same root as "lucidity." She is a centuries-old Yule goddess who drives out the demons of winter. A tarot reading would be useful today. For best results, dress all in white and wear a traditional red silk ribbon or sash around your waist. Dress your altar in white and burn twelve white candles. Decorate your altar with pictures of eyes. Before you throw your tarot spread, burn a stick of bay incense for the goddess. Say:

> Through the darksome night
> Visions come a-winging.
> Lo! Tis the queen of light
> Joyfully singing.
> Solstice is drawing nigh
> Candles are gleaming
> Welcome are visions
> And luminescence.

A clear message should come to you.

Lily Gardner-Butts

Notes:

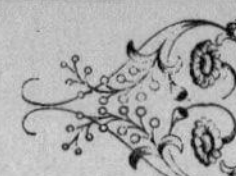

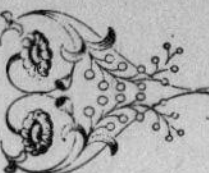

December 14
Thursday

4th ♎

Color of the day: Turquoise
Incense of the day: Musk

Nostradamus Divination Ritual

Today is the birthday of the prophet Nostradamus. In honor of him, perform a divination. Place a dark cloth on a table. Have a finger bowl of water on the table. Get out your favorite divination tool. Light a few candles, and turn out the lights. Rinse your fingers in the bowl, and say: "I wash myself of all confusion and distractions. I cleanse myself from selfishness. I come with pure intent." Hold your divination tool over one of the candles, saying: "O spirit of prophecy, today grant me clear vision. Let me see clearly through the veils. Give me strength to accept the truth and wisdom to make choices based on my vision." Perform your divination. At last hold your divination tool over a candle, and say: "Thanks, O spirit, for the insights you have given."

Luci Sophia Zain

Notes:

December 15
Friday

4th ♎
☽ → ♏ 5:42 pm

Color of the day: Rose
Incense of the day: Almond

Gingerbread Spell

Add a warm spicy note in your relationships this month with the follow recipe.

Gingerbread Cake

1 1/2 cups all-purpose flour
1/2 cup brown sugar
1/2 tsp. ground cinnamon
1/2 tsp. ground ginger
1 tsp. baking powder
1/2 tsp. baking soda
1 stick butter, melted
1/2 cup dark molasses
1 egg
1/2 cup water

In a bowl, combine the flour, brown sugar, cinnamon, ginger, baking powder, and baking soda. When mixed, add the butter, molasses, egg, and water. Using an electric mixer, beat on medium speed until everything is well combined. Beat on high speed for another two minutes. Pour the batter into a greased baking pan, and bake in a 350-degree oven for forty minutes or until a toothpick comes out clean. Cool for ten minutes before serving. Serve it with either vanilla bean

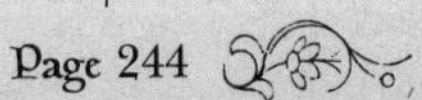

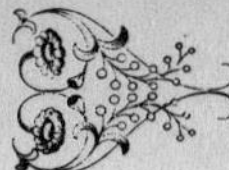

ice cream or whipped cream for an extra yummy treat.

Laurel Reufner

Notes:

December 16

Saturday

Hanukkah begins

4th ♏

Color of the day: Gold

Incense of the day: Coriander

Dreidel Spinning Ritual

Hanukkah is the Hebrew festival of lights. It lasts for eight days. Dreidel, a type of spinning top, is not only a favorite game at this time of year, but it is also an object rich in symbolism. We can use something similar for divination at this time of year. Get yourself some clay or colorful modeling compound. Form it into a cone with three flat sides near the top. Be sure to give it a handle in the center of the top so you can spin it. Paint three symbols or words on the sides—such as "yes," "no," and "maybe." When it is dry and ready to use, light at least eight candles around the table where you will play. Hold the top and ask your question. Then spin it to see what comes up.

Kristin Madden

Notes:

December 17

Sunday

4th ♏

Color of the day: Gold

Incense of the day: Cinnamon

Unbirthday Ritual

Why should birthdays happen only once a year? To celebrate your unbirthday, write your name in all the varieties that you use on a small piece of paper. Place that paper in a small box and wrap it with festive paper. Now, gather three colored birthday candles, a cupcake, and several lengths of colored ribbon. Place the first candle in the cake and make a wish. Do the same with the second and third candles. Light them, and take the box and hold it in front of you, chanting: "I am special and I declare today is my day." As you

chant, tie a bow around the box. With each loop, think about your own special qualities. Place the box next to your plate and sing your birthday song. Blow out the candles. Eat the cake, and keep the gift on your altar as a constant reminder that you are special every day.

Gail Wood

Notes:

Holiday lore: Saturnalia was the Roman midwinter celebration of the solstice, and the greatest of the Roman festivals. It was traditional to decorate halls with laurels, green trees, lamps, and candles. These symbols of life and light were intended to dispel the darkness of the season of cold. The festival began with the cry of "Io Saturnalia!" Young pigs were sacrificed at the temple of Saturn and then were served the next day. Masters gave slaves the day off and waited on them for dinner. Merrymaking followed, as wine flowed and horseplay commenced. Dice were used to select one diner as the honorary "Saturnalian King." Merrymakers obeyed absurd commands to dance, sing, and perform ridiculous feats. It was also a tradition to carry gifts of clay dolls and symbolic candles on the person to give to friends met on the streets.

December 18
Monday

4th ♏
☽ → ♐ 4:10 am

Color of the day: Silver
Incense of the day: Peony

Season of Quiet Spell

Winter is the season of introspection and wisdom. Its cold, quiet days give us a chance to rest after the spring and summer seasons of growth and expansion. Now we may meditate on chances taken, lessons learned, and other subtle changes. This is a perfect time for scrying. For this spell, you will need three candles—one each of black, white, and blue—a black bowl, and some snow or ice. Fill the bowl with snow or pieces of ice. Light the candles and set the bowl in front of them, saying:

> Light and water,
> Son and daughter,
> Dancing in winter's glow;
> Ice and fire,

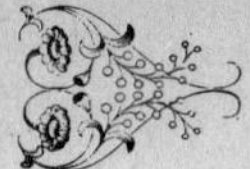

Grant desire.
Show me what I would
know.

Watch for images in the flicker of candlelight on the melting ice. Pay attention to the symbolism of the shapes you see. When the bowl's contents have melted completely, blow out the candles and pour the water outside.

Elizabeth Barrette

Notes:

December 19
Tuesday

4th ♐

Color of the day: Gray
Incense of the day: Sage

Seeking Inspiration Spell

Sometimes in our various creative endeavors, we run out of ideas, power, and vitality. We need motivation to help us pursue our artistry. To seek the power of inspiration, we tap into the Moon's dark, introspective magic. Find a quiet place now, and surround yourself with the tools of your creativity. Gather pens, clay, brushes, or whatever it is you work with or seek to work with. Handle each one with loving care and envision yourself producing beautiful works of art with them. When you are ready, light some frankincense for transformation. As you breathe in the scent, see yourself busy at your creative work. Know that the creative part of you sees that you are watching. Ask what it is that you are creating, then listen. As you listen, you feel all the blockages and impediments fall away. You are now clean, fresh, and inspired.

Gail Wood

Notes:

December 20
Wednesday

4th ♐

New Moon 9:01 am

☽ → ♑ 7:22 pm

Color of the day: White
Incense of the day: Cedar

Mothers' Dream Pillow Divination

Tonight is the Norse Festival of Modresnach, or the Anglo-Saxon Mother Night. It is also called the

Night of the Mothers in Germanic tradition, and it is from this holiday that many of our modern Yule and Christmas traditions derived. For instance, evergreen trees were decorated with lights to represent Yggdrasil, the Tree of Life, on which Odin hung. Feasts and presents celebrated the gifts that the goddesses give their earthly children. In modern Pagan tradition, it is seen as a time to honor the Mother before the New Year is born. Older customs remember the mothers who have passed from this world and the wisdom that may still share with us. Thus, this is considered the best night for having insightful dreams about the coming year. Fill a bag or small pillow with lavender flowers, mugwort, and hops. Also add some sweet marjoram for dreams concerning present and future romantic relationships. If you are pregnant, use lavender alone. Before you go to bed, smell the bag and place it beside your pillow, asking:

> Dear mothers,
> I thank you for your
> guidance and wisdom.
>
> On this long, dark night,
> I ask that you fill my dreams
> with visions.
>
> Grant me the guiding
> light of future truths.
> Blessed Be.

Lady MoonDance

Notes:

December 21

Thursday

Yule – Winter Solstice

1st ♑
☉ → ♑ 7:22 pm

Color of the day: White
Incense of the day: Vanilla

Thin Veil Spell

The Winter Solstice marks the beginning of the returning light of the Sun. It is the shortest day and longest night. In pre-Celtic Ireland, a wonderful ancient tomb and fairy mound called Brug na Boinne, located near modern Newgrange, contained a passageway which was aligned with the Sun on the Winter Solstice. On this day, sunlight streamed into the back of the sacred site. Like other sacred days, the Winter Solstice is a time when the veil between the worlds is thin, and contact with the gods may be auspicious. A ritual sleep or vision quest prior to the solstice morning ceremony may bring you visions of what is to grow in your life. Before bed, recite these words

   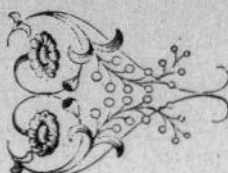 

inspired by the Scottish "Lullaby of the Snow" until you fall asleep:

> Cold, cold this night,
> Lasting this night my
> sleep.
> My eye is closed,
> My sleep is heavy,
> Bring visions of my soul
> to me.

Sharynne NicMhacha

Notes:

Holiday lore: The Yule season is a festival of lights, and a solar festival, and is celebrated by fire in the form of the Yule log—a log decorated with fir needles, yew needles, birch branches, holly sprigs, and trailing vines of ivy. Back porches are stacked with firewood for burning, and the air is scented with pine and wood smoke. When the Yule log has burned out, save a piece for use as a powerful amulet of protection through the new year. Now is a good time to light your oven for baking bread and confections to serve around a decorated table; sweets have an ancient history. They are made and eaten to ensure that one would have "sweetness" in the coming year. Along these lines, mistletoe hangs over doorways to ensure a year of love. Kissing under the mistletoe is a tradition that comes down from the Druids, who considered the plant sacred. They gathered mistletoe from the high branches of sacred oak with golden sickles. It is no coincidence that Christians chose this month to celebrate the birth of their savior Jesus. Now is the time when the waxing Sun overcomes the waning Sun, and days finally begin to grow longer again. In some Pagan traditions, this struggle is symbolized by the Oak King overcoming the Holly King—that is, rebirth once again triumphing over death. And so the holly tree has come to be seen as a symbol of the season. It is used in many Yuletide decorations. For instance, wreaths are made of holly, the circle of which symbolized the wheel of the year—and the completed cycle. (*Yule* means "wheel" in old Anglo-Saxon.)

December 22

Friday

1st ♑

☽ → ♒ 4:49 pm

Color of the day: Purple

Incense of the day: Dill

Magical Firewood Spell

This is the season for building a fire and enjoying some time by

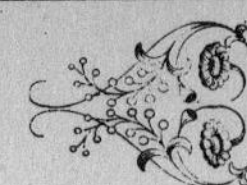

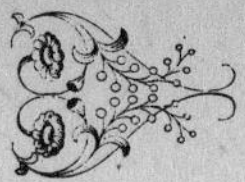

the hearth. Fires also play an important role in spell-casting. To increase the power of a ritual fire, consider the magical meanings of the following woods.

Apple: Burn applewood when working love, past-life, or fertility spells.

Ash: Ash burns very hot. Use when you need to add energy to a spell.

Birch: Burn to connect with the Goddess.

Hawthorn: Burn to fulfill a wish, or to work with the fairy realm.

Hickory: An excellent wood to burn if you need to break a curse.

Maple: Burn for peace and prosperity.

Oak: Burn during health and fertility spells, or to connect with the God.

James Kambos

Notes:

December 23

Saturday

Hanukkah ends

1st ♒

Color of the day: Blue
Incense of the day: Violet

Orange Pomander Recipe

Now is a time of festive activities centered on presents, food, and gathering with friends and family. Why not make an orange pomander that captures the scent of the season for yourself and a friend? To make two pomanders, you will need two oranges, one-quarter cup of whole cloves, ribbon, and three tablespoons each of ground cinnamon, nutmeg, cloves, and ginger. Combine the ground spices and set the mixture aside. Stud the cloves into the fruit. Place the cloved oranges onto a foil tray and cover the fruit with the spices. Take some ribbon and wrap around the orange. Make sure you leave enough ribbon to hang up the orange. Allow the oranges to dry out with the spice mixture for two weeks. After two weeks, the oranges will have shrunk noticeably. The spicy, clove-based aroma will attract success and protection. Hang the pomander in your cupboard in the New Year.

Emely Flak

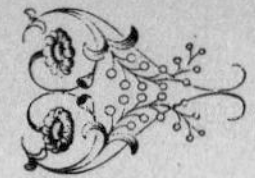

Notes:

December 24

Sunday

Christmas Eve

1st ♒

☽ → ♓ 8:43 pm

Color of the day: Amber
Incense of the day: Sage

Home Safely Spell

During the holidays, we often get visits from distant relatives that we don't see at any other time of the year. This spell is aimed at bringing your loved ones home to you safely. Create a small altar. Take a white candle and write the names of your loved ones who are traveling to you on it. Place it in the center of the altar. Surround the white candle with colored candles, such as brown for protection, yellow for quick thinking, red for energy, and blue for peace. Light the white center candle, saying: "May my family be blessed with protection." (Light the brown candle.) "Clear thinking." (Light the yellow candle.) "Vitality and energy." (Light the red candle.) "And peace and harmony." (Light the blue candle.) Finish by saying: "May the God and Goddess bless my loved ones as they make their way to me. With harm to none, so mote it be."

Olivia O'Meir

Notes:

December 25

Monday

Christmas

1st ♓

Color of the day: Ivory
Incense of the day: Chrysanthemum

The Pancha Ganapati "Hindu Christmas" Ritual

Although in India non-Christians generally do not observe the Christmas holiday, many celebrate a modern Hindu festival called Pancha Ganapati, which is regarded as the "Hindu Christmas." Pancha Ganapati begins on December 21 and runs through to the 25. During this time, families and friends share a togetherness and exchange gifts. Pancha means

"five-faced," and Ganapati is one of the names of Lord Ganesha in the aspect of "Lord of Categories." The Western traditional Christmas pudding is of course substituted with Indian variations, as are other common holiday snacks and foods. In observance of Pancha Ganapati, a home shrine is erected for five days in a family's living room. The shrine includes a statue of Lord Pancha Ganapati or a picture of Ganesha. Decorations include tinsel, flashing fairy lights, flowers, and other meaningful items. Offerings include modaka balls, Ganesha's favorite sweet, palm sugar, milk, incense, ghee lamps, candy, flowers, fruit, Indian cakes, and homemade sweets. Each day, a traditional Hindu tray of offerings is prepared and offered by children to Pancha Ganapati. The kids are also given gifts on each of the five days. These are placed on the shrine and not opened until December 25. The statue of Pancha Ganapati is usually dressed by children in different colors of clothing during each day of the five-day festival. On December 21, the color is golden yellow, and royal blue is used on December 22. Ruby red is used on the third day. On December 24, he wears emerald green, and on Christmas Day, Pancha Ganapati is adorned in a brilliant orange robe. It is believed that he blesses all who pay homage at his shrine by bestowing 365 days of smooth transitions, success, abundance, prosperity, happiness, and health. Some families go on outings and picnics, and the generally engage in joyful activities. Instead of the usual Western musical fare—along the lines of "Jingle Bells," "Rudolph the Red-Nosed Reindeer," or "Santa Claus Is Coming To Town," Hindus use Indian songs in praise of Lord Ganesha, as well as sacred hymms and relevant Sanskrit chants. It is probably no coincidence that while Santa Claus is carted around in a sleigh pulled by eight reindeer, Lord Ganapati's vehicle is called "Mushika," the mouse. Both "vehicles" have an uncanny knack for traversing in and out of tight corners, nooks, and crannies. If bulky Santa Claus whooshes down a chimney laden with gifts, so can Lord Ganapati with his big belly bestow blessings in unlikely locations across the Indian subcontinent.

S. Y. Zenith

Notes:

 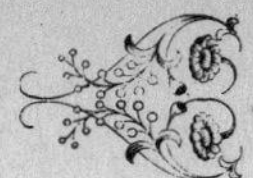  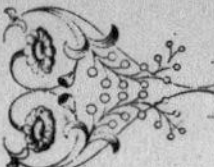 

December 26

Tuesday

Kwanzaa begins

1st ♓

Color of the day: Maroon

Incense of the day: Gardenia

Home Protection Spell

Take a picture of your house, snapped on a happy day. In the room where you feel the most energy, stare at the photo, visualizing a protective white aura around it. Then place the photo inside a box that has a lid. Repeat this chant three times:

> In all the days to come,
> This home be guarded,
> My will be done.
>
> From fire, disaster,
> or robbery,
> This home be safe.
> So mote it be!

Place the photo in the box and close the lid. If you like, tie it securely with white thread or ribbon for extra assurance. As long as the lid remains closed and the box stays in your house, your home will be protected.

Nancy Bennett

Notes:

December 27

Wednesday

1st ♓

☽ → ♈ 12:04 am

2nd Quarter 9:48 am

Color of the day: Brown

Incense of the day: Neroli

End of Year Spell for Fruitful Business

To close that last deal of the year or to achieve that last key goal, you will need a piece of silver such as a coin or pendant, a square of orange silk, a piece of fool's gold (iron pyrite), some bayberry oil (for money), a yellow candle, a bay leaf, and some silver thread. You will also need to find a nearby fruit tree. Anoint the candle with bayberry oil and light. In the orange silk, place the other ingredients while asking for Felícitas to help with closing the deal or with fulfilling your goals. Tie up the silk pouch of herbs and metal with the silver thread. Hang the bag in the fruit tree. Be sure that this tree is close to where you live or work, so the spell's energies can affect you daily. If no fruit tree is available near where you live or work, place the pouch in a bowl of oranges that you can take to work. Think of the spell each time you eat an orange to make the deal or project fruitful.

Boudica

Notes:

December 28
Thursday

2nd ♈

Color of the day: Purple
Incense of the day: Geranium

Wishing Well Spell

Have you ever felt the urge to throw a coin into a pool or fountain? These wishing spells are not just for kids. We can all benefit from this simple money magic. Choose a coin that you can release without any second thoughts. If you can't part with a silver dollar so easily, try a dime or a penny. Soak the coin overnight in water with as much salt as you can get to dissolve in it, along with a tablespoon of lemon juice. If the coin is not totally clean by the next day, rub it with a paste of salt and water to get it nice and shiny. Carry the coin with you in a pocket or in a special pouch. When you see a pool or fountain, hold the coin in your right hand and say to yourself:

> Silver coin,
> I set you free.
> Into this pool;
> I release thee.
>
> Boundless as drops
> In the sea,
> Unlimited wealth
> Now comes to me.

Throw the coin into the water

Kristin Madden

Notes:

December 29
Friday

2nd ♈
☽ → ♉ 3:08 am

Color of the day: Coral
Incense of the day: Nutmeg

Wishbone Talisman

As the new year approaches, we consider dreams we want to come true, and we make our wishes known to those around us. There is an easy way to obtain a talisman that helps our wishes manifest. The wishbone is a forked bone formed by the fusion of the clavicles of most fowl. Save a wishbone from your turkey feast, or request one from a friend if you are vegetarian. Clean the meat off the

bone by boiling it in a pot of water. Make sure an adequate amount of water is used. Boil this for twenty minutes. Sanitize the bone by setting it in a bowl and covering it with a some bleach dissolved in water. Place the bowl in a sunny spot for one full day. Then rinse and dry the wishbone. Hang it on a nail in the kitchen, above the hearth, or above your altar, or carry it in mojo bag or pierce it and string it around your neck. You don't have to break it ritualistically for wishes to come true. Using it, intact, as a talisman will also attract wishes, remind you of any resolutions, hopes, and dreams for the new year.

Stephanie Rose Bird

Notes:

December 30

Saturday

2nd ♉

Color of the day: Indigo

Incense of the day: Lavender

No Let-Down Spell

This is the let-down season for many. To lift your spirits, celebrate now with a ritual meal. Buy or prepare one of your favorite meals, and serve it on your best dishes. Use a pretty tablecloth, placemat, and cloth napkins, or buy paper party linens. Set the table as if a favorite celebrity or other VIP were coming to have a meal with you. Before eating, wash your hands as an act of purification. Ask: "O lord and lady, join me in my meal today. I celebrate your love and power, and I celebrate myself." Eat your meal consciously and mindfully. Enjoy every nuance of the food and ambiance. After finishing, express your gratitude for your meal, saying: "I thank all of the spirits and energies that contributed to my enjoyment of this meal." As a transition from your ritual meal to your normal routine, clear the table, wash the dishes, and put them away.

Luci Sophia Zain

Notes:

December 31

Sunday

New Year's Eve

2nd ♉

☽ → ♊ 6:16 am

Color of the day: Orange
Incense of the day: Poplar

Bring in the New Spell

Invite your family and close friends for a late night feast tonight. Have everybody bring a worn item of clothing. Make a scarecrow by stuffing the clothing with pieces of paper on which each person at the party has written old habits or sad memories they wish to rid themselves of. In some cultures, people add a few firecrackers to add more excitement to the spell. Carry the scarecrow out of doors and burn it. Visualize the old habits and memories going up in smoke. At the stroke of midnight, eat twelve grapes to symbolize the twelve months of the new year, then make twelve wishes. When this is done, the youngest person at the party should stand in the front door and ring in the new year, and the oldest person in the group should stand at the back door and ring out the old year.

Lily Gardner-Butts

Notes:

 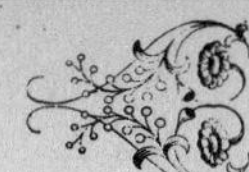   

A Guide to Witches' Spell-A-Day Icons

 New Moon Spells

 New Year's Eve, Day

 Imbolc

 Valentine's Day

 Ostara, Easter

 April Fool's Day

 Earth Day

 Beltane

 Mother's Day

 Father's Day

 Litha

 Lammas

 Mabon

 Full Moon Spells

 Jewish Holidays

 Samhain, Halloween

 Thanksgiving

 Yule, Christmas

 Sunday Health Spells

 Monday Home Spells

 Tuesday Protection Spells

 Wednesday Travel Spells

 Thursday Money Spells

 Friday Love Spells

 Saturday Grab Bag

Daily Magical Influences

Each day is ruled by a planet that possesses specific magical influences:

Monday (Moon): peace, healing, caring, psychic awareness, and purification.

Tuesday (Mars): passion, sex, courage, aggression, and protection.

Wednesday (Mercury): conscious mind, study, travel, divination, and wisdom.

Thursday (Jupiter): expansion, money, prosperity, and generosity.

Friday (Venus): love, friendship, reconciliation, and beauty.

Saturday (Saturn): longevity, exorcism, endings, homes, and houses.

Sunday (Sun): healing, spirituality, success, strength, and protection.

Lunar Phases

The lunar phase is important in determining best times for magic. Times are Eastern Standard Time.

The waxing Moon (from the New Moon to the Full Moon) is the ideal time for magic to draw things toward you.

The Full Moon is the time of greatest power.

The waning Moon (from the Full Moon to the New Moon) is a time for study, meditation, and little magical work (except magic designed to banish harmful energies).

Astrological Symbols

The Sun	☉
The Moon	☽
Mercury	☿
Venus	♀
Mars	♂
Jupiter	♃
Saturn	♄
Uranus	♅
Neptune	♆
Pluto	♇

Aries	♈
Taurus	♉
Gemini	♊
Cancer	♋
Leo	♌
Virgo	♍
Libra	♎
Scorpio	♏
Sagittarius	♐
Capricorn	♑
Aquarius	♒
Pisces	♓

The Moon's Sign

The Moon's sign is a traditional consideration for astrologers. The Moon continuously moves through each sign in the zodiac, from Aries to Pisces. The Moon influences the sign it inhabits, creating different energies that affect our daily lives.

Aries: Good for starting things, but lacks staying power. Things occur rapidly, but quickly pass. People tend to be argumentative and assertive.

Taurus: Things begun now do last, tend to increase in value, and become hard to alter. Brings out an appreciation for beauty and sensory experience.

Gemini: Things begun now are easily changed by outside influence. Time for shortcuts, communications, games, and fun.

Cancer: Stimulates emotional rapport between people. Pinpoints need, supports growth and nurturance. Tend to domestic concerns.

Leo: Draws emphasis to the self, to central ideas or institutions, away from connections with others and emotional needs. People tend to be melodramatic.

Virgo: Favors accomplishment of details and commands from higher up. Focus on health, hygiene, and daily schedules.

Libra: Favors cooperation, compromise, social activities, beautification of surroundings, balance, and partnership.

Scorpio: Increases awareness of psychic power. Precipitates psychic crises and ends connections thoroughly. People tend to brood and become secretive under this Moon sign.

Sagittarius: Encourages flights of imagination and confidence. This Moon sign is adventurous, philosophical, and athletic. Favors expansion and growth.

Capricorn: Develops strong structure. Focus on traditions, responsibilities, and obligations. A good time to set boundaries and rules.

Aquarius: Rebellious energy. Time to break habits and make abrupt change. Personal freedom and individuality is the focus.

Pisces: The focus is on dreaming, nostalgia, intuition, and psychic impressions. A good time for spiritual or philanthropic activities.

Glossary of Magical Terms

Altar: a low table that holds magical tools as a focus for spell workings.

Athame: a ritual knife used to direct personal power during workings or to symbolically draw diagrams in a spell. It is rarely, if ever, used for actual physical cutting.

Aura: an invisible energy field surrounding a person. The aura can change color depending upon the state of the individual.

Balefire: a fire lit for magical purposes, usually outdoors.

Casting a circle: the process of drawing a circle around oneself to seal out unfriendly influences and raise magical power. It is the first step in a spell.

Censer: an incense burner. Traditionally, a censer is a metal container, filled with incense, that is swung on the end of a chain.

Censing: the process of burning incense to spiritually cleanse an object.

Centering yourself: to prepare for a magical rite by calming and centering all of your personal energy.

Chakra: one of the seven centers of spiritual energy in the human body, according to the philosophy of yoga.

Charging: to infuse an object with magical power.

Circle of protection: a circle cast to protect oneself from unfriendly influences.

Crystals: quartz or other stones that store cleansing or protective energies.

Deosil: clockwise movement, symbolic of life and positive energies.

Deva: a divine being according to Hindu beliefs; a devil or evil spirit according to Zoroastrianism.

Direct/Retrograde: refers to the motions of the planets when seen from the Earth. A planet is "direct" when it appears to be moving forward from the point of view of a person on the Earth. It is "retrograde" when it appears to be moving backward.

Dowsing: to use a divining rod to search for a thing, usually water or minerals.

Dowsing pendulum: a long cord with a coin or gem at one end. The pattern of its swing is used to predict the future.

Dryad: a tree spirit or forest guardian.

Fey: an archaic term for a magical spirit or a fairylike being.

Gris-gris: a small bag containing charms, herbs, stones, and other items to draw energy, luck, love, or prosperity to the wearer.

Mantra: a sacred chant used in Hindu tradition to embody the divinity invoked; it is said to possess deep magical power.

Needfire: a ceremonial fire kindled at dawn on major Wiccan holidays. It was traditionally used to light all other household fires.

Pentagram: a symbolically protective five-pointed star with one point upward.

Power hand: the dominant hand, the hand used most often.

Scry: to predict the future by gazing at or into an object such as a crystal ball or pool of water.

Second sight: the psychic power or ability to forsee the future.

Sigil: a personal seal or symbol.

Smudge/Smudge stick: to spiritually cleanse an object by waving incense over and around it. A smudge stick is a bundle of several incense sticks.

Wand: a stick or rod used for casting circles and as a focus for magical power.

Widdershins: counterclockwise movement, symbolic of negative magical purposes, and sometimes used to disperse negative energies.

Spell Notes:

Call for Submissions

We are looking for magical daily lore for next year's *Witches' Spell-A-Day Almanac.* If you have lore or history to share about a day or holiday, we'd like to hear about it.

Writers: Daily lore pieces should be 100 to 150 words long, and focus on the folklore, historical information, or trivia particular to a calendar day or holiday. We are looking for unique and interesting lore that is timely, revealing, and intriguing.

Submissions should be sent to: annualssubmissions@llewellyn.com

or

Witches' Spell-A-Day Submissions
Llewellyn Worldwide
P.O. Box 64383
St. Paul, MN 55164

(Please include your address, phone number, and e-mail address if applicable.)

If you are under the age of 18, you will need parental permission to have your writing published. We are unable to return any submissions. Writers and artists whose submissions are chosen for publication will be published in the 2007 edition of the *Witches' Spell-A-Day Almanac* and will receive a free copy of the book.